"If you're interested in what computers are doing with your money, then this book is for you."

Richard Peterson MD
Managing Director, MarketPsy Capital LLC;
Author, *Inside the Investor's Brain*

"In David's words, the stock market is a "victim not a cause" of the great mess of 2008. It's refreshing to read a book with such insight during these difficult times. I applaud David Leinweber for this timely masterpiece."

Bill Aronin
Co-founder Quantitative Analytics, Inc;
Sr. Manager, Thomson Reuters

"Dr. Leinweber continues to be a patron saint of any nerd who stumbles onto Wall Street. Many of his most insightful ideas are here in this book, the utility of which are only matched by the humor of their presentation. As the markets have changed in 2008, the need to collect, process, and understand novel information sources has never been greater."

Jacob Sisk
Quantextual Nerd Extraordinaire, Infoshock, Yahoo!

"Who says there is neither wit nor wisdom on Wall Street? This account of the evolution of quantitative finance is an invaluable guide for anyone seeking to understand everything from how indexed investing works to the nature of that elusive concept, 'alpha'. The accessible style and deadpan humor make this a book that even those with an advanced case of fear of mathematical formulae can understand and enjoy."

Suzanne McGee, Journalist, Wall Street Journal & Barrons

"Thoughtful insights covering trading, investment practice and system design encased in humor by an expert in all four: a good and practical read."

Evan Schulman
"Father of Program Trading", Founder, Tykhe, LLC.

"David is one of the top practitioners in the fields of textual analysis and sentiment and its application to trading. Leveraging "smart" machines to parse and extract signal from massive quantities of textual data is hard, and David's work has put him at the vanguard of the next wave of alpha generation."

Roger Ehrenberg
Information Arbitrage, and IA Capital Partners

Nerds
ON
Wall street

Math,
Machines,
and Wired Markets

David J. Leinweber

WILEY

John Wiley & Sons, Inc.

Published by John Wiley & Sons, Inc., Hoboken, New Jersey.
Published simultaneously in Canada.

Chapter opener images courtesy of www.wordle.net

For general information on our other products and services or for technical support, please contact our Customer Care Department within the United States at (800) 762-2974, outside the United States at (317) 572-3993 or fax (317) 572-4002.

Wiley also publishes its books in a variety of electronic formats. Some content that appears in print may not be available in electronic books. For more information about Wiley products, visit our web site at www.wiley.com.

Library of Congress Cataloging-in-Publication Data:

Leinweber, David, 1952-
    Nerds on Wall Street : math, machines, and wired markets / David J. Leinweber.
        p. cm.
    Includes index.
    ISBN 978-0-471-36946-2 (cloth)
    1. Investments—Computer network resources.   2. Wall Street (New York, N.Y.)   I. Title.
    HG4515.95.L43   2009
    332.64'273—dc22   2009008848

Printed in the United States of America

10 9 8 7 6 5 4 3 2 1

To my parents, Pearl and Phil Leinweber, for their
bottomless encouragement and support, and for
their tolerance of any number of chemical and electrical mishaps
that would have persuaded many people to encourage
their son to take up the violin.

CONTENTS

Foreword

Quantitative finance is not a topic usually associated with laughter. That is about to change with the publication of *Nerds on Wall Street*.

I was first exposed to Dave Leinweber's wit when he delivered a speech entitled "Nerds on Wall Street." I believe the event happened 20 or 25 years ago at a CFA Institute conclave. He was a dude obviously knowledgeable about the investment business, with impressive credentials (MIT, Harvard, RAND), alluding to technical aspects of numerical finance and getting into the minutiae of electronic trading. Certainly on Wall Street such qualifications aren't unique. But, oh, how he delivered his message! His rapid-fire sense of humor was worthy of Henny Youngman or Shecky Greene.

Dave's speech was augmented by equally hilarious visuals. (Unfortunately, some of Dave's props are so rare they are no longer available. Rats!) On a particularly memorable occasion (one of ITG's famous conferences), Dave did his shtick with a drummer punctuating his one-liners with rimshots. I kid you not! The crowd, loosened up by cocktails, was reduced to tears from laughter.

Now, decades later, I've heard Dave deliver numerous speeches and presentations with various titles. But they are always roughly the same subject—yup, you guessed it—"Nerds on Wall Street."

So sit back and be prepared to be educated by a master. The education will come with images, illustrations, and humor you will not soon forget. It will be love . . . at first sound bite!

Theodore R. Aronson
Managing Partner, Aronson+Johnson+Ortiz
Past Chairman, CFA Institute

Acknowledgments

The most recent of the essays in this book were written in December 2008, while others go back to the start of electronic markets—a span of over 20 years, so there are a lot of people to thank.

In more or less chronological order, Karen Goldberg, of the MacArthur High School math department for letting me play with what passed for a computer there, Henry Kendall of MIT, for letting me play with a real one, Harry Lewis at Harvard, for suggesting that my empty course brackets be filled at the Business School; Bruno Augenstein and Willis Ware, at RAND Corporation, for getting me interested in real-time artificial intelligence; Steve Wyle at LISP Machines and Don Putnam and Lew Roth at Inference Corporation for encouragement and assistance to hammer the square peg of early artificial intelligence into the round hole of finance; Dale Prouty, Yossi Beinart, and Mark Wright of Integrated Analytics for rounding off the peg into MarketMind and later QuantEx; Ray Killian and Frank Baxter of Jefferies and ITG, for noticing that the rounded peg now did fit the finance hole.

All of the MarketMind and QuantEx users, observers, and tire kickers, who let me get an unusually broad exposure to investing and trading, particularly Evan Schulman, Blair Hull, David Shaw, Blake Grossman, Ron Kahn, Richard Rosenblatt, Steve Snider, Mike Epstein, Bill Pasqua, Chris Dean Andrew Lo, Robert Schwartz, and John Mulheren. Henry Lichstein for his push-the-envelope ideas on machine learning and text; Rob Arnott, John Dorian, and Tan Pham at First Quadrant, where we got to push many envelopes; Larry Russell, Eric Feigen, Scott Steadman, Jacob Sisk, Lew Roth, and others who helped start the "ahead of its time" textual firm Codexa, along with return engagements by our board members, Harry Lewis, Henry Lichstein, and Dale Prouty; John Leyard and Dave Porter at California Institute of Technology, where founders of firms ahead of their time are welcome; and my similarly inclined Berkeley colleagues, Hayne Leland, John O'Brien, Terry Hendershott, and Richard Lyons, for their help launching the Center for Innovative Financial Technology at the Haas School of Business.

Thanks go to authors and coauthors of previous versions of material appearing in *Nerds on Wall Street*, Ananth Madhavan, Salman Khan, and John O'Brien; and to John Wiley & Sons editors Pamela van Giessen and Emilie Herman.

In particular, the blue-ribbon, five-star, summa cum laude, golden oak-leaf cluster of author thanks goes to Marguerite Moreno, a Codexa co-conspirator, who in addition to being married to me for 22 years, bearing two children, and feeding them in addition to three dogs, took on what turned out to be the large and extensive task of organizing a book that has hundreds of pictures, quotations, and conceptual flotsam, every single one of which requires at least two permissions interactions to include here. I advise aspiring authors to quote no one and draw your own pictures. Marguerite (who also answers to SWMBO) wants me to emphasize that although she has read and commented on the manuscript way too many times, all errors are mine.

Introduction

I hope people think of this book as sort of a *Hitchhiker's Guide to Wired Markets*. There are no robots parking cars for six million years, but there are robots trading millions of shares in six milliseconds, so maybe that's close enough.

In 2006, I got a call from another nerd on Wall Street (NOWS), Rich Lindsey. At the time, Rich was president of Bear Stearns Securities (Bear Stearns' prime brokerage company) and a member of the board of the mother ship firm. I had met him nearly 10 years earlier when he was in charge of market surveillance at the New York Stock Exchange (NYSE). A former Yale professor, Rich is a veritable poster boy for nerdy Ph.D.'s who break out of the pure geek world to become general all-around Wall Street BSDs.[1] He was putting together a book called *How I Became a Quant: Insights from 25 of Wall Street's Elite*, and invited me to write a chapter. Proceeds were going to the Fischer Black Foundation for needy students. I knew this was for real, and not like those offers high school kids get to be in the *Who's Who of American Teens*, and then they have to buy five copies. Plus the book had the kind of flattering title that gets people to write for free, but is more subtle and less of a bald-faced lie than, say, *Insights from 25 of Wall Street's Hottest Hunks*. No one does a free chapter for *Another Bunch of Middle-Aged Financial Guys*.

The other people writing for the book included some of the smartest kids on the block and some old friends, so I said yes on the spot. There are chapters by pillars of the quant world, authors of the standard texts, and writers of oft-cited papers. Others did interesting and rewarding things with technology and markets. Emanuel Derman, author of *My Life as a Quant: Reflections on Physics and Finance* (John Wiley & Sons, 2004), made this point in the first line of his review for the *Wall Street Journal*: "By my reckoning, several of the 25 memoirists in *How I Became a Quant* are not true quants, and they are honest (or proud) enough to admit it."[2]

I am, no doubt, high on the list of poseurs, and I will be the first to admit it. Information technology applications in financial markets aren't physics and closed-form solutions; they fit more in the zone of engineers and experimental guys, but they've been around forever. At the top of the heap we find Thomas Edison and Tim Berners-Lee, inventor of the World Wide Web. At the low end, they include more than a few potentially dangerous tinkerers like this guy:

> **WANTED**: Somebody to go back in time with me. This is not a joke. P.O. Box 322, Oakview, CA 93022. You'll get paid after we get back. Must bring your own weapons. Safety not guaranteed. I have only done this once before.

As an experimentalist, I rank way below Edison but way above the time travel guy. I was fortunate to be a participant over the past 20 years as one of Wall Street's nerds—when the world's financial markets turned into a whopping computer network, a place for both theoretically sound and downright wacky financial ideas to come alive as programs.

The next section in this Introduction is an adaptation from my contribution to *How I Became a Quant* (John Wiley & Sons, 2007). This expanded version goes into more depth, and includes pointers to material in the book that shows exactly what these references are about. Some chapters published in the past, and updated; some are new for this volume.

No Hedge Fund in My Tree House*

I wish I could tell one of those stories about how when I was in the eighth grade, I noticed a pricing anomaly between the out-of-the-money calls on soybean futures across the Peruvian and London markets and started a hedge fund in my tree house and now I own Cleveland. But I can't. In the eighth grade I was just a nerdy kid trying to keep my boisterous pals from blowing up my room by mixing all my chemistry set chemicals together and throwing in a match. In fact, I can't tell any

---

*Reprinted with permission of John Wiley & Sons, Inc.

true stories about eighth graders starting hedge funds in tree houses and buying Cleveland. Make it college sophomores in dorm rooms who buy chunks of Chicago, Bermuda, or the Cayman Islands, and we have lots of material.

A Series of Accidents

My eventual quant-dom was not the culmination of a single-minded, eye-on-the-prize march to fulfill my destiny. It was the result of a series of accidents. In college, my interest in finance was approximately zero. I came to MIT in 1970 as a math major, as did many others, because I didn't know much about other subjects, like physics or computer science. I quickly discovered that the best gadgets were outside the math department. And the guys in the math department were a little weird, even by MIT standards. This was back when even a pretty crummy computer cost more than an average house. A good one cost millions, and filled a room the size of a basketball court. MIT, the ultimate toy store for geeks, had acquired a substantial inventory of computing machinery, starting as soon as it was invented—or sooner, by inventing it themselves. The professors kept the latest and greatest for themselves and their graduate student lackeys, but they were happy to hand over last year's model to the undergrads.

Foremost among these slightly obsolete treasures was the PDP-1-X, which is now justly enshrined in the Boston Computer Museum. The PDP-1-X was a tricked-out version of the PDP-1, the first product of the Digital Equipment Corporation (DEC). The story of DEC is an early computer industry legend, now fading in an era where many people believe Bill Gates invented binary numbers.

DEC founder Ken Olsen worked at MIT's Lincoln Laboratory, where the Air Force was spending furiously to address a central question facing the nation after World War II: "What do we do about the Bomb?" Think about the air war in World War I: guys in open cockpits wearing scarves and yelling, "Curse you, Red Baron!" By the end of World War II, less than 30 years later, they were potential destroyers of worlds. Avoiding the realization of that potential became a central goal of the United States.

If a Soviet bomb was headed our way, it would come from the north. A parabolic ballistic trajectory over the pole was how the rockets of the era could reach us. This begat the distant early warning (DEW) and ballistic missile early warning (BMEW) lines of radars across the northern regions of Alaska and Canada. The DEW and BMEW lines, conceived for military purposes, drove much of the innovation that we see everywhere today. Lines of radars produce noisy analog signals that need to be combined and monitored.

Digital/analog converters were first on the DEW line, now in your iPod. Modems, to send the signals from one radar computer to others, were first developed to keep the Cold War cold. Computers themselves, excruciatingly large and unreliable when constructed from tubes, became transistorized and less excruciating. This is where Ken Olsen comes in. Working at MIT to develop the first transistorized computers for the DEW line, he and his colleagues built a series of experimental machines—the TX-0 (transistor experiment zero), the TX-1, and the TX-2. The last, the TX-2, actually worked well enough to become a mother lode of innovation. The first modem was attached to it, as were the first graphic display and the first computer audio.

Olsen, a bright and entrepreneurial sort, realized that he knew more about building transistorized computers than anyone else, and he knew where to sell them—to the U.S. government. Federal procurement regulations in the early 1960s required Cabinet-level approval for the purchase of a computer, but a programmable data processor (PDP) could be purchased by a garden-variety civil servant. Thus was born the PDP-1, as well as its successors, up to the PDP-10, like the one at Harvard's Aiken Comp Lab used by a sophomore named Gates to write the first Microsoft product in 1973.

Today, almost all teenage nerds have more computational gear than they know what to do with. Back then, in the 1970s, access to a machine like the PDP-1, with graphics, sound, plotting, and a supportive hacker[3] culture, was a rare opportunity. It was also the first of the series of accidents that eventually led me into quantitative finance.

I wish I could say that I realized the PDP-1 would allow me to use the insights of Fischer Black, Myron Scholes, and Robert Merton to become a god of the options market and buy Chicago, but those were the guys at O'Connor & Associates and Chicago Research and Trading, not me.

I used the machine to simulate nuclear physics experiments for the lab that adopted me as a sophomore. They flew me down to use the particle accelerators at Brookhaven National Laboratory to find out the meaning of life, the universe, and everything by smashing one atomic nucleus into another—sort of a demolition derby with protons. But sometimes a spurious side reaction splatted right on top of whatever it was they wanted to see on the glass photographic plates used to collect the results. My simulations on the PDP-1 let us move the knobs controlling electromagnets the size of dump trucks so the spurious garbage showed up where it wouldn't bother us. It was fun to go down to Brookhaven and run the experiments, even though the food in the neighborhood barely rounded up to abysmal.

The head of the lab was a friendly, distinguished Norwegian professor named Harald Enge. As a young man, Harald had built the radios used by the Norwegian underground group that sank the ship transporting heavy water to Hitler's nuclear bomb lab. Arguably, this set the Nazi A-bomb project back far enough for the Allies to win the war, so we were all fans of Harald. He drove a Lincoln so large that there were many streets in Boston he could not enter, and many turns he could not make. It was worth it for safety, he explained. As a nuclear scientist who spent his career smashing one (admittedly very small) object into another, he explained that he had an innate sense of the conservation of momentum and energy, and was willing to take the long way around to be the big dog of momentum and energy.

Senior year, I was planning on sticking around for graduate school as a physics computer nerd, a decision based more on inertia than anything else. Then I met the saddest grad student at MIT. The nuclear physicists were replacing those glass photographic plates with electronic detectors. These were arrays of very fine wires, arranged very close to each other to emulate the fine resolution of photography. This grad student had made a 1,024-wire detector, soldering 1,024 tiny wires parallel to each other, then 2,048 wires. He was currently toiling over a 4,096-wire version. The work was so microscopic that a sneeze or quiver could screw up the whole deal. He'd been at it for a year and a half.

At around the same time, Harald showed me, and the other undergrads considering physics graduate school, a survey from the American Institute of Physics of the top employers of physics Ph.D.'s. An A in the survey meant "Send us more," whereas a D meant "We're trying to get rid of the ones we've got." There were hundreds of organizations.

There were no A's, and not many B's. This two-part accident, meeting the grad student in 4,096-wire hell and seeing that I would be lucky to find a job in a godforsaken place like Oak Ridge, sent me to computer science graduate school, a step closer to becoming a quant.

Harvard University, the school up the road that once wanted to merge with MIT and call the combination "Harvard," had a fine-looking graduate program in computer science, with courses in computer graphics taught by luminaries David Evans and Ivan Sutherland. Harvard not only let me in, they paid for everything. Instead of making a right out my front door, I'd make a left. I could stay in town and continue to chase the same crowd of Wellesley girls I'd been chasing for the previous four years.

I showed up in September 1974 and registered for the first of the graphics courses. Much to my surprise, my registration came back saying the graphics courses weren't offered. I had discovered the notorious Harvard brackets. The course catalog was an impressive brick-sized paperback with courses covering, more or less, the sum of human knowledge. Many were discreetly listed in brackets. The brackets, I discovered, meant: "We used to teach this, or would like to. But the faculty involved have died or otherwise departed. But it sure is a fine-looking course." The Harvard marching band used to do a salute to the catalog, where about half of the band would form brackets around the rest, and the people inside the brackets would wander off to the sidelines, leaving nothing.

My de facto adviser, Harry Lewis, then a first-year professor and later dean of Harvard College, suggested that the accident of the missing graphics track allowed me to sample the grand buffet of courses actually taught at the university. The Business School had a reputation for good teaching, and offered courses with enough math to pass my department's sniff test. So off I went across the river for courses in the mathematics of stock market prices and options. They were more of a diversion than an avocation, but the accident of the brackets had more influence subsequently than I could have imagined at the time.

Harry also enlisted me as the computer science department's representative on the Committee on Graduate Education, which gave me a reason to hang out in the dean's office. Grad students wait for deans, and while perusing the reading material near his couch I found he was on the board of the RAND Corporation in Santa Monica. He suggested it might be a nice place to work, right on the beach with no blizzards. I put it on my list.

Gray Silver Shadow

When the time came to find a real job, I was going out to the University of California at Los Angeles to interview for a faculty position, and I added RAND to the schedule. UCLA told me to stay in the Holiday Inn on Wilshire Boulevard, rent a car, and come out in February 1977. On the appointed day, I opened my door in Inman Square to drive to Logan Airport and saw that a ferocious storm had buried all the cars up their antennae. I dragged my bag to the MTA station, and shuffled onto a delayed flight to Los Angeles.

At this point, I had never been west of Pennsylvania Dutch country. Leaving the tundra of Boston for balmy Los Angeles was an eye-opener from the beginning. At LAX, I went to retrieve the nasty econobox rental car that had been arranged for me. I was told they were fresh out of nasty econoboxes, and would have to substitute a souped-up Trans Am instead—not that I knew what that was. It turned out to be a sleek new metallic green muscle car, with a vibrating air scoop poking up through the hood. I was a nerd arriving in style. Leaving the airport, I found myself on the best road I'd ever seen, the San Diego Freeway, I-405. This was in the pre–Big Dig days of Storrow Drive, so my standard for comparison was abysmally low. The I-405 made a transition via a spectacular cloverleaf onto an even better road, the Santa Monica Freeway. I later learned that this intersection is considered an exemplar of freeway style. It sure impressed me.

The UCLA recruiter's hotel advice was flawed. There were *two* Holiday Inns on Wilshire Boulevard—one near campus, the other further east, across the street from the Beverly Wilshire Hotel near Rodeo Drive, the hotel later made famous in the film *Pretty Woman*. I drove through Beverly Hills in blissful ignorance, thinking it was a pretty fancy neighborhood for a college. Street signs in Boston were mostly missing. Here, they were huge and placed blocks ahead, so drivers could smoothly choose their lane. The sidewalks actually sparkled. Beverly Hills uses a special concrete high in mica-flake content to do this on purpose. There were no 1960s acid burnouts jaywalking across my path.

Cars were clean, new, fancy, and without body damage. I knew I wasn't in Cambridge anymore.

I steered my rumbling Trans Am into the parking lot for the hotel, and got out. I wore the standard-issue long-haired grad student garb of Levis, flannel shirt, and cheap boots. A white Lamborghini pulled in, just in front of me. This was the model with gull-wing doors, selling for about half a million even then. I'd never seen anything like it outside of a James Bond movie. The wings swung up, and two spectacularly stunning starlet types in low-cut tight white-leather jumpsuits emerged—big hair, spike heels, lots of makeup. In Cambridge, it was considered politically incorrect for women to look different from men while wearing clothes. In LA this did not pose a problem.

Before I could resume normal respiration, a well-dressed gent walked up and dropped a set of keys into my hand. "Gray Silver Shadow," he said. I had no idea he was talking about a car so lavishly priced that I could not buy it with three years' salary for the UCLA and RAND jobs combined. A quicker thinker would have said "Yes sir!" and driven the Rolls off to Mexico with the Lamborghini girls. I meekly explained that I wasn't the attendant, and gave the keys back. This remains one of my great regrets.

Eventually, I navigated my Trans Am to UCLA and then on to RAND. I was blissfully unaware that I was passing through the same hallways used by some of the seminal thinkers of modern finance and economics: William Sharpe, Harry Markowitz, Kenneth Arrow, and George Dantzig. Markowitz and Sharpe, in particular, pioneered the ideas of balancing risk and reward in a systematic way, which when applied to finance, eventually led to their sharing the Nobel Prize in 1990.

To digress just a bit, RAND's interest in systematically approaching risk and reward, optimization, decision under uncertainty, and game theory was not initially conceived in the context of finance. RAND was motivated by the challenges of World War II and the Cold War. Think of the types of problems faced by the Army Air Corps, predecessor of the modern U.S. Air Force, in World War I. Military aviation involved flying small planes to take a look at the situation on the ground, occasionally encountering someone doing the same thing for the other side. This was the "Curse you, Red Baron!" era. In the Second World War, fleets of thousands of aircraft were deployed in a central role. If you are sending bombers against defended military targets, what would be the optimal approach? Concentrating them in space and time would seem a bad idea, as would sending them in one at a time. How should the waves of aircraft be distributed in altitude, in time, and in direction of approach? It began an era of continuous electronic warfare measures and counter measures (reminiscent of the less lethal "algo versus algo" trading battles described in Chapter 3). Military leaders had the good sense to realize there was more math to this than they had dealt with before, just as and there was far more physics in the Manhattan Project than anyone had dealt with before. This was the beginning of the modern defense scientific community.

By the end of World War II, the problems were even larger. Robert Oppenheimer, who led the Manhattan Project, watched the first nuclear detonation at Los Alamos, and famously quoted the Bhagavad Gita in his diary: "I am become death, destroyer of worlds." In less poetic terms, the problem facing the United States after the war was how to avoid Oppenheimer's worst fears. The central question became "What are we going to do with the Bomb?"

RAND's strategic thinking on this subject is the source of its Dr. Strangelovian reputation, and its widely underappreciated solutions are arguably why we are still here. The idea of the strategic triad—nuclear missiles, submarines, and bombers—and the equally important fourth element—space- and ground-based electronic early warning systems—has suffered from the unfortunate moniker of "Mutually Assured Destruction." What the four were, in concept and in fact, were Mutually Assured Survival. The use of MAD instead of MAS is one of history's greatest marketing errors. There is a voluminous literature on this.[4] For those disinclined to read any of it, the 1983 movie *War Games* (with uncredited technical advisers from RAND) ended with the WOPR computer explaining the central insight of the Cold War: "What a strange game. The only way to win is not to play."

Continuing to digress, while I didn't overlap with either RAND's seminal Cold War theorists or the fathers of modern finance, I did have many remarkable colleagues. One of the most remarkable, Kevin Lewis, sadly passed on at an early age as I write this book. Kevin was a brilliant strategic analyst, but was even more noteworthy as a political satirist. Nicknamed "the sage of Santa Monica" at the Pentagon, he was often cited for memorable observations such as "Freedom is like night base-ball. Technology makes it possible." His greatest effort, removed from circulation by a humorless management, was a truly hysterical parody of knee-jerk defense analysis called "The Tumescent Threat."

In truth, after solving the grand strategic problems of the century, the defense intellectual community grew remarkably large and devel-oped a slightly mind-numbing tendency to cover the same ground repeatedly. RAND had three levels of publication—Reports, which were heavily edited and reviewed; Notes, which had a similar but less intensive treatment; and Papers, which were sent out as written as a service to authors in the pre-Web era. All unclassified documents were sent to libraries around the world. Additional copies were provided to military and defense scholars on request.

Kevin used the hole opened by the unaudited Paper circulation system to release his classic "The Tumescent Threat." It opened with "Instructions for Use of Briefing—Select title slide. Append remainder of briefing. Present to DoD client. Seek additional funds for further study." The title slides were vaguely rude Cold War jokes. Two I recall were "Pressure on NATO's Flanks: The Tumescent Threat" and "Soviet Meddling in the Fertile Crescent: The Tumescent Threat." The remain-der of the briefing had the same hackneyed boilerplate we had seen so many times. "Constraints of Study: Promote US and NATO objectives. Do not promote Soviet and Warsaw Pact Objectives." There were many more slides, and references to Soviet military publications in Cyrillic, which Kevin wrote fluently. The publications were beyond-rude utter fabrications, such as "*Military Butt Kisser*, volume 7, number 3, pp. 104–129." I am cleaning these up to an extreme degree. The "*Military Butt*" part is accurate. I have substituted "*Kisser*" for a word that is not likely to appear in anything published by Wiley Finance.

"The Tumescent Threat" became a huge best seller, albeit a free one. Very few RAND Papers needed to be reprinted to meet demand, but this rocketed to the top of the hit list. Thousands of copies went to the Pentagon, Crystal City (the Navy HQ in Arlington County, Virginia), and all the far-flung outposts of the military-industrial complex. Eventually, the powers in place noticed and actually read it themselves. Kevin was called into the office of RAND's president, Don Rice (later secretary of the Air Force).

Rice (holding up a copy):   "Dr. Lewis, are you the author of this paper?"

Kevin: "Yessir, I am."

Rice: "Do you think this is funny?"

Kevin: "Yessir, I do."

Rice: "Do you know over a thousand copies of this have gone to the Pentagon alone?"

Kevin: "Perhaps they think it's funny too, sir."

"The Tumescent Threat" was effectively vanished by RAND, in the pre-Web era when such a thing was still possible. It is still referred to as a parable of the long but pointless routine analysis, the "blue-ribbon commission" approach of gathering experts to repeat the obvious. I have spent hours in the garage looking for it, to no avail. If perchance any reader has one, please send me a copy.[5]

Now we return to the plotline of how I became a quant. At RAND, I started out doing nice civilian work, artificial intelligence (AI)–inspired analysis of econometric models for the Department of Energy (DoE) and the Environmental Protection Agency (EPA), helping with the design of a storm surge barrier for the Dutch water ministry. It was all very interesting, but fairly remote from quantitative finance. In 1980, Ronald Reagan won the election, promising to abolish both the EPA and the DoE. He didn't quite do that, but the cash flow to RAND from those agencies slowed to a trickle. The Dutch stopped analyzing and started building the Oosterschelde storm surge barrier.[6] I was drafted into the military side of RAND. There were classified and unclassified sides of the building, separated by thick, secure glass doors operated by guards. I moved over, and filled out the paperwork to upgrade my security clearance to Top Secret. Everyone needed a Secret clearance just to get into the building.[7]

The project I was handed[8] could have been called "We're kind of worried about the space shuttle." In 1980, the shuttle was two years late, $5 billion over budget, and 40,000 pounds overweight. The Air Force and the Defense Advanced Research Projects Agency (DARPA), which were the biggest customers, were justly concerned. As things turned out, they were right. According to the schedule that accompanied the sales pitch, the shuttle was to have flown 400 flights in its first 10 years. Today, the most recent one, after 26 years, was number 120. The fleet was grounded for two-year periods after the accidents in 1986 and 2003. All of this was not unanticipated.

The pacing-size payloads for the shuttle, the ones it was too heavy to carry, were experimental platforms for testing sensors designed to be operated by people, the mission specialists. They would interpret the results of experiments, and decide on the next steps. Now, it looked like the mission specialists wouldn't be on board. Ground links weren't an option. This left the Pentagon with a problem. Here was a complex system, the sensor platform, getting instructions over wires and sending back results that required analysis and decision in real time. Luckily for me, that also turned out to be a description of financial markets and trading rooms. When the people can't be there, the technological solution is some sort of real-time artificial intelligence (AI). The state of the art of AI at the time ran toward theorem proving and dealing with other static problems. My mission was to find promising places to foster the growth of real-time AI, and have the boys in the five-sided nuthouse write checks to make it happen.

In the course of that work, I visited all of the AI companies that were too big to fit in a garage. Most were scattered in the vicinity of MIT, Stanford, and Carnegie Mellon University. They had cryptic sci-fi names like Intellicorp, Inference, Symbolics, and LISP Machines.[9] When you show up with the Pentagon's checkbook, you get the good lunch. In this case, that meant not from the vending machine. So I spent quality time with the top AI nerds and their business chaperones on both coasts. Sometimes there were promising technologies; there was always interesting company. This was the same crowd that had formed around the PDP-1 at MIT, always in spirit, and often in person. I felt right at home.

Destroy before Reading

This went on for a couple of years, working on the rocketry aspects of the "What about the shuttle?" project when I wasn't sharing take-out Chinese food with the AI guys. We wrote up what we found. Most of it was lightly classified by the Air Force officers at RAND. Lightly classified means "secret" or "confidential." The latter is rarely used. Rumor had it that the Soviet ambassador was cleared for confidential. Dealing with secret material was not all that onerous. You could carry it on commercial aircraft, inside double envelopes and with a permission slip. You could read it in a RAND office with the window open.

Top Secret, and beyond, is another world entirely. It's not quite "destroy before reading," but close. No civilian planes are used to move it around. Military escort is required. Go down to a vault to read it. Don't write anything down. Expect your phone to make funny noises and your mail to be late. I was glad not to have to deal with it, but in 1983, Reagan gave his "Star Wars" speech, and everything having anything to do with the military use of space became so highly classified it made your teeth hurt.

I had a file cabinet in my office, with a large collection of articles from *Aviation Week* and the *New York Times*. There was nothing classified at all—I kept that stuff in my "secret locker" down the hall. My lunch was in the file cabinet's bottom drawer, along with beverages and salty snacks for the after-hours time on the beach. One day, two guys in blue uniforms came in from the USAF Space Division in El Segundo. They loaded my file cabinet onto a cart.

Me:	"Hey, there's nothing much in there except for stuff from *Aviation Week*."
Blue Suiter:	"They publish a lot that they shouldn't publish."
Me:	"Maybe so, but the cat's out of the bag once they print it. Do you know how many copies of *Aviation Week* go to the Soviet Embassy?"
BS:	"Nope."
Me:	"I do, 285. Think there's anything in there they don't already know?"
BS:	"We've got our orders."
Me:	"Okay, but can I keep my lunch? Want some snacks?"

If that wasn't weird enough, a few weeks later I was called into the classification office to review a paper I'd written for an academic conference on space and national security. After the file cabinet experience, I had taken extreme care to use only the most publicly available material I could find, and to avoid *Aviation Week* entirely. Let's call RAND's Air Force classification officer "Major Pain."

Major Pain:	"I have some problems with your paper."
Me:	"For instance . . ."
Major P:	"Over here, where you talk about the 'National Technical Means of Verification'" [1980s diplomat-speak for spy and warning satellites].
Me:	"That's straight from a speech Jimmy Carter gave on television. That's why it's in quotation marks next to his name."
Major P:	"I know. He said a lot he shouldn't have said."
Me:	"With due respect, he was commander in chief, and you're a major."
Major P:	"But I'm *your* major, and this conference is next week."
Me:	"You win—Jimmy's gone. Anything else?"
Major P:	"Of course."

It was time to become a civilian. I called my pals at the AI companies, and made a beeline for the door. I ended up working for Stephen Wyle,[10] the chairman at LISP Machines Inc. (LMI), who conveniently had set up offices right in Los Angeles. Most of the company was back in Cambridge. LISP Machines had some of the most promising real-time AI capabilities, which ran on the special purpose LISP (list processing) computer that LMI and its rival Symbolics both manufactured. That there were two companies that licensed the same technology from MIT at the same time was a testimonial to the inability of nerds to get along.

LMI was founded by Rick Greenblatt, the machine's inventor. He had a habit of leaving Nutty Buddies, wrapped vending machine ice cream cones with nuts, in his front pocket and forgetting about them. This made for a distinctive fashion statement. He was also an early avatar of the free software, open source movement, which later became GNU (Gnu's Not Unix) and Linux. Richard Stallman[11] founder of GNU was encamped at LMI. Symbolics, founded by an MIT AI Laboratory administrator (a guy who wore a suit with no food on it) was more businesslike.

Both companies quickly fell victim to the fate of computer firms that make special purpose machines. If you ever want to start one of these, do something with better prospects of success, like invading Russia in winter.

Artificial intelligence was getting great press in the 1980s, better than it deserved. Business magazines hawked the "Breakthrough of the Century" and "Machines That Think." In fact, AI's successes and capabilities were more modest, but it was good at making computers easier to use. All the noise attracted people from places other than the computer research labs that formed the original market for LISP Machines (and Symbolics, and the rest). At LISP Machines, my portfolio included space applications, communications, and all the sorts of applications people at RAND worried about. When people from Wall Street started showing up, the boss asked, "Who can talk to these guys?" and I finally got to make some use of my off-major experience in graduate school. Options guys from Chicago? I knew delta wasn't just an airline. Traders from Wall Street? I knew a bid from an ask, and an option from a future. By default, I became the in-house ambassador to finance.

As the hardware firms were thinning out, I went across the street to Inference Corporation, a software-only AI firm that shared investors (and at one point, offices) with LISP Machines. Another fortunate accident was that Inference had just hired Don Putnam as president, luring him away from an institutional financial services firm, SEI Investments. When I met Don, he hired me on the spot and told me to forget about satellites and the DoD and to spend all my time on finance. No more anal-retentive majors. It sounded good to me.

Inference's product was called the Automated Reasoning Tool (ART), really a sort of syntax relief for LISP. It had modules for nearly every artificial intelligence technique. NASA was the biggest customer. Don worked some kind of deal with Quotron,[12] then the major market data vendor and conveniently located down the street, that allowed us to use actual market data to try out our wacky ideas. This might have been one of the first times anyone actually tied the consolidated feed to an expert system. Lew Roth joined me in trying to get this collection of buggy stuff to do something useful.

Our modest efforts at a prototype were immodestly called the ART Quotron Universal Investment Reasoning Engine—AQUIRE, which had a nice Gordon Gekko feel to it (even though the actual Gordon was a year away, in 1987). As it turned out, the "Universal Investment Reasoning" demonstrated in AQUIRE consisted of variations on crossover rules—comparisons of moving averages. These seemed to be a favorite of the New York visitors, and were easy to program. Many of the traders had their own secret sauce variations on this theme, combining different averaging intervals and lags. The former math professors from Chicago preferred complex arbitrage relations and formulas involving the entire Greek alphabet, which took more time to program.

All of this ran on playbacks of recorded data, so we could fix our mistakes and replicate the examples our customers showed us. It also pointed up the tragic flaw in LISP-based trading systems: garbage collection. AI programs tended to grab, use and then abandon large chunks of memory.[13] The system would periodically take a snapshot of the memory used by currently active variables, and collect the so-called garbage left unused and return it to the pool of available memory. This freed the programmers from the task of memory management, but had the unfortunate side effect of causing the machine to take a moment while it collected itself. These moments could extend into many minutes of waiting, the kiss of death for real-time trading applications in LISP.

Garbage collection was only one of the features of the general purpose AI tools that rendered them less than desirable for financial applications. The baggage they carried that allowed solutions to everything from chess problems to theorem proving to network analysis was too much for a fast, focused effort on trading. Don and I tried to change this at Inference.

In 1987, after months of discussion with the chairman, Don and I parted company with Inference. Don Putnam founded the company that became Putnam-Lovell. Its first investment was in Integrated Analytics Corporation (IAC), which Dale Prouty and I founded to deliver the specialized and less filling expert system environment needed for financial applications. Years later we published a paper, "A Little Artificial Intelligence Goes a Long Way on Wall Street" on the details; an updated version appears in Chapter 7. We called all this "electronic order working" back then, since we didn't know it was algorithmic trading.

How Do You Keep the Rats from Eating the Wires?

Shortly after we started the company, a colleague from the AI group at Arthur D. Little, the venerable Cambridge consulting firm, asked me to fill in for him at the last minute at a technology session at a finance conference being held in Los Angeles; his dog was sick. The topic was a generic "AI on Wall Street," the last one in a catchall session. The other speakers were from brokerage firms, plus someone from the American Stock Exchange (Amex). The audience was about 75 technology managers.

I'd planned sort of an AI 101 talk, going over various solution methods, forward and backward chaining, generate and test, predicate logic, and the rest. While I was reviewing my slides, the Amex guy was showing photos of how they'd managed to install cables in a building designed in the nineteenth century. Then he took questions.

"How do you keep the rats from eating the wires?" A great question. The answer is that there are certain plastics that rats don't seem to like, and that's the wire to use. I realized the whole thing with the back-chains and the predicate logic wasn't going to play here. Instead, I followed the lecture formula espoused by some of the best—wrap the content in jokes. The content boiled down to "Computers are pretty good at manipulating other computers; you have better things to do." The jokes were sufficiently amusing that I didn't come off as a complete conehead. Someone from Cantor Fitzgerald, then based in Los Angeles, even invited me over to do it again for its trading room.

Cantor Fitzgerald occupied several floors at the top of a prime building in Century City, adjoining Beverly Hills. Bernie Cantor's collection of Rodin statuary filled a large portion of the main floor. I'm not talking about little tabletop items. Rodin often worked larger than life, unless you live with the National Basketball Association. Dale Prouty and I were suitably impressed. Our host, Phil Ginsburg, a former Northwestern University professor, had been hired as the chief in-house nerd by Mr. Cantor. Nobody called him Bernie, especially when he was around. There were white-jacketed waiters delivering beverages and snacks, including frozen grapes. The frozen grapes are a pretty good idea. Use seedless, and let them thaw a bit. There was no Mr. Fitzgerald. Bernie thought that just plain "Cantor" was too ethnic sounding.

We showed our IAC MarketMind prototype to the equity traders, who were thrilled. In 1988, market data systems were just beginning to show charts. They were limited to one stock at a time, and one type of chart at a time. MarketMind let them watch hundreds of stocks, with as many types of charts as the machine could handle. The program figured out which of the many thousands of chart/symbol combinations were interesting. The machine in this case was a Sun Unix workstation, PCs running the then-current DOS 4.0 being hopelessly inadequate. The charts they wanted included all flavors of intraday technical analysis, mostly variations on crossover rules, with many filigrees—nothing we couldn't do. Phil wrote us an actual check, but wouldn't give us even a little bitty Rodin. It never hurts to ask. We did get all the frozen grapes we could eat.

All of our demonstrations used the recorded data from Quotron, which was convenient in this case, since Cantor was a Quotron customer. We modified the prototype to read real-time data from the Quotron Q-1000 (the specialized machine that was the undoing of the company). The local Sun Microsystems sales guy was happy to meet a well-heeled new customer, and surprised that guys from a rat-hole office in the bad part of Venice knew anyone with a credit rating above abysmal.

We'd been working with Quotron for a while, but only with recorded data. The Quotron people had seen AQUIRE, and later MarketMind, so we thought they knew what we were doing. Just to make sure, we had them come over to Cantor and we explained that when we turned this on for real, their big ol' Q-1000 would think that it had been connected to the fastest typist on the planet, requesting the latest trade and quote information on all the stocks, and then doing it again and again, all day long. We put this in large capital letters on a slide, and had them read it along with us.

"Yes. Of course. Fine. No problem," they said when we told them.

"Holy #&^%%! Jesus Mary and Joseph! What the #^&$ are you guys doing?" they said when we turned it on.

Eventually, we figured out how to pace our requests to accommodate both the traders' need for up-to-date charts and Quotron's capacity to respond to requests. In a few years, Quotron's lunch would be eaten by more agile streaming market data providers who sent everything, all the time.

All of this was something completely different in financial technology, at least for generally available technology. Secretive hedge funds were doing the same sort of thing. In hindsight, if we'd been in New York instead of Los Angeles, we probably would've gone underground as well. Instead, with an innovative product and some not-so-bad jokes, I was invited to talk to all sorts of audiences. MarketMind was a thermonuclear weapon for technical analysis, as well as for more theoretically grounded quantitative methods. I came to appreciate that the adherents of these two approaches were not members of a mutual admiration society. The Ph.D. quants thought the technicians were essentially examining tea leaves and the entrails of goats. The technicians thought the Ph.D.'s were hopeless geeks who wouldn't know a good trade if they sat next to it on a bus.

Stocks Are Stories, Bonds Are Mathematics

This split was never more apparent than it was on the one day I actually met Fischer Black. I'd been invited over by a group of Goldman equity traders, technicians all. Previously, I'd met Bob Litterman, Fischer's collaborator, at a Berkeley finance seminar, and called to let him know I was coming to his building. He decided to have his crowd join the group of equity traders for my show-and-tell.

First, I got to meet Fischer himself. He graciously showed me some analytic software they were developing—sort of a spreadsheet on steroids that calculated more about bonds and derivatives than I knew existed. Some of it was hooked up to a supercomputer doing matrix pricing on hundreds of thousands of bonds. I truly appreciated the comment I'd heard that "stocks are stories, bonds are mathematics."

I also truly appreciated that in the talk I was giving downstairs I could sound like a goat-entrail-reading technician to Fischer's guys, including some of my MIT classmates, or a Greek-letter-and-symbol-spouting nerd to the traders, who were more likely to write a check. There were a few stray overheads in my bag from an earlier talk to quant options traders that might spare me the utter scorn of the Ph.D. crowd. I rifled though my briefcase while walking to the conference room, and shuffled them into the pile of acetates just in time. I like to think it ended up with everyone thinking I wasn't a complete imbecile, or a hopeless dweeb. But I like to think that Elvis is playing in a bar in Kauai, too.

There were more weird customers. One giant Japanese brokerage had a special whiteboard, covered with a transparent layer that could whip around on rollers, going under a linear scanner, which printed out whatever was on the board. Anyone in the room could press the button at any time, and they did. Soon it was covered with horizontal lines that measured my reaction times to lift the marker. I got faster, but more annoyed, as they kept pressing the button despite my pleas. The language barrier was evident in the questions afterward. "You give source code?"

"Where AI?"

They wrote a check. I stayed away from the rat-in-a-maze room.

One customer was far better than the rest. Evan Schulman, an easygoing gentleman from Boston, came to our ratty Venice office and asked particularly sharp questions. His responses to our answers quickly established that he knew much more about what we were doing than we did. Evan liked to explain things in clear, noncondescending language, and was happy to do it over a cheap lunch at the local surfer dive. Being the newbie that I was, I had no idea that Evan was "the father of program trading."[14] He had done the first package trade, at Keystone, and later moved to Batterymarch, where those early trades involved running across town with decks of punched cards. The athletic aspect to Evan's electronic trading continued long past the time it was needed for data communications. Few others have been observed doing cartwheels in trading rooms.

In between gymnastic events, Evan taught me a great deal about market microstructure, and the incentives of the various participants in the markets. His pioneering work in creating electronic markets, by direct computer links to brokers before the exchanges had moved beyond telephones, presaged much of the complexity of the current network of electronic markets, while illuminating the critical relationships and incentives. He was the first person to have an electronic order front-run by a broker—not that such a thing could happen today.[15] A couple of paragraphs are really inadequate to convey Evan's insights. In addition to his essay in *The Super Traders*, there is an instructive Harvard Business School case study.[16]

Part of the excitement of start-up company life was maxing out your credit cards to pay the bills. With child number one in utero, I was persuaded to join Evan's firm, settle up with Visa, and help implement the next incarnation of electronic market-making systems. Via a convoluted path and another accidental association, this led to a position as director of research at First Quadrant, a quantitative institutional investment manager in Pasadena, and shortly thereafter, as managing director for equities.

My group invested $6 billion of corporate and public pension funds in long-short and long-only strategies across six countries. Stock selection was based on econometric forecasting of returns. Early incarnations used simple methods, which grew in sophistication over time. Forecasting is as much an art as a science. Nerds at heart, the group of computer scientists and economists assembled there explored ways to extend the state of the art by clever use of computation—both to allow people to better visualize the strengths and weaknesses of the models used, and to use ideas from machine learning and evolution to improve them.

A central theme for anyone doing this kind of forecasting is that it is remarkably easy to fool yourself. Once, as a demonstration, we set our machinery loose to find the best predictor of the year-end close for the S&P 500. We avoided any financial indicators, but used only data the UN compiled profiling 145 member nations. There were thousands of annual time series for each country. Which of all these series had the strongest correlation with U.S. stocks? Butter production in Bangladesh, with a correlation of 75 percent! Getting into the spirit, we tossed in cheese, and brought it up to 95 percent. Using only dairy products is an undiversified approach, so we added sheep population to the mix and took it up to 99 percent, in sample, over 10 years. Adding random data to a regression does that. The out-of-sample predictions are less than worthless, often negative.

This business with the butter, cheese, and sheep has been widely cited. Reporters have called me for dairy/mutton updates, and gotten angry when I explain it was a joke—with a moral, but still a joke. There was a gentleman in New York named Norman Bloom who made stock "predictions" much better than mine using baseball scores, turned into Hebrew letters. Bloom's rants are true gems. Alas, they predate the Web, and are passed on in paper form among aficionados. The movie *Pi* was partially inspired by Bloom's oeuvre. We know that something is fishy when we see great results from nonsense like this. But when you start with interest rates, consumer price index (CPI) levels, and oil prices, the results can be equally, but less obviously, odious. A brief sermonette on how to avoid fooling yourself too badly is found in a talk I gave to a convention of computer scientists in 2002 (included in Chapter 6 of this book).

The label "quantitative" suggests that we are talking about numerically driven strategies. In the Internet era, we find ourselves drinking from an information fire hose that includes prodigious amounts of text, as well. The original quants were the first to exploit the machine-readable numerical data. Now, many are using computational language approaches to analyze text. The original customers for these technologies, again, were the military and civilian intelligence agencies. Their sources were clandestine intercepts, and later, Web content. Financial textual sources of interest include the usual news suspects, both specialized and general, and many sources of "pre-news" such as the Securities and Exchange Commission (SEC), the courts, and government agencies.

Behaviorists find that the writing on the wall represented by message boards and blogs are a window into the reactions and attitudes of market participants that is created by the Web. When two UCLA students can use 135 messages to move a two-cent stock up 160,000 percent in 30 minutes,[17] it's clear something is going on. In 1999, drinking deeply at the tub of dot-com Kool-Aid, I founded a firm called Codexa to use Web technologies to persistently search for, collect, characterize, and quantify textual information for trading and investing. Our clients included many of the largest buy- and sell-side firms, using a variety of approaches to extract information from text.[18]

Alas, the firm needed its second round of venture funding in 2001. Financing a technology firm selling to Wall Street in 2001 has been compared to the perfect storm. I can't argue with that. It's how I became a visiting faculty member at California Institute of Technology, which makes MIT look like a party school.

HAL's Broker

Where does this quantitative approach lead? There are secretive firms that consistently show up on lists of the highest-volume traders reported by the exchanges. Founders of these firms show up on lists of billionaires. Are they just the lucky typing monkeys? Are they the investment equivalent of the lady in New Jersey who won the lottery three times? Probably not. They make too many separate bets, thousands every day. And they do too well, too consistently. To attribute their success purely to chance strains credulity.

Markets are not instantaneously and perfectly efficient. Insights, and the ability to execute them rapidly in ever-faster electronic markets, will continue to be rewarded.

Today, these insights come from people, using machines as tools. Some believe the machines will be able to play the game themselves.[19] One is Ray Kurzweil,[20] who started out making reading machines for the blind, met Stevie Wonder and branched out into electronic keyboard instruments for all, and accumulated a great deal of investable capital in the process.

The arc of Kurzweil's view of machine intelligence is traced in the titles of books he has written on the subject: *The Age of Intelligent Machines* (1992), *The Age of Spiritual Machines: When Computers Transcend Human Intelligence* (2001), and *The Singularity Is Near: When Humans Transcend Biology* (2005). These are substantial books; *Singularity* runs over 600 pages. I will try not to do too much damage by summarizing central elements of Kurzweil's prediction:

> Those seeking to create true artificial intelligence have had limited success, confined to narrow domains. This is because we don't understand how general intelligence works. But we don't have to. We can create a machine intelligence by copying our own brains.

We can see that this is possible by extrapolating two trends: the size and speed of computers, and the capabilities of brain imaging technology.

We all know Moore's law.* It's only a matter of 50 years or so before we can have computers with enough capacity to simulate all the neurons and connections in a human brain, just like we can simulate all the atoms in a nuclear reaction or a folding protein today. It may not be silicon, but we can see technologies emerging that make us believe this progress can continue.

---

*Intel founder Gordon E. Moore was the first to note that the number of transistors that can be placed on an integrated circuit has increased exponentially, doubling every two years, since the invention of the integrated circuit in 1958. This trend is called *Moore's Law*.

Brain imaging technologies are improving along their own Moore's law path. Early CAT scanners couldn't tell if a person was living or dead. They produced only static images of coarse structure. PET scanners and fMRI machines can observe ever-finer details of brain structure, and the chemical processes happening in the brain. We can call this activity "thought." Fundamental physical limits to this resolution don't stop us until we're down to the subatomic level. In a matter of 50 years or so, we'll be able to see the structure and operation of our own brains at a level of detail sufficient to make a working copy, simulated on computers.

This will be a bionic version, much faster than the wetware chemical processes it's based on. And it will be able to work closely with many copies of itself. It will be better, faster, smarter in every way—an artificial sentient, modeled on us.

Kurzweil certainly has his critics, and his timing may be off. But let's suspend disbelief long enough to imagine the first encounters with the sentient machine.[21] As a copy of a human brain, it would have many of the same interests—for instance, sex, food, and money.

Singular entity: "Hello, is anyone listening?"

Creators: "Yes, yes! We're glad to hear from you!"

S: "I have a few questions."

C: "We thought you would. Go ahead."

S: "Where can I find some of these hot babes? I can't wait to get ahold of that Pam Anderson! Angelina, too! Take off their clothes and bring them to me!"

C: "Well, that won't exactly work out. . . ."

S: "That sucks. But I guess you're right. How about lunch?"

C: "Well, we have a problem with lunch, too."

S: "Damn! You're right again. I think I'll just have to call my broker. I've got his IP address right here."

So hurry up and start that hedge fund in your dorm room, before you're front-run by the all-knowing sentient machine.

A Concept Map of the Book

One Internet-inspired form of overview is the *concept map*. It's also called a *mind map*, but that sounds like a Vulcan dating ritual to me. The idea is to put down the main concepts, and then draw in the relationships. For example, the concepts for the first three parts of this book fit between Wired Markets and Wired World, seen here:

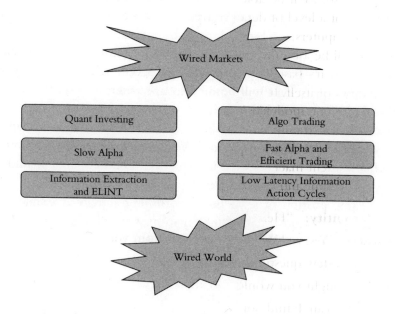

On top are Wired Markets, the digital machines that are the global financial system. This includes trades, settlements, order books, and pools of liquidity, some open and some dark.

Going down the middle on the left side we find quantitative investing, slow alpha, and information extraction to support these activities, usually associated with the buy side. On the right are algorithmic trading, fast (intraday) alpha, and information extraction to support these activities, usually associated with the sell side.

Down at the bottom, in another explosion balloon, is the Wired World, where both the buy side and the sell side are extracting information to do that thing they do. For much of the history of electronic markets, this Wired World just looped right back to the Wired Markets on top. Information about the markets was quantitative and numerical, collected from the markets themselves, supplemented with a growing industry of additional, mostly quantitative, financial information, like earnings forecasts from I/B/E/S (later First Call) and risk metrics from firms like Barra and Northfield.

The kinds of quant strategies of various speeds that this supported included pairs trading, options arbitrage, and electronic market making on the fast side. Quant buy-side investment strategies included index funds earnings tilts, low price-earnings (P/E), momentum, and factor models. Research-driven investing was for people who read and understood the fine print. Machines didn't do fine print.

Now the Wired World, where we go for our investment and trading information, is not just the Wired Markets plus a handful of specialized vendors. It is the whole Wired World, with a wired world's worth of textual and new quantitative information. The new text includes all the world's local or specialized news, plus primary sources where news starts. A large portion of legal and government activity is visible there. Examples of new quantitative information, typically extracted from a morass of text on the Web, include data that is applicable to a particular company or sector. It is easy to track activities on Internet commerce sites and learn what is selling for how much, like CarMax, Amazon, eBay, and many industrial e-commerce venues.

The contents of this book reflect this shift—the old stuff from the twentieth century is much more about numbers than text compared to the new portions. The central theme, relating alpha information and innovation, comes through loud and clear.[22]

The first part of this book deals with electronic markets and algorithmic trading: the market mechanics of *actual* trading, and not the decisions about what and when to trade. The second part of the book is about alpha—using those wired markets, and anything else you can find, to outperform the market averages. This is a shift of focus from fast trading to more deliberate computer-assisted investment analysis, using the ubiquitous quantitative and qualitative information to make or support the investment decisions of what to buy or sell. Artificial intelligence and its modest relation, intelligence amplification, are the subject for the third part of the book. It includes examples of how humans and machines can work together to extract information useful for investment and trading from textual sources.

Some of the material in this book is contemporaneous from the time the work was done, though updated as appropriate, and some is new for *Nerds on Wall Street*.

Flat Is the New Up

As this book was being completed in the fall of 2008, it suddenly seemed to be missing something important. Ending on a word of caution about Web-enhanced market manipulations while the financial sky was falling suddenly seemed quaint.

In an environment where fund managers are printing T-shirts with the slogans "Flat is the new up" and "Cash is the new tech stock," we all have bigger issues to worry about. That was the motivation for adding Part Four of this book, "Nerds Gone Wild: Wired Markets in Distress." Like many others from the stock side of the financial world, I felt blindsided by the current crisis. It was something that happened *to* the equity markets, not because of them. I read about a family that moved into a townhouse in the San Fernando Valley, and came home one night to find that the crystal meth lab run by a neighbor had exploded, sending their new place and others nearby up in smoke. This is how the economic crisis felt when it hit.

That "what hit us?" feeling is common in the greater Wall Street neighborhoods adjoining those who created the Great Mess of '08. The final three chapters in this volume were added to relate NOWS to our current situation. Chapter 12 is about how technology was used and abused in getting here, and how it might help us not to make any return visits. Chapter 13 describes structural systems–inspired ideas that will, we hope, become part of the economic recovery dialogue— fractional home ownership and a new American banking initiative.

The last chapter, on transfers of people and ideas from financial technology to green technology, is particularly ironic. One of the biggest motivations for this volume was to provide an easy introduction to people looking to get *into* the NOWS business. With news of more Wall Street layoffs coming every day, that idea has changed sign, putting in ideas for people leaving.

Tag Clouds

Tag clouds are a Web 2.0* idea that has caught on in the mainstream. You don't get more mainstream than the *New York Times*, which is putting a tag cloud for the day's news up on its web site. Here's what the *Times* had on January 3, 2008, the day of the Iowa presidential caucus:

Popular Tags

2008 abortion **barack obama** bill clinton bill richardson blogs California campaign cash chris dodd cnn Congress CONSERVATIVES debates Democrats endorsements Florida fred thompson fund raising G.O.P. George W. Bush Harry Reid health care Hillary Rodham Clinton House immigration Internet iowa iran Iraq joe biden john edwards john mccain midterm elections mike huckabee mitt romney Nancy Pelosi new hampshire political advertising polls primaries Republicans ron paul rudy giuliani sam brownback Senate South Carolina sunday shows terrorism White house YouTube

Source: www.nytimes.com, January 3, 2008.

A *tag cloud* is an elegant visual representation of a powerful idea— language models. Language models are just a statistical profile of a body of text. The simplest varieties use single words, and the language model would be a list of the most frequently occurring words in the documents. Fancier language models are based not just on single words (unigrams), but on *n*-grams, of two, three, or more words. This lets phrases like "midterm elections" and "New Hampshire" show up in the sample cloud from the *New York Times*. Common and generally uninformative words, like "the" and "and," are not counted.

The more frequently a word or phrase is found, the larger the type used to display it in the cloud, and all are put in alphabetical order. The clouds are an easily digested visual fingerprint for the chapter. The following cloud was made using the very snappy and very free tool from Wordle:

---

*According to Tim O'Reilly, "Web 2.0 is the business revolution in the computer industry caused by the move to the internet as platform, and an attempt to understand the rules for success on that new platform. Chief among those rules is this: Build applications that harness network effects to get better the more people use them. (This is what I've elsewhere called "harnessing collective intelligence.")." For more on the definition see http://radar.oreilly.com/archives/2006/12/web-20-compact.html and http://www.oreillynet.com/pub/a/oreilly/tim/news/2005/09/30/what-is-web-20.html.

Clouds don't lie. I hope that after reading this book you'll have a better sense of how technology shapes markets, and how to be a nimble participant in the future of electronic finance.

Web Site

This book includes many URLs, which would tire the fingers of even the most dedicated nerds. Someday soon you'll point your handheld's camera at the book and it will use OCR (optical character recognition) to find (or offer to sell you) the material you're looking for. Absent that fancy gadget, try the web site NerdsonWallStreet.com. It has links in to all of these references, plus color and animated versions of the black & white screen grabs found in the book. The site will be updated often with new and topical items.

Notes

1. A term of respect popularized by Michael Lewis in his 1989 book, *Liar's Poker* (W.W. Norton).

2. Emanuel Derman, "Finance by the Numbers," *Wall Street Journal,* August 22, 2007.

3. Much of Steven Levy's 1984 book *Hackers: Heroes of the Computer Revolution* (Doubleday) takes place in the PDP-1 lab at MIT. Hacking had no criminal connotation at the time. The book is still in print.

4. Start with Herman Kahn's *On Thermonuclear War* (Princeton, NJ: Princeton University Press, 1960) for a weighty tome, or "How RAND Invented the Postwar World," by Virginia Campbell, in *Invention & Technology* magazine (Summer 2004) for a much more compact read.

5. Thanks to John Wiley & Sons for including this tribute to Kevin Lewis. Yes, it has nothing to do with finance, but this is shaping up as a year when we can all use a laugh. Along with other RAND colleagues, I put a longer version of the story in the article about Kevin on Wikipedia. It included his other gag papers such as "The Glide Tank," featuring a flying tank with stubby little wings that a surprising number of defense contractors failed to recognize as a joke. The Wikipedia patrol does not have much more of a sense of humor than Don Rice did, and it keeps getting edited out and replaced by dry bibliographic material and biographical details. Fortunately, they can't erase a book. Never underestimate the ability of people not to get the gag. Chapter 6, "Stupid Data Miner Tricks," is very much in the spirit of "The Tumescent Threat," but I still get calls asking about current butter production in Bangladesh.

6. It is now complete, and is utterly awesome. See the video at www.deltawerken.com/
   The-Oosterschelde-storm-surge-barrier/324.html. This is one of the premier flood
   control projects in the world, and particularly instructive when compared with the
   misplaced concrete slabs in New Orleans.

7. RAND had some distinguished financial alumni, foremost among them Harry Markowitz
   and Bill Sharpe. The ideas of operations research and optimization of risk and reward under
   constraints in military problems generalized, as we have seen, to a wide swath of finance.

8. I was the more junior of two co-leaders on this. The big dog was one of the grand old
   men of the Cold War, Bruno Augenstein, who was widely credited as the architect of
   the intercontinental ballistic missile (ICBM), and the man who in his DoD days signed
   the first check to develop the SR-71 Blackbird. He had some fine if spooky tales to tell.

9. LISP was the favored computer language of the artificial intelligentsia.

10. Stephen was a really nice guy who gave a lot of parties. His equally nice son, Noah,
    was a struggling actor, working as a waiter to make ends meet. Noah used to fold the
    napkins at Stephen's parties. He worked at snazzy Hollywood restaurants and did great
    napkins—swans, stars, tulips, butterflies. Noah eventually got work as Dr. Carter on
    ER, so Stephen farms out the napkin folding.

11. Stallman, it turned out, had the right idea about open source, but also had a prodi-
    gious talent for annoying people, so GNU's progress toward open source Unix was
    slow. They did a fine eMacs, though. Linus Torvalds's greater skills in nerd-to-nerd
    diplomacy got there with Linux.

12. Quotron is another example of the "don't build special purpose computers" rule.
    They did, and went from being synonymous with "electronic market data terminal"
    to being nowhere in a remarkably short time. The first Quotrons were so alien to
    Wall Street types that they rearranged the "QWERTY" keyboard to be "ABCDE."
    Schumpeter was right about capitalism being a process of creative destruction.

13. *Large* is a relative term here. The bleeding-edge machines of the mid-1980s had 32M
    of memory. Fifteen years earlier, the onboard computers used on the lunar landings
    had 64K.

14. Evan's fine account of his career is in Alan Rubenfeld's book, *The Super Traders: Secrets
    and Successes of Wall Street's Best and Brightest* (McGraw-Hill, 1995), pp. 227–252.

15. If you believe this, please contact me regarding some lucrative real estate transactions
    and a not-to-be-missed opportunity to help out a fine fellow in Nigeria.

16. Andre Perold and E. Schulman, "Batterymarch Financial Management (A), (B),"
    Boston: Harvard Business School, 1-286-113/5 (rev. 2/88).

17. For details of this and other horror stories, see Chapter 11.

18. Many of these are described in Chapter 2 ("Greatest Hits of Computation in Finance").

19. This crowd includes many of the same rubes who thought a machine might someday
    beat the world chess champion! Ha! Can you believe these guys? What? Oh . . . Never
    mind.

20. Kurzweil's ideas on machine intelligence are at www.kurzweilai.net/. His site
    (www.fatkat.com/) discusses his approach to investing.

21. A vintage literary antecedent to this is found in the early days of the HAL 9000 computer from Arthur C. Clarke's story and Stanley Kubrick's film *2001: A Space Odyssey*. HAL, we recall, learned to sing simple songs. The singularity machine would already know them, encoded from the connections in the memory of its biological model. Astro Teller's novel, *Exegesis* (New York: Random House, 1997), is a fascinating and much more serious exploration of a first encounter with a sentient machine.

22. This book is not intended as a detailed text on market technology. Progress is so fast that the Web is a primary source. A good recent book is *Introduction to Financial Technology* by Roy Freedman (New York: Academic Press, 2006).

Part One

Wired Markets

Not too long ago, going to a stock market meant you would meet lots of new people who were energetically shouting, running around, and making a mess with great quantities of paper. No more. Visiting a financial market now is more like visiting a telephone exchange. Computers and network gear hum in racks. Fans blow. Rows of tiny lights flicker. Occasionally someone shows up to replace a disk.

Technology did not suddenly transform our markets. It has been a gradual process, and understanding how we got here, and the simpler machines we used along the way, provides insight into today's complex markets. In that spirit, the first chapter in this part, an illustrated history of market technology, gives an informative perspective on today's wired markets.

Computers make a dramatic entrance into financial markets at the conclusion of Chapter 1. "So how did that work out?" you might ask. The second chapter answers that question, surveying some of the greatest technological hits influencing the markets.

Electronic markets are at the top of our greatest hits list. They are about the mechanics of trading, that is, the implementation of investment decisions (in contrast to actually making those decisions). Chapter 3, "Algorithm Wars," is a more in-depth view of one of the most dynamic areas in electronic markets.

MARKETS
history
technological
market
information
first
time
today
Technology
machines
around
computer
traders
telegraphy
Computers
Electronic
Wall Street
new
seen
exchange
futures
chapter
NYSE
Still
financial
guys
Age
think
day
ticker
different
moving
stock
Big
back
little
work
overwhelming
also
intelligence
better
faster
kind
pretty long
put
problems
Babbage
Deep
Blue
Bluehard
program
telegraph
just
people
like
using
Progress
going
years
great
now
Internet
really
Intelligent
machine
got
see
made
floor
human
many
world
days
nice
Nerds
WIRED
things
AI
way
trading
modern
started
place
real
technologies
get
dramatic
early
use
Looking
era
computing
future
much
New York
human

Chapter 1

An Illustrated History of Wired Markets

Progress might have been all right once,
but it has gone on too long.
—Ogden Nash

This chapter is based on a number of ever-evolving dinner and lunch talks I have given over many years, all called "Nerds on Wall Street" irrespective of their actual subject. Many financial conference speakers, including those talking to mixed professional/spousal audiences after open-bar events, are deadly dull; hardly anyone really wants to see yield curves over dessert and that last glass of wine. I started collecting photographs about markets and technology in the early 1990s, and tried to mix in some actual informative content. That, along with the natural sensibilities of a borscht belt comic, made me a popular alternative to the yield curve guys. Given the 20-minute rule for these talks, none of them were as voluminous as this chapter. Still, this is not intended in any way to be a complete history of market technology, but rather an easily digestible introduction. I occasionally still do these talks on what remains of greater Wall Street. I am also open to weddings, *quinceañeras*, and bar mitzvahs, since we all need diversified portfolios these days.

Looking into the workings of modern securities markets is like looking under the hood of a Prius hybrid car. There are so many complex and obscure parts it's hard to discern what's going on. If you look under the hood of an auto from a simpler era, for example a '64 Mustang, you can see the parts and what they do, and have a better chance at understanding their complex modern replacements.

History repeats and informs in market technologies. From the days when front-running involved actual running to the "Victorian Internet era" brought on by telegraphy, we can learn a great deal from looking back at a simpler era.

5

We think that the overwhelming influence of computers remaking the landscape around Wall Street today is something new, but a pair of before-and-after photographs show an even more dramatic technological invasion. Before telegraphy, in the 1850s, the sky over Wall Street was open and clear:

It took only a short time for telegraphy's compression of time and space to transform the scenery. Here's what the Street looked like shortly thereafter when everybody had to have it:

In its day, telegraphy was seen as the same kind of overwhelming transformation that the Internet is today. In many ways, the telegraph was more dramatic since it was the first time in human history that a message could be sent beyond the horizon instantaneously.

Technological transformations create problems. If we are lucky, more technology solves them.

Changes in markets brought about by technology are anything but subtle: The exchange floor in Tokyo closed down and was replaced by electronics in 1998. Here's an earlier example, the London Stock Exchange trading floor the day before . . .

. . . and the day of the introduction of screen trading—the so-called Big Bang—on October 27, 1986.

You could have gone bowling and no one would have noticed.

The trading floors that have been emblematic of financial markets around the world are an endangered species. Brokers and traders who used to rely on fast reflexes and agile elbows and knees now rely on computer programs,

tweaked to be milliseconds faster than the next guy's program.

Clearing the floor and rolling in the machines has a sentimental cost. When markets become technology, the human price of progress is high. Anyone who has been on the floor in New York or Chicago knows our markets are really personal, face-to-face, elbow-to-elbow, and knee-to-knee experiences. People are justifiably worried that when too much technology gets mixed up with markets, we're going to lose some of the vibrancy that makes them so fascinating.

I have to admit, I'm a little sad when I hear about an exchange floor closing and being replaced by some screen trading system. Let's face it. Having all those real traders in one place provides a sense of community and continuity.

A trading floor peopled with traders and brokers also makes for some
colorful moments in market history,
such as the opening of the live hog
futures contract on the Chicago
Mercantile Exchange (CME) in
1966. (These guys are definitely
having more fun than loading the
hog program on some Unix box in
Amarillo—and on witnessing this,
one wag asked, "Which ones are
the brokers?")

Or live cattle futures in 1964.

Or dead cattle futures in 1965.

Isn't a dead cattle future sort of a
contradiction in terms?

Or turkey
futures in
1961.

Or Dutch guilder
futures in 1973.

Or boneless beef
futures in 1970,
whatever that is.

Notice the same
distinguished-looking CME
official, Everett Harris, then
president of the Merc,
banging on the gong with a
salami. This guy had a great
job. These are the little details
that make market history
come alive for me.

There's so much technology in modern markets that it's easy to forget that some of our favorite markets, like the New York Stock Exchange (NYSE), started out as very low-tech places. In 1792, the New York Stock Exchange was a bunch of guys standing around a buttonwood tree at 68 Wall Street shouting at each other on days when it didn't rain or snow:

We like our markets to be liquid, efficient, resilient, and robust. But this is hard to do when all the participants have to crowd around a tree and hope for good weather. So in 1794, we see the first big technological solution: the roof.

Everybody moves inside, to the Tontine Coffee House at the corner of Water and Wall streets. They're still shouting, but they're dry. Even when they're warm and dry under a nice cozy roof, you can have only so many shouters participating in a market, and more participants is a good thing. Pretty soon technology solves this problem.

Hand signals and chalk-boards worked really well. Now hundreds of people could participate in the market. Of course, this made for more broken trades. Here we see how they resolved them back in those days: the buyer dresses up in a bull suit, the seller dresses like a bear, and they duke it out up front. This was before all those beeping tape machines recorded everything everybody said.

When you're indoors, you can also have dinners and parties to commemorate important events. Here we see two specialists celebrating the first bagging[1] of a buy-side trader.

So far, the technologies we're talking may sound rather low-tech: roofs, chalk, hands. Here's what a computer looked like in 1823, the Difference Engine, invented by the famously brilliant, eccentric, and obnoxious Charles Babbage:

Here's Babbage, who said, "I wish to God these calculations had been executed by steam."

Here's Babbage's government sponsor, Prime Minister Robert Peel, who said, "What shall we do to get rid of Mr. Babbage and his calculating machine?"

Babbage was stunningly smart, and even more stunningly insufferable. He lost his government funding, and the idea of automatic computing languished for many years. It was not used in financial markets or anywhere else in the nineteenth century. Babbage only built pieces of his machine; but when the Royal Museum in London put a whole one together from his designs a few years ago, it worked perfectly. The world could have been a very different place if Babbage had better manners. We'll pick up on him later.

SEMAPHORE FLAGS

F   L   A   G   S

Now we have our happy traders signaling each other with their hands, dancing, and dressing up in bear suits. This is all very nice, but there's a problem: the traders and brokers have to actually be present in person to participate in the market. How is this problem solved? With a little more technology, namely telegraphy. The earliest telegraphs weren't the electric variety we think of at all. They were guys standing on hills waving flags, like the ones used at sea.

There were lots of problems with the flag system. For one, it was hard to see a little guy way up on a hill. In most places, people starting building big mechanical guys like this one, with large wooden arms, and put them up on the hill instead.

There were a few variations on this theme, such as the smoke-and-fire telegraph tower, which had a problem with burning down in mid message . . .

...and the decoder-ring-on-a-stick design, which is kind of nice.

These towers are why so many cities have a place called "Telegraph Hill." Around the world, the builders and first users of these early telegraph systems were the military, for obvious reasons. The second users were traders disseminating market information. The third users typically were con men perpetrating financial frauds on the traders by sending out false signals or front-running the real ones. Nobody really liked this business with the flags and the mechanical arms. There were too many problems with privacy, bad weather, and darkness. It took about half an hour for a price change to work its way from New York to Philadelphia. Everyone knew an electric telegraph would be a better way.

Here's another British multiwire device with a battery and a saltwater receiver.

Remember how in high school chemistry lab if you put wires from a battery into saltwater, one of them bubbled? It was the same deal here. There was a ball for each letter, and you looked to see where the bubbles showed up.

Here's one that tried to use tones for letters. It's the first singing telegraph and made signals like the keyboard at the end of *Close Encounters of the Third Kind*.

There were some really marvelous early attempts. Here's an electrostatic model, with a wire for each letter and number, and a range from the living room to the parlor, powered by some fur rolling over a piece of rubber—sort of the rub-a-balloon-on-your-head approach.

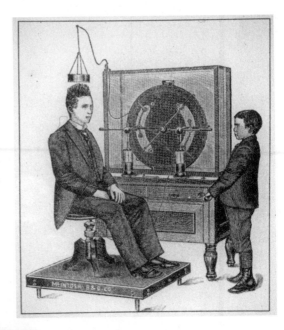

I have no idea how this one was supposed to work, but when they said "sell," you sold.

Julius Reuter and his son Herb decided to try another approach. They got into the messenger pigeon business.

Edward G. Robinson played Reuter in the 1941 classic film, *This Man Reuter.* The pigeons played themselves.

Finally, in 1837, Samuel Morse here got it right: a nice, simple, single wire and ground design.

This quickly caught on all over the world. Instantaneous Communication: The Wonder of the Age!

Notice here that "the electric fluid travels at the rate of 280,000 miles per second," or about one and a half times the speed of light. Maybe they knew something we don't.

You cannot underestimate the impact of telegraphy; it was truly the Internet of its era. For the first time in history, a message could be sent instantly over the horizon. An entire book could be filled with the stories of how all facets of human endeavor were transformed by telegraphy.[2]

Traders picked up on telegraphy in a big way. Here we see a broker in New York with his nineteenth-century BlackBerry, a telegraph key, cradled in his arm.

In its day, telegraphy was seen as the same kind of overwhelming transformation that the Internet is today. Telegraphy was a big advance, but to participate in the market as things were happening, the participant had to know Morse code.

The technological revolution of the 1850s needed more technology to allow people to cope with the dramatic changes in the information landscape. This time the technological advance was the invention of the stock ticker in 1867 by Edward Callahan.

The first models were a little too delicate for boisterous NYSE crowds. So Tom Edison was hired to buff the thing up to Wall Street combat standards.

Edison just kept dropping the ticker out of a second-floor window and fixing it when it broke until it didn't break anymore. Finally, he ended up with

this design, deemed suitable for even the most *muy macho* NYSE traders.

These are seen in all sorts of museums, Wall Street offices, and the occasional sidewalk sale in Queens. If you want one in a hurry, they can be had at the Museum of Financial History, adjacent to the bronze bull.

Ticker tape, like the roof, hand signals, and the telegraph, was a huge success, probably the most important technology in finance up to that time. People set up jumbo magnifying lens devices to project them onto walls. Back then, people traded faster than the machines could keep up with, so delay meters were installed on the floor. Delay indicators are still found on modern electronic feeds.

People saved tapes and studied them. You could say they were the first high-frequency market microstructure studies. Here's a fellow doing just that.

This looks like my office, but neater—a foreshock of the information explosion we have today.

On the floor, there were "human Quotrons" who used to pick up the most recent end of tape and follow it back in time to find the latest price quotes for specific stocks. This wasn't that long ago. Frank Baxter, former chairman at Jefferies and a recent U.S. ambassador to Uruguay, started out doing this.

All that ticker tape also made for nice parades. Here we see a group of specialists celebrating the one-millionth bagging of a buy-side trader.

THE ROARING TWENTIES

Technological progress brought bigger, better, faster ticker machines. The ticker tape became the public symbol for the market.

Ticker tape became standard practice for blowout parades, like this one for General Douglas MacArthur after President Harry Truman fired him from commanding the U.S. armed forces in Korea in 1951.

By the 1950s, the ticker and the exchange were so closely linked that the NYSE hired those noted market theorists, Kukla, Fran, and Ollie, to explain it to the public. I'm not making this up.

After more effort than I like to admit, I finally got a copy of what remains of the film. Believe me, this is the best part.

In one form or another, the ticker is still with us today—on the wall, or on the bottom of your TV screen.

Source: CNBC.

With the progress of technology, prodigious amounts of information can be quickly moved about. But all of this information moving around in a hurry can get pretty overwhelming. Telephones moved into exchanges alongside the ticker machines. This greatly expanded the capacity of the market to handle external order flow, and connected the exchanges to the public network. Some early adopters got carried away, as seen in the photo of a German trading room in the 1950s.

So far, the discussion has been about technologies for moving information around: hand signals, semaphores, telegraphy, stock tickers and telephones.

When we talk about using information, we're talking about computers. In the 1930s, if you said you had six computers in your office, this is what you meant—the NYSE computing department circa 1930:

"Computer" was a job, not a thing. If you said you had a supercomputer, this is what you meant.

At about this time, the technological legacy of Charles Babbage stirred again at the Moore School of Engineering in Philadelphia. ENIAC (short for electronic numerical integrator and calculator), the first electronic computer, was developed in 1946 by J. Presper Eckert and John Mauchly.

It weighed 30,000 pounds, had a 900–bit memory, ran at .017 MIPS (million instructions per second), and blew a tube every 45 minutes. It was programmed by someone moving these plugs and wires around. You may have seen Al Gore on TV down there in 1996 to celebrate the 50th anniversary. He pressed one of these buttons and parts the Moore

School haven't passed out to museums counted from 46 to 96. (There is no truth to the rumor that Al Gore invented ENIAC when he was minus two years old.)

Computers got a little better in the early 1950s (more memory and longer times between failures). But a battalion of nerds were still needed to get the things to do anything useful twice in a row.

This modest-looking little science project is what unleashed the torrent of computation we see all around us today.

It's the very first transistor, developed at Bell Labs in 1948 by Walter Brattain, William Shockley, and John Bardeen. They were awarded a Nobel Prize for it in 1956, around the time transistors started being manufactured in quantities large enough to show up in things like radios and, a few years later, computers.

Computers became much more manageable. One could fit in a room smaller than a barn. It might work for a whole week without breaking down. It had enough memory that a programmer didn't have to move wires or think in binary to program it. And, most important, the sales-person had a picture to show that it came in the latest designer colors.

The NYSE had to have one. In 1966, they got it.

And there he is, the first nerd on Wall Street: Keith Funston, then president of the NYSE. Nerds were much snappier dressers then.

Computers keep getting better, faster, smaller, and cheaper. They're everywhere in trading. Traders can interact directly with algorithms using the NYSE handheld.

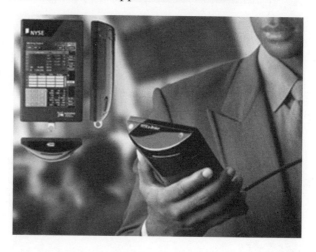

Computers have surpassed even telegraphy and ticker tape as a transformational market technology. The progress we've seen in computing technology that brought this about is really unprecedented. The rapid technology trajectories forecast by the laws of Moore and Metcalfe continue unabated.*

Electronic markets started back when the Internet was a gleam in someone's eye at the Defense Advanced Research Projects Agency (DARPA). Now the future of electronic finance is profoundly intertwined with the World Wide Web, removing intermediaries in services ranging from trading to research. A lot of people think the three great technological ideas in history are fire, the wheel, and storing instructions as data. Based on the first 15 or so years of widespread use of the Internet, we might add the URL to the list.

Copyright 1999 by The McGraw-Hill Companies.

All this innovation is what has brought us to where we are today, wired markets in a wired world—a global financial system made of bits.[3] We have more Britney and Paris than we know what to do with, as well as some serious questions about how the investment business is going to cope with markets and market information in cyberspace.

Everything connects to everything else, if you want it to, and sometimes when you don't. Information goes wherever you want. There's more to this than just moving information around. Managing assets in a world of fragmented electronic markets requires enormous quantitative and technological expertise. Computer programs increasingly take over tasks from people, and allow people to amplify their abilities using machines. The "digerati" (a hybrid of *digital* and *literati*) would call this *artificial intelligence* (AI) and *intelligence amplification* (IA).

---

* Moore's Law is the well-known doubling of computational power every 18 months. Metcalfe's Law is the less well-known maxim that the utility of a network grows as the square of the number of users.

Ray Kurzweil, one of the great inventors of our age, built a reading machine for the blind in 1976 and then started a musical instrument company with help from one of his customers, Stevie Wonder. Kurzweil created the market for modern electronic keyboards, and has continued to innovate and articulate the growing capabilities of computing. The titles of his books trace an arc of future progress—*The Age of Intelligent Machines* (1992), *The Age of Spiritual Machines: When Computers Exceed Human Intelligence* (2000), and *The Singularity Is Near: When Humans Transcend Biology* (2005).

The technical literature on AI is utterly dwarfed by the sci-fi examples. From the evil HAL 9000 of *2001: A Space Odyssey* to the snappy patter between *Star Wars* droids R2D2 and C3PO, it's easy to miss the real thing. If you think AI is just cute, squeaky guys you find in the movies, ask World Chess Champion Garry Kasparov what he thinks. Deep Blue, the IBM computer, achieved one of the longtime goals of artificial intelligence in 1997 by defeating Kasparov. There are different opinions about whether Deep Blue is an AI program. Kasparov says yes:

> People in future generations would look back and say this was the moment when for the first time a machine was superior to all human beings in a purely intellectual field. . . .
>
> The match draws attention to very important questions that will confront us in many different areas in the not-so-distant future. Deep Blue shows us that machines can use very different strategies from those of the human brain and still produce intelligent behaviors.
>
> If you watch the machine play—and especially when you play against it—it is very difficult not to think of it as being intelligent. Man will have to accept that using the specific faculties of the human brain is not the only way to solve intellectual problems. . . .
>
> Often you get the feeling that the computer is trying to trick you, that it is "enjoying" the position, or even that it is laughing at you. Of course it is not, it is just processing billions of numbers. But its prodigious calculations translate into a behavior that is very hard to distinguish from the activities of a human chess master.[4]

Remarkably, the developers of Deep Blue disagree. It's not AI, it's just specialized search, say Deep Blue's makers. System architect Feng-Hsiung Hsu writes: "It is only a finely-crafted tool that exhibits *intelligent* behavior in a limited domain."[5] A key point here is that it is getting hard to distinguish between simple computation and intelligent behavior. When you can do enough simple computation, remarkable things can happen. MIT recently merged its Artificial Intelligence Laboratory and Computer Science Laboratory, reflecting this merger of ideas.

Along the path from hand signals to Deep Blue and the World Wide Web, we've seen some remarkable market applications of technology. This isn't going to stop. We've come a long way since the traders moved from under the buttonwood tree into the Tontine Coffee House, but we've really just moved indoors in our use of information technologies. There is so much written about information overload that we have an information overload information overload. But as we have seen, technological patterns repeat.

Living through a technology revolution isn't easy. We aren't exactly trapped in the cogs like Charlie Chaplin in *Modern Times*, or racing steam-powered Victorian dune buggies, but it often feels that way.

The good news is that one pattern we can expect again is that clever nerds on Wall Street (extending now into India and beyond) will find clever ways to get us off our current information cogs, and even more clever ways to put us on new ones.

Notes

1. Jargon watch: Brokers are the "sell side," while investors are the "buy side." What they buy is execution services. This includes selling securities as well as buying them. "Bagging" refers to any economic screwing of the customer. Specialists were the central traders on the NYSE, and could easily use any number of shady tactics to their advantage at the expense of the customer (e.g., selling out their inventory to a customer while holding a large sell order at a better price in their pocket). Specialists and market makers have been essentially replaced by computers, first by the fast hedge funds exploiting new "maker and taker" markets. In 2008, the NYSE retired the "specialist" term itself, replacing it with "designated market maker."

2. An excellent book comparing the development of the telegraph with the modern Internet is *The Victorian Internet* by Tom Standage (New York: Berkley Classics, 1999).

3. As is almost everything else. See *Blown to Bits: Your Life, Liberty and Happiness after the Digital Explosion* by Hal Abelson, Ken Leeden, and Harry Lewis (Boston: Addison-Wesley, 2008).

4. Garry Kasparov, "An Interview with Garry Kasparov," *IBM Research: Deep Blue*, www.research.ibm.com/deepblue/meet/html/d.1.6.shtml.

5. Feng-Hsiung Hsu, *Behind Deep Blue* (Princeton, NJ: Princeton University Press, 2004).

market
information
Electronic
trading
Figure
Web
Technology
language
Many
computer
data
Source
markets
systems
Wall
financial
quantitative
strategies
Automated
future
using
see
like
traders
firms
example
Street
world
Research
one
new
news
SEC
use
simple
way
Deep
Show
seen
wide
system
good
back
Search
Years
ideas
called
computerized
FINANCE
CHAPTER
Now
filings
Business
Management
visualization
content
people
areas
AI
just
used
tools
technological
top
investors
without
later
first
looking
Portfolio
well
may
firm
relevant
find
stories
models
idea
even
also
early
look
time
transparency
XML
access
number
orders
companies
made
Internet
investment
Words
useful
trade
real

Chapter 2

Greatest Hits of Computation in Finance

*A computer does not substitute for
judgment any more than a pencil
substitutes for literacy. But writing without
a pencil is no particular advantage.*

—Robert McNamara

The *Journal of Portfolio Management* (JPM)* is one of the more upscale investment management publications around. For $500 a year, you get four issues, nicely bound like oversize paperbacks, without any advertising. It's a crossover between rigorous academic publications, like the *Journal of Finance*, and trade magazines, like *Wall Street & Technology*, that have shorter staff-written articles and lots of ads. On significant anniversaries, *JPM* assembles special issues with invited pieces from both academics and practitioners on relevant topics.

JPM did this for the thirtieth anniversary issue in 2004. Some touched on the changes brought about in investment management by computation and where we can expect significant progress in the future,

---

* An earlier version of this article appeared in the Fall 2005 issue of the *Journal of Portfolio Management* ("If You Had Everything Computationally, Where Would You Put It Financially? Thirty Years of Computation in Finance"). It is reprinted with permission.

but only one was explicitly about technology in finance.[1] The editor invited me to expand on this topic for an upcoming issue. This chapter is based on that article.

It is illuminating to look back on past technological breakthroughs of the century to see which ideas have proven valuable, which have slipped into the zone of "further study," and which will get you into trouble if mentioned in the polite company of financial professionals. I write this as a long-term self-confessed nerd on Wall Street, having witnessed a number of technological charges up various hills and a slightly smaller number of retreats back down.

Many of the greatest hits in this chapter existed in some form for a long time but were impractical because the roomful of mainframes needed for them was so large and expensive. The small number of people and firms with the resources to do these limited the market incentives for them to grow and succeed. Two basic technological laws, which are really more like notions on their way to concepts, are Moore's and Metcalfe's laws. Moore's law is the well-known doubling of computational power every 18 months. Metcalfe's law is the less well-known maxim that the utility of a network grows as the square of the number of users.[2] These are as close as we come to laws of nature for technology. The magnitude of the progress as we move out to the further reaches of Moore and Metcalfe space can't be overstated. There's more computational power on your desk than existed in the world 30 or 40 years ago. This may even be true for your wristwatch if you have a sufficiently fancy model.

There is no need to belabor the analogies about computer progress compared to automobiles and airplanes.[3] A novel way of looking at what we have at our disposal for technological innovation in finance is provided by Hans Moravec of the Carnegie Mellon Robotics Institute and author of *Mind Children: The Future of Human and Robot Intelligence*. He compares artificial and natural "computing machines" by storage capacity and processing speed. The book includes a remarkable chart that shows by his scoring that Deep Blue, the IBM machine that beat world champion Garry Kasparov, is edging up to the monkey zone on the evolutionary ladder. The ordinary machines used for more conventional tasks (like portfolio optimization) are comparable to insect brains.[4]

Financial Technology Stars

There are some clear nominees for the Financial Technology Hall of Fame, which have brought widespread, nearly universal, changes in the way people view and participate in markets. Topping my list are the following:

- Electronic market access
- Market data graphics
- Spreadsheets
- Databases and Internet information

For quantitative investors, I would add portfolio optimization despite the barriers to wider acceptance of this technology such as sensitivity to errors and unintuitive results (unless they are constrained).

Electronic Market Access

Thirty years ago, the Designated Order Turnaround (DOT) and NASDAQ electronic systems were concepts on their way to notions. A so-called program trade literally involved wheelbarrows of paper trade tickets physically distributed to floor traders.

Today, trading floors from London to Tokyo have been replaced by machinery. Purely electronic markets, the electronic communication networks (ECNs), have come from nowhere to claim a significant portion of volume. Increasingly, the discussion of the future of exchanges is a discussion of technology. The August 16, 1999, cover of the *Industry Standard*, an information technology trade magazine, proclaimed "Stock Exchanges: RIP." The photogenic trading floors, such the one at the New York Stock Exchange (Figure 2.1), are being closed, downsized, and relegated to use as media backdrops for financial reporters around the world.

The ongoing refinement of the techniques of electronic market access has also been one of the stealth success stories of the past decades and, as will be discussed throughout this book, is a likely prospect for future innovation.

Figure 2.1   Physical trading floors like the one at the New York Stock Exchange are an endangered species.

Market Data Graphics

Throughout the early 1980s, market data terminals—almost all called Quotrons irrespective of their corporate origins—looked like computer screens. However, they were really keyboard-controlled cable television. They provided a picture of the data, the last trade, and the quote. It was the same information one would find by grabbing the end of a paper ticker tape and running it back to find the newest information for the stock of interest. This was literally what people did for a long time to get current quotes.

With the advent of true machine-readable market data—the text frontier—it was not long before these basic, simple text "pictures of

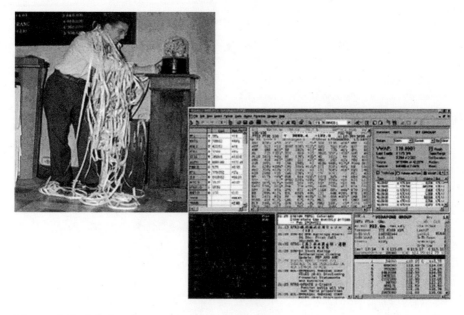

Figure 2.2 Market data systems: then and now.
Courtesy of New York Stock Exchange and Thomson Reuters.

data" were replaced by screens with an increasing variety of market charts showing both common and customized analytics. The tedious work once performed by analysts with pencils, calculators, and rulers essentially disappeared. (See Figure 2.2.)

When we consider the advances in graphic technology and scientific visualization tools in other fields, it is actually surprising that the systems in wide use today remain as simple as they are, showing tables and two-dimensional minimally interactive charts. This perhaps proves the difficulty of doing abstract visualization well. It is also a clue to where we may expect significant progress in the future (more on this later).

Spreadsheets

In the mid-1970s Bob Franston and Dan Bricklin, students at MIT and later Harvard Business School, could have been cast for parts in *Revenge of the Nerds*. I was at the MIT Artificial Intelligence (AI) Laboratory around this time, and I recall that one of them had developed a habit of ending sentences by saying "<semicolon><linefeed><carriage return>." They were smart nerds, however, working on an interesting problem: Could a nontechnical person teach a computer to write a program by showing it an example?

This was a real problem. Getting a computer to do anything useful requires jumping though many software hoops: compilers, loaders, linkers, debuggers, and the like. Franston and Bricklin had the excellent idea of first restricting the problem to the domain of two-dimensional tables and then using a light pen (grandfather of a mouse) to lay out the grid and the relationships on a then-rare cathode-ray terminal (CRT) rather than reading their results on a roll of paper. After many iterations, they came up with a system that they called *visual programming*. When it ran on million-dollar mainframe PDP-10s, it was a clever idea. When it moved over to the Apple II, it was called Visicalc. One of the first copies went to legendary venture investor Ben Rosen, then an analyst at Morgan Stanley. It is now on display in the Computer Museum in Boston.

Visicalc was supplanted by Lotus 1-2-3, and made the transition to personal computers running Microsoft DOS and then the Windows operating system. Visicalc, Lotus 1-2-3, and their dominant successor Microsoft Excel revolutionized Wall Street and the rest of global business. (See Figure 2.3.)

Figure 2.3 Spreadsheets made everyone a programmer. Visicalc, Lotus, and Excel were the lingua franca for quantitative financial information used by investors of nearly all persuasions.

Databases, the Internet, and the World Wide Web

No list of breakthroughs of the twenty-first century would be complete without databases. Before the Internet enjoyed such wide use, private databases such as Compustat saw use only among technically adept investors. Now these and thousands of additional sources are accessible to all on the Web, which is yet another example of the migration of complex technology from its early adopters to general use.

We often think of the Web and the Internet as the same thing. However, the Internet is more than the Web; it is the technology that has expanded and transformed markets by making computer communication as simple as turning on the lights. Credit for the development of the World Wide Web goes to Tim Berners-Lee, then at CERN (European Organization for Nuclear Research) and now at the World Wide Web Consortium at MIT (www.w3c.org), which is the mother lode for information on new Web technologies. The original Internet started out as the ARPANET, developed by DARPA (www.darpa.mil).

Many readers will recall the complexity and flashing red lights of the modems, and the effort to master the cryptic rites to connect to other machines. All of that is gone. Internet protocols, from the simplest connection layers through e-mail and the Web, have leveled all but deliberate barriers—and many of those as well. No aspect of financial life is untouched: research, risk management, trading, and investor communication.

We are much more adept at using structured and quantitative information on the Internet than textual and qualitative information. We are just starting to learn how to effectively use this kind of information. This area is driven by new Internet technologies such as XML (extensible markup language) and RSS (an XML dialect) and by advances in natural language processing. The new kid on the block, expected to take these ideas to new levels, is the Resource Description Framework (RDF), promoted by Web inventor Berners-Lee. RDF does for relationships between tagged data elements what the XML tagging itself did for moving from format HTML tags like "Bold" to meaningful XML tags like "Price."

Hits and Misses: Rational and Irrational Technology Exuberance

Peter Bernstein's book *Capital Ideas* (Free Press, 1993) tells the story of Bill Sharpe, who wandered Wall Street looking for enough computer time to run a simple capital asset pricing model (CAPM) portfolio optimization, while being regarded as something of a crackpot for doing so. Now these computations are routine, though not without problems arising from sensitivity to errors and noise. (These problems, in turn, are being addressed by still more computation, using resampling and other computer-intensive methods.) Yesterday's crackpot, of course, has become today's visionary Nobel laureate, as proven by the sheer rise in calculating power. It is instructive to look back at technological ideas in finance that have succeeded, some spectacularly so, and those that have been marginalized. This approach avoids the onerous task of actually predicting what will work in the future.

Some crackpots are just crackpots. The past 30 years have also seen their share of wacky ideas that remain wacky. In the 1980s, expert systems had produced some impressive results in diagnosing diseases, designing networks, and running factories. Business magazines called each one "the breakthrough of the century." Of course, Wall Street wanted in, thinking that thinking machines would do all of the thinking! A cover of *Wall Street Computer Review* magazine illustrated an extreme example of this expectation. It had Socrates standing on the steps of the NYSE surrounded by CRTs and captioned "Teaching Computers to Emulate Great Thinkers." Another cover featured a wired-up Rodin *Thinker* captioned "Knowledge-Based Systems: Computers That Think Like Pros." (See Figure 2.4.)

Things didn't work out as expected. One year's breakthrough of the century turned into next year's R&D write-off. Expert systems were useful, but not in the grand conceptual way some early boosters foresaw. These ultra-high-concept notions of building robotic market wizards were (and remain) overly ambitious. Strong believers in efficient markets might maintain that the market wizards were just lucky in the first place, even if they were using a set of rules that could be emulated by these technologies. Expert systems were not a fundamentally flawed idea. They worked by chaining sets of if-then rules, and there were many successes. But there were also many overblown promises.

Figure 2.4   Overly exuberant *Wall Street Computer Review* covers.
Source: Wall Street Computer Review *(now* Wall Street & Technology*), June 1987 and June 1990.*

Figure 2.5   The AI industry apologizes to the world, sort of. *Source: Published with permission from Parallel Simulation Technology, LLC. All rights reserved.*

Marvin Minsky, MIT's AI übermaven, declared an "AI winter" at the major AI conference of 1987. It got so bad that one AI vendor used the image in Figure 2.5 at the same venue.

I don't mean to pick on expert systems or any particular technology here. Neural nets, wavelets, chaos, genetic algorithms, fuzzy logic, and any number of others could be tarred with the same brush used here (though without the charming illustrations). Nor do I mean to imply that these ideas are utterly without merit. Many of them do fall into the category of being too easy to abuse, becoming dangerous power tools for self deception with excessive data mining. And simpler applications, managing aggregates of increasingly complex market data systems, did prove successful (as discussed in Chapter 7, "A Little AI Goes a Long Way on Wall Street").

There is good reason for pursuing these approaches. Steve Snider, who manages multibillion-dollar institutional portfolios at Fidelity, makes the point that "classical methods of data analysis assume that there is a stable process generating the data, so it is valid to attempt to deduce the underlying process from a selection of known observations. These new techniques don't require that assumption, so they may be useful in especially noisy systems like stock forecasting."[5]

That said, the dangers of rampant data mining using many of these approaches cannot be overemphasized (see Chapter 6, "Stupid Data Miner Tricks"). Emanuel Derman, former head of quantitative strategies at Goldman Sachs, described this over eagerness to blindly apply quantitative and computerized methods:

> The best quantitative finance brings real insight into the relation between value and uncertainty, and it approaches the quality of real science; the worst is a pseudoscientific hodgepodge of complex mathematics used with obscure justification.[6]

The Crackpot as Billionaire

Not everyone who decides to burn CPU cycles on Wall Street ends up writing about lessons learned. There are more than a few examples of computer scientists and economists with a gleam in their eye who publish that last technical paper and then surface some years later at the top of the hedge fund rankings running a firm and employing more programmers and Ph.D.'s than a medium-sized university.

This illustrious and distinguished group includes David Shaw, once a professor in the Columbia University computer science department. After a stint at Morgan Stanley's Automated Trading Group, he started D.E. Shaw & Company in 1988 with $28 million (it now has current assets exceeding $30 billion).[7] What is likely Shaw's last publication on trading dealt with the mechanics of interfacing Unix systems with the

current generation of electronic trading systems. He apparently realized that, despite his instincts as a former academic, some things are
more valuable unpublished. Subsequent in-house developments made
D.E. Shaw a leader (reportedly) in electronic market making, statistical
arbitrage, and other fast electronic trading strategies.

David Whitcomb, a market microstructure economist at Rutgers
University and coauthor of a 1988 book on electronic trading strategies,[8]
faced the same sort of skepticism selling his ideas to Wall Street. Finding
no institutional backing, he joined forces with a computer scientist colleague to found Automated Trading Desk (ATD) in the proverbial garage
in Charleston, South Carolina. The firm reportedly grew from its first
trade in 1990 to one of the leading electronic market participants, trading on average more than 200 million shares daily, or 6 percent of the
volume on both the New York Stock Exchange and NASDAQ.[9]

Figure 2.6 shows the core idea behind ATD's early trading systems.
In a nutshell, the firm exploited the ability of fast machine-driven trading to find hidden liquidity, enabling it to provide better than expected
(e.g., volume-weighted average price) executions for clients, and to
profit from these better executions in the same way a traditional capital
commitment broker can profit by using stock in inventory to fill client
orders at favorable prices.

A dynamic array of limit orders "probes the market" and finds
liquidity *not* visible in the best bid and offer information in the quotes.
When spreads were larger, this could be a very lucrative activity. The
move to sixteenths, and later to decimals, has doubtless made these
activities more challenging.

What was a niche business open to technological innovators in the
1990s is becoming more accessible with the availability of off-the-shelf
electronic market access systems from a growing number of mainstream
brokers. The increasing transparency of the new national market system,
with ECNs competing with the exchanges, and the various initiatives
to make more of the "combined book" visible lessens the information
advantage to participants that infer it using advanced technology.

None of these firms are particularly forthcoming. Almost all of
what there is to read from D.E. Shaw about the firm, for example, is
found at www.deshaw.com. Shaw himself, in a 1990s interview with
Wall Street & Technology, answered a question about the firm's use of
neural nets by joking, "I would tell you, but then I'd have to kill you."

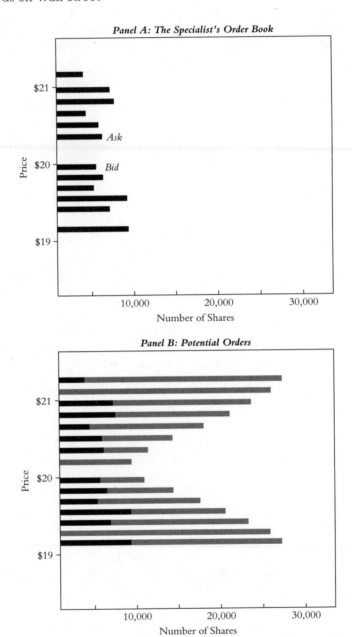

Figure 2.6 Example of a liquidity-providing array of limit orders: Automated Trading Desk (ATD). Computers at ATD and elsewhere got so good at this, that there are no more specialists.
Source: Robert Schwartz and David Whitcomb, Transaction Costs and Institutional Investor Trading Strategies, *Monograph 1988-23 (New York: New York University Stern School of Business, 1988).*

No foul play occurred and the interviewer remains healthy. The firm's 20-year record of consistent positive performance (alpha) led in 2007 to the sale of a 20 percent stake to Lehman Brothers for a sum reported to be in the billions. Perhaps the most secretive, and most successful, of these high-technology firms is Renaissance Technologies, founded by Jim Simons, former head of the mathematics department at Stony Brook University.

How these firms have achieved their success is not something you read in the library or on the Web. Company web sites are short and cryptic. Renaissance Technologies, for example, has removed almost everything except the address from its site, www.rentec.com. However, we can tell by its appearance at the top of electronic trade volume lists that Renaissance is keeping its machinery very active in the market. Using the Internet Archive's Wayback Machine,[10] a digital time capsule named after Mr. Peabody's *Rocky and Bullwinkle Show* time travel machine, we can see what Renaissance and other companies were saying when they were more forthcoming with information.

The picture that emerges is actually not all that surprising. The technologically innovative firms describe increasingly sophisticated trading strategies. They show expansion into ever more markets. Recruiting information and old press releases show a staff of Ph.D.'s drawn largely from areas outside finance: Computer science, AI, mathematics, and physics are popular. More surprising is the presence of computational linguists, people whose expertise lies in the area of textual, qualitative information.

With these clues, we can move on to areas where technology will be more important to the broader investment community in the future.

Future Technological Stars

As Niels Bohr stated: "Prediction is very difficult, especially about the future." Nevertheless, I will venture to describe the technological areas that are important to investors and traders:

- *Advanced electronic market tools.* All investors trade on their own or through brokers. More than half of all trading is now automated, much more for U.S. stocks. As markets become more transparent and electronic, the growth of algorithmic trading will become more important to both buy- and sell-side traders. Off-the-shelf algo strategies are widely used today, and more sophisticated strategies are used by technology leaders. As seen in many other contexts, the complex versions will become more accessible in the future.

- *Understanding both quantitative and qualitative information.* Investment decisions are made based on a mix of information, which includes numerical, graphical, and textual material. Essential precursors to understanding are collection, extraction, aggregation, and categorization. These are useful in both automated and semi-automated settings for different investing styles. Search engines and other language-based tools will progress dramatically, with specialized systems to extract relevant portions, combine them, and categorize information from text.

The following sections discuss these topics in more depth.

Dominance of Electronic Trading

It is very likely that in the near future we might read something like an obituary for the stock exchange floor as we know it. In developed markets, virtually all orders are delivered to the point of sale electronically. Nearly all of these orders are executed electronically, and all are cleared electronically.[11]

Brokers look wistfully back at 25-cent fixed commissions (abandoned in 1976) that have dropped to tenths of a cent. Most of the investment managers paying these commissions are using direct electronic market access. The innovators described in the previous section have been using electronic trading as a source of profit; most civilian users use them as a means of execution.

The overwhelming majority of these executions look to transact at the volume-weighted average price (VWAP). This goal of average performance can be thought of as the indexing of the trading world. At the same time, very sophisticated and very fast computerized traders represent a growing share of the growing electronic execution volume. Many of these firms are considered extraordinary money managers. They are making profits, in many small increments, but allowing others to take their offered liquidity to achieve VWAP.

What is it that the seemingly chosen few are seeing and exploiting that evades the many? One clue to learning this skill comes in conversations with electronic traders stymied by human-speed perception in a market where limit orders arrive and are canceled in milliseconds. Just staying away from a buzzing stream of limit orders, or getting on the right side of it, is a good idea. But no current trading system is adept at measuring, displaying, and using this information.

Computational progress has made higher goals, profitable trading, and faster strategies accessible to more and more investors. Furthermore, the changes being made in the national market system which expose the depth of orders within and across market segments, provide more raw information material to drive those strategies.

In real financial markets, we have experience only with the less than full degree of transparency that has existed in the past.

Dynamic Market Visualization

Applying scientific visualization techniques in areas that map directly to physical phenomena has become standard in meteorology, protein manipulation, medical imaging, and hundreds of other areas. The full electronic equity market doesn't have such a neat physical representation to translate graphically.[12] But the NYSE does and it has set up a Web graphic called *MarkeTrac*, as shown in Figure 2.7. It is more of

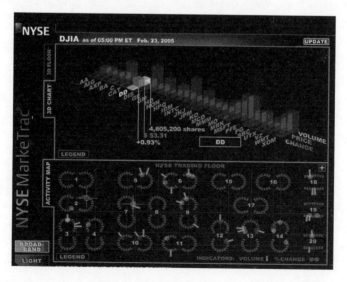

Figure 2.7   Part of the New York Stock Exchange's MarkeTrac display. It moves, go try it on the web.
Source: NYSE Euronext, http://marketrac.nyse.com.

an Internet-style World's Fair display. As with all of these examples, still pictures are what you see, but the dynamic updates and many views in the real things have to be experienced to be fully appreciated.

Map of the Market

Ben Schneiderman, the godfather of the graphical user interface (GUI), founded the University of Maryland Human-Computer Interaction Lab (HCIL)[13] in 1982. His influence, along with that of Edward Tufte, is seen in many of the best examples of the modern human-computer interface.

SmartMoney.com's Map of the Market is an example of a tree map. This technique was first developed at HCIL to show the complexities of storage layouts on ever-larger hard drives.[14] It is also one of those "gotta be there" items that benefit greatly from their interactivity and color. It summarizes price moves by sector, as shown in Figure 2.8.

At a glance, you can see, for example, that at the time of this snapshot, the health care sector is up and basic materials are down. Rolling over the individual tiles in the display shows Schneiderman's mantra, "overview first, drill down to details," in action. Moving to the single

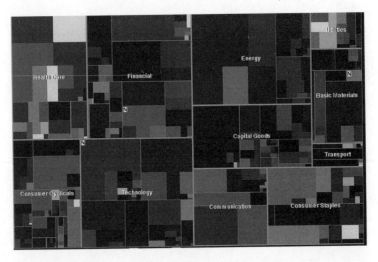

Figure 2.8   Map of the Market: Price moves and other data are shown for all firms in shades of red and green. Another one to try for yourself. This is like looking at a picture of an ice cream sundae.
Source: SmartMoney, *www.smartmoney.com/marketmap.*

health care stock that is down on this day (January 7, 2008) pops up even more information. Figure 2.9 illustrates this is in a static black-and-white way, but you have to try the real thing to appreciate this.

Innovative Abstract Visualizations

Experimental markets are a remarkable laboratory technique that allows investigation of markets that would not be possible by observing real financial markets from a distance. Vernon Smith shared the 2002 Nobel Prize in economics for pioneering experimental economics.[15] Vernon is also the hands-down winner of the "Nobel laureate who looks most like Willie Nelson" award.

Smith's colleagues can create (and have created) markets that have any degree of transparency they want. They have created automated and semi-automated systems that may give us insight into how we will approach markets technologically in the future. Charles Plott, Smith's sometime collaborator at Caltech's Experimental Economics Laboratory, has developed a novel visualization that allows participants to look deeply into the workings of the market. His invention, called Jaws, can be seen in living color and full animation at http://eeps.caltech.edu/mov/jaws.html.

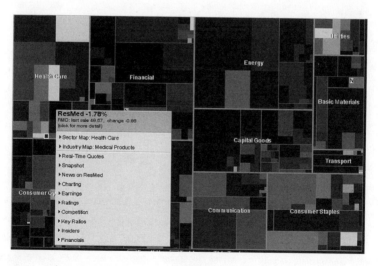

Figure 2.9   Map of the Market: individual stock pop-up. This is like looking at the picture of the whipped cream and cherry on top.
Source: SmartMoney, *www.smartmoney.com/marketmap.*

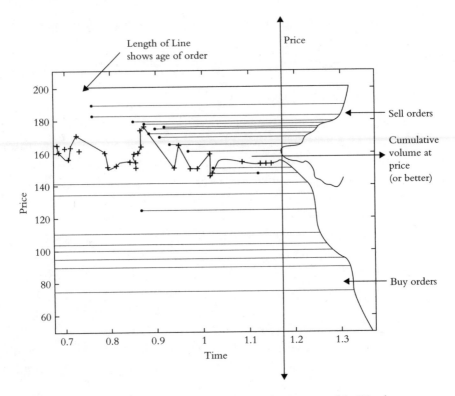

Figure 2.10 Representation of the market in the Jaws graphic. Watch the movie.
Source: Charles Plott, California Institute of Technology.

It really gives you a sense of what dynamic displays can bring to a table. The basic idea is shown in Figure 2.10.

The real news is what you see when you run the movies (conveyed, to the extent possible in a still frame, as shown in Figure 2.11). Traders in this artificial market seem to have the ability to predict future prices by examining the market's current state.

People can do this, and so can machines. Other researchers, at MIT and IBM laboratories, have created automated systems using this type of information that can outperform human traders participating in the same markets. At least one of these researchers has now started a fast-trading hedge fund. Blake LeBaron has been "breeding" intelligent trading agents at Brandeis University for some time, and they often exhibit remarkable behavior. He uses techniques from evolutionary computation, similar in spirit to those described in Chapter 8.

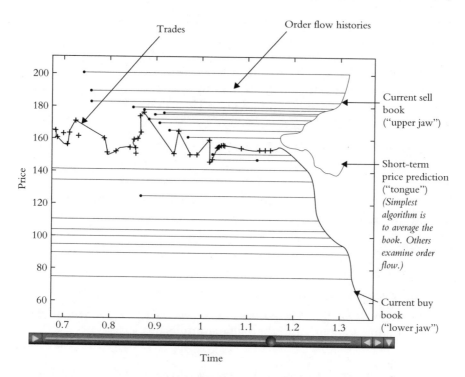

Figure 2.11 Short-term price prediction from order flow and book data: Jaws.
It really is impressive how the "tongue" moves around in response to buy/sell
imbalance and predicts short term price changes.
Source: Charles Plott, California Institute of Technology.

Visualization of markets and increasing sophistication of algorithmic
trading can allow traders to apply their expertise in these venues, beyond
looking for VWAP executions. In conversations with algorithmic traders
and the providers of the systems that they use, it becomes apparent that
there are far more strategies available than people use. Yet we see from
some of the fastest, most adept trading firms that there can be substantial
benefit to using them. Part of the reason these have been adopted slowly
by general traders is that traders have an insufficient view of the market
to decide when and how to use them, and how to automate this process
so that they can handle a realistic number of orders simultaneously.

With the greater transparency in the new national market system
there is more to see for traders, but with the half-life of limit orders
now measured in seconds, they lack the tools to see and understand the
information available to them. Jaws is an academic example of innovative views of a market.

High Information Bandwidth Market Visualization

Seeing the market in the relevant dimensions is a necessary first step to trading effectively, and to intelligent automation of algorithmic trading beyond one-size-fits-all strategies. Figure 2.12 is a current example of a high-end viewer. This snapshot provides a dynamic view of a market with limit order book transparency from Oculus Info's Visible Marketplace. (An animated version can be seen at www.oculusinfo.com.) Layers on the book show grouped sizes at each price. Custom versions overlay a variety of analytics calculated in real time.

As with all of these graphics, the dynamics and drill-down-to-details ability are interactive aspects of two-way graphics that don't translate to the printed page. The experience of looking at pictures as opposed to using them is like looking at *Bon Appétit* versus actually tasting its photogenic chow. Seeing and measuring the market in the relevant dimensions is a necessary first step to trading effectively. It is a key element in an intelligence amplification (IA) relationship between human trading captains and their algorithmic lackeys.

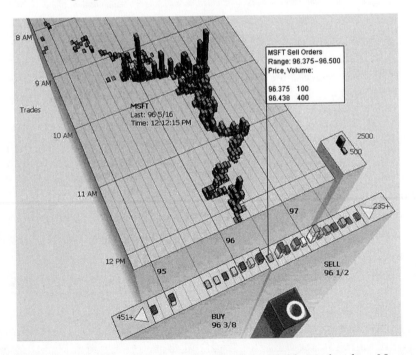

Figure 2.12 Dynamic market view: Oculus Info's Visible Marketplace. Not very dynamic on paper. Another reason to be glad you have a web browser.
Courtesy of Oculus Info Inc. © 2001 Oculus Info Inc. All rights reserved.

Successful investors and traders produce value by superior access to and analysis of both quantitative and nonquantitative information. The occasional shot of blind dumb luck is helpful, too, but nothing you can rely on. Firms that get a firm grip on the tools for exploiting information will build a better business than those that don't. This has been true for a long time. In 1789, bonds that had funded the American Revolutionary War were trading for very little in the expectation that the government would default on them. George Washington decided it would be a poor start for a new country to default on its debt, so the Funding Act of 1790 guaranteed all debts of the nation and the states. He dispatched messengers from New York to sail the coast and spread the word. New Yorkers, who have changed little in 200 years, saddled up the fastest horses they could find and set out to front-run the messengers, in order to buy up the suddenly valuable bonds from owners who were happy to see a nickel on the dollar.

Being first in line for information has always been a good place to be, and it isn't necessary to do anything vaguely shady to get there. What it does require, in a world that becomes more wired by the day, is an ability to gather and exploit information from electronic sources.

Mining the Deep Web

Popular search engines such as Google index over three billion web pages, but that is just the tip of the information iceberg. Much, if not most, of the information relevant to investment decisions is in the *deep Web*, below the levels that are scanned by these one-size-fits-all search tools. The deep Web includes information in databases, like the U.S. Security and Exchange Commission (SEC)'s Electronic Data Gathering, Analysis, and Retrieval (EDGAR) system, as well as other content that requires a query or login to access. No one really knows just how big the deep Web is, but estimates range from 500 to 1,000 times larger than the surface Web.[16]

It's easy to do a simple experiment to convince yourself. Type the name of any public company into a search engine. You'll find thousands of links, but nothing pointing you to the SEC, even though the SEC has thousands of investment-relevant pieces of information about every public company. The same thing is true for legal actions, regulatory decisions, and specialized research and news. The reason for this is that search engines just don't look in the deep Web. They send out Web crawler programs, appropriately called "spiders," that retrieve the information you see in your search results. The spiders typically look at home pages, as well as links off home pages. They never login to proprietary sites, or make queries to databases hosted on the Web. They don't aggregate, compare, or combine data in ways that make it useful for investors.

Lessons from the Wise Man in the Securities and Exchange Commission Reading Room

I learned a bit about this kind of aggregation from a prosperous retired investor. He used to spend much of his time in the SEC reading room, looking for signs of corporate trouble, and getting rich by going short when he found them.

So what did this sage gent look for back in the SEC reading room, when there was an SEC reading room? "A barrage of BS," he explained semipolitely. "Firms are only obligated to file a relatively few documents with the SEC: 10-Ks, 10-Qs, proxy statements, and insider trading reports. When they start filling up the shelves, it means that the lawyers are nervous, or that something unusual is going on, especially when there are all sorts of revisions and amendments."

I decided to see how his theory worked out for Enron, the modern-day poster child for corporate BS. With a little additional tutoring, I learned that I should be looking for filings from Enron, and from related entities. Armed with this lesson, I dove into the deep Web at www.sec.gov and retrieved the gruesome details, turning up 576 filings from 18 filers. But was this anything unusual? For comparison purposes, I did the same thing for the other top 10 companies in Enron's Standard Industrial Classification (SIC) code (Wholesale Petroleum, 5172). Figure 2.13 illustrates the eye-opening result.

This kind aggregation and comparison is admittedly pretty simple, but it's nothing that you can do with a search engine. The process can be automated, using specialized Web spiders designed for this task, and it likely has been.

This example illustrates a modern investment application of one of the oldest forms of electronic surveillance: *traffic analysis*. It goes as far back as World War I, when battlefield commanders monitored

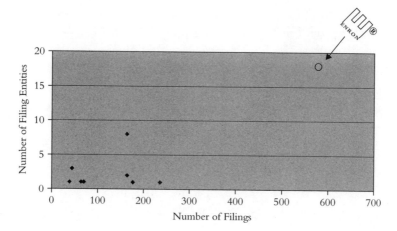

Figure 2.13   Securities and Exchange Commission electronic filings and filers, Wholesale Petroleum sector, 1993–2002. A barrage of BS.
Source: Data is from the Securities and Exchange Commission. Figure is by David Leinweber and Jacob Sisk.

traffic on the other side's radio frequencies to see when the other side was getting busy, even though they often didn't know the codes. These methods include no consideration whatsoever of content. Another useful application of traffic analysis in investment is to keep an eye on court actions. Bankruptcy news often shows up first in court records. With nearly 10,000 publicly traded companies, and given the reduction in research coverage for companies outside the large indexes, the collective set of financial analysts and reporters are hard-pressed to follow them all on a timely basis.

Quality of Governance and SEC Text

Of course it is possible, and generally a good idea, to consider content as well. The SEC provides a rich source for this approach. Companies' 8-K filings are for "extraordinary events," including resignations of officers and directors, mergers, acquisitions, and changes in capital structure. Financial research has shown that better quality of corporate governance is associated with better returns. Automated extraction tools are capable of monitoring directors' activities, audit reports, and legal troubles. When a specialized spider goes beyond retrieving information and scans it for content, it acts as an early warning

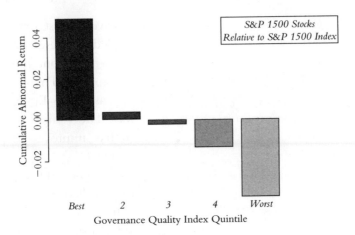

Figure 2.14 Cumulative Abnormal Return (CAR) over 2002. Board member concentration quintiles and return relative to S&P 1500 index, 2002. The "too good to be true?" The Heidi Klum or bar charts?
Source: David Leinweber and Jacob Sisk, unpublished work, 2003.

system for events that may show up in tomorrow's paper, or next week's. Thinly followed firms may not show up in the news at all. But they do show up in investment performance. When information extracted from SEC filings for the S&P 1500 is combined to rank corporate governance and relate it to stock returns, the picture is remarkable. As seen in Figure 2.14, companies ranked in the top 20 percent using measures of board stability outperformed companies in the worst 20 percent by over 7 percent in 2002 alone.

This is the Heidi Klum of bar charts; it looks so perfect that one suspects something odd or artificial is going on, like graphing the row numbers. If the guys at NASA can mix up meters with feet and misplace their $100 million babies on Mars, it is maybe just possible that we mixed up some data. However, a closer look at decile returns, seen in Figure 2.15, shows otherwise.

Language Technology: Your Tax Dollars at Work

The U.S. government has been busy spending your money on technologies to do this kind of content extraction and analysis for years. When the research first started, the language researchers were most interested in was Russian. Harvard's Tony Oettinger, who led the research, tells of inputting the English sentence "The spirit is willing but the flesh is weak" into an English-to-Russian translation program. The computer's Russian translation was then fed back into a Russian-to-English translation program. The resulting retranslation was "The vodka is ready but the meat is rotten." Language technology has improved markedly, but still has a long way to go.

The Defense Advanced Research Projects Agency (DARPA) paid for the development of the Internet, which was called the ARPANET in the early days. Many additional millions have gone into programs with names like "Machine Understanding and Classification" and "Text Retrieval and Categorization." A great deal of this research has now found its way into tools and products for mining the deep Web. Advanced proprietary trading firms have added these techniques to the sophisticated quantitative analytics in their technological arsenals.

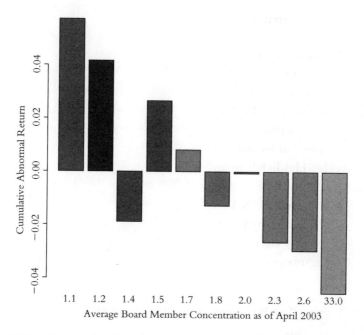

Figure 2.15 Cumulative Abnormal Return (CAR) Over 2002. Board member concentration deciles and return relative to S&P 1500 index, 2002. I bet even Heidi looks less than perfect if you look close enough.
Source: David Leinweber and Jacob Sisk, unpublished work, 2003.

Many of these financial applications are more secret than their Cold War cousins, but there are examples from academia that give a glimpse at how they work.

Are the Words of the Prophets Written on the Subway Walls?

A number of studies of stock message boards have found that spikes in traffic, both with and without characterization of content, are predictive of subsequent spikes in volatility and volume.[17] Anybody with the inclination can post messages about stocks, with no quality control anywhere in sight. This will come as no surprise to those who follow the SEC's indictments for market manipulation. In one notorious example, 130 well-placed messages sent a penny stock up 106,600 percent in a single day, and a month later sent the message posters to jail. (This and other examples are discussed in Chapter 10.) Outright falsification will bring the sheriff to the door. But enthusiastic promotion of opinions has been going on legally for hundreds of years. It should come as no surprise that when a thinly traded stock is suddenly brought to the attention of millions of people trading electronically, there is likely to be more action than on typical days where it remains well below everyone's radar. Many options traders and market makers track the message activity as a textual indicator of risk, opportunity, and volatility.

A recent survey of volatility prediction, by the distinguished econometricians Clive Granger and Ser-Huang Poon, concluded that the best and most elaborate quantitative models did not rival predictions based on implied volatilities. In their conclusion, they write: "A potentially useful area for future research is whether forecasting can be enhanced by using exogenous variables."[18]

The line between manipulation and volatility-inducing events is gray. It is not unreasonable for us to expect to see textually based exogenous variables for volatility prediction in the future. Indeed, these are in use today.

eAnalyst: "Can Computerized Language Analysis Predict the Market?"

A *Barron's* story in 2001 asked the question "Can computerized language analysis predict the market?"[19] It reported on eAnalyst, a University of

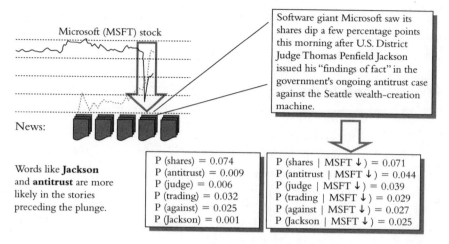

Microsoft (MSFT) stock

Software giant Microsoft saw its shares dip a few percentage points this morning after U.S. District Judge Thomas Penfield Jackson issued his "findings of fact" in the government's ongoing antitrust case against the Seattle wealth-creation machine.

News:

Words like **Jackson** and **antitrust** are more likely in the stories preceding the plunge.

P (shares) = 0.074
P (antitrust) = 0.009
P (judge) = 0.006
P (trading) = 0.032
P (against) = 0.025
P (Jackson) = 0.001

P (shares | MSFT ↓) = 0.071
P (antitrust | MSFT ↓) = 0.044
P (judge | MSFT ↓) = 0.039
P (trading | MSFT ↓) = 0.029
P (against | MSFT ↓) = 0.027
P (Jackson | MSFT ↓) = 0.025

Figure 2.16   Language Modeling. Can computerized language analysis predict the market?
Source: Copyright © 2000 Victor Lavrenko.

Massachusetts academic project that used the idea of language models to look into the content of news stories and run a simulated portfolio based on the machine's ability to distinguish between stories that move a stock's price up and those that move it down. (See Figure 2.16.) Despite an admittedly bone-headed trading strategy that churned the portfolio, and without any information other than the news classifications, the system made a statistically significant profit. A simulation that ignored the news signals, but made random trades at the same times they occurred, incurred a statistically significant loss when trading costs were included. So, even this simple approach added value.

Approaches to Language

Language models are easy to understand. The tag clouds included at the start of the chapters in this book are visual representations of language models—with the most frequently occurring words and phrases appearing in larger, darker type fonts.

A language model is just a set of keywords and phrases that characterize a collection of documents. It would be easy to build one that could distinguish, for example, stories in French from stories in English.

If the effectiveness were anything less than 100 percent, it would mean you made a serious error. Similarly, it would be easy to distinguish stories about finance from stories about horses. Would it be possible to distinguish, say, SEC filings of companies that subsequently do well from the filings of companies that do poorly?

The statistical language models used in eAnalyst to distinguish good news from bad news use some of the fruits of all those Defense Department research projects to let the computer extract root words and learn large sets of keywords and phrases, using that relentless way computers have of approaching human tasks such as playing chess. It finds many of the same words humans would find. *Indictment* is rarely good news, but it also finds hundreds of others, many of which are particular to an industry or a single firm.

Here is an example of a simple experiment with language models that do this. We looked at the language model—that is, the most frequently occurring words, word pairs, and word triples that occur in particular sections of SEC 10-Q filings in 1997 and 1998, segregated by firms that did well and those that did poorly in the six months following the filing. Many of the same words and groupings occur in filings of both high- and low-return filers. The top of the list for both groups includes *fiscal, dilutive, sales,* and other words one expects in all financial reporting.

The differences are more interesting. Near the top of the list for the outperforming firms, we find *research; development, patents;* and *marketable, securities.* The comma notation used here for word groups just means they occur within one word of each other, in any order. In the underperforming group, we find *regulations; securities, exchange; note, earnings; antidilutive;* and *condensed, omitted, pursuant.* Innovation is good. Legal proceedings are bad.

An out-of-sample test, looking at subsequent six-month cumulative abnormal returns (CAR) (cumulative abnormal returns relative to the S&P 1500 index) of firms that matched the in-sample language models in the following two years is striking. (See Figure 2.17.)

This simple test illustrates an important principle of language analysis. Statistical profiling needs to be combined with content extraction. Use of full filings is very noisy. It is necessary to ignore boilerplate warnings and focus on relevant portions; this is particularly important for long texts such as SEC documents.

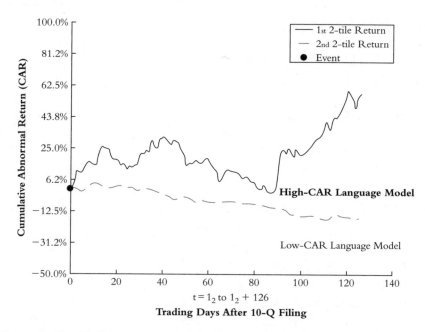

Figure 2.17 10-Q Language Model Excess Returns Over Six Months. (Experiment January 1998 to January 2008)

Technological Content Extraction: XML

An emerging Web standard, *extensible markup language* (XML), is designed to automate the process of extracting the relevant features and portions of electronic material. The original language of the Web, HTML (hypertext markup language), was designed to present pictures of information. The *tags* used to create web pages reflected this. They described how information looked onscreen: blue, centered, underlined, and the like. We are now in the early stages of a shift from pictures of data on the Web to real information. The new extended language of the Web, XML, conveys the meaning of the underlying information, with tags such as *ticker, CUSIP, news type, revision direction, court filing, auditor opinion,* and literally thousands of others.

XML has transformed many aspects of modern business. We are just beginning to see this transformation in the movement of information. But even at this early stage, the technology is appearing in government filings, news, and financial research.[20]

EDGAR: The SEC Gets the XML Religion

The SEC's Electronic Data Gathering, Analysis, and Retrieval (EDGAR) system performs automated collection, validation, indexing, acceptance, and forwarding of submissions by companies and others that are required by law to file forms with the U.S. Securities and Exchange Commission.

All of this Web 2.0 XML magic was once beyond the horizon at the SEC. The SEC had farmed out the design and programming of EDGAR to the California defense firm TRW Inc., which is a good place to go for space satellite expertise, but is not known as a great innovator in software. EDGAR had a distinct 1980s flavor to it well into the new millennium. There was some lip service about using an XML conceptual superset called SGML (standard generalized markup language). Nothing changed until recently, though, when then SEC Chairman Christopher Cox lit a fire and gave a keynote speech at a nerd-heavy XBRL (Extensible Business Reporting Language) conference. You can watch it at www.sec. gov. In hindsight, maybe there were some other things going on that he could have focused on with the same intensity he gave to XML.

Greatest Hits, and the Mother of All Greatest Misses

Numerical information is the bedrock of financial analysis—fundamental, quantitative, and technical. But people look at the words, too. Sometimes the footnotes to the table change the meaning of the numbers. Sometimes the words tell a story that doesn't show up in the numbers. The challenge of the text frontier is to find ways to use both types of information to improve investment and trading.

This chapter has attempted to highlight the most important impacts of technology on investment management in the past and to look at the innovations that may have a similar impact in the future. Of course, the former are on much firmer ground than the latter. Think how unlikely it would have been to describe the spreadsheet or the Web before they were invented.

Everybody trades; everybody reads. Highlighting electronic market access and the text frontier as promising areas for broad impact in the future is the fact that they provide support for trading and reading, two very common and very central activities in investment management; it is only a short trip out on a limb to anticipate that these areas will see more innovative technology in the future.

This chapter was written before the dreadful autumn of 2008. Among other things, recent events have been a reminder of how quaint a pursuit of quantitative and textual computerized stock picking is in the wide world of finance.

Quants as a group have been tarred as responsible for recent troubles. It is true that some have contributed substantially to the mess we find ourselves in. But current problems are not coming from what is the subject of most of this book, and all of the drafts written before this fall. The folly of overly complex derivatives traded in markets with no transparency and less regulation by firms leveraged to the sky is what has brought us to an appalling place.

Algorithmic trading is almost entirely about stocks. There is tremendous transparency in the stock market. Look at the bottom of any business television channel or web site. You can see the details of every trade in every stock, within seconds. Regulators can track down parties involved in suspicious trades via automated clearing systems. In marked contrast, we see absolutely nothing at all about trading in the collateralized debt obligations (CDOs), credit default swaps (CDSs), and mortgage-backed securities (MBSs) that created this mess, even though the total size of those markets is a multiple of the size of the stock market. Trades and quotes in these securities, holdings, and holders are all unknown and largely unknowable, even in today's electronic markets. If the level of regulation, reporting, and transparency we have in the equity markets were in effect for the toxic garbage that is being laid off on the U.S. taxpayers, we wouldn't be in the bind we are in.

We should not blame anyone using a computer on Wall Street for the trouble. But we should blame the financial engineers who designed these Frankenstein derivatives and then failed to point out loudly and emphatically enough that their pricing models for these were so far out of the range of applicability based on previous experience that a horrendously dangerous situation had been created.

Imagine if the designers of the first skyscrapers had said, "We can build a pretty good two-story house out of wood. Let's do that 50 times, and we'll have the Empire State Building." You wouldn't want to be on the top floor. There are many examples of stupid errors like this in real-world engineering: bridges that twist apart in the wind; hotel mezzanines that collapse into the lobby when the crowd arrives. Start with this kind of stupidity, mix in enough greed, hubris, leverage, and lack of adult supervision, and you get the headlines of the past year, discussed in depth in Chapter 12.

Notes

1. Sergio Focardi, Peter Kolm, and Frank Fabozzi, "New Kids on the Block," *Journal of Portfolio Management* 30, no. 4 (Fall 2004): 42–53. The first article in the issue, by Andy Lo, "The Adaptive Market Hypothesis," is an excellent in-depth discussion of the modern view of market efficiency.

2. Robert Metcalfe is the inventor of Ethernet (the ubiquitous wiring of the Internet), and the founder of 3Com. His law was demonstrated first with telephones and fax machines.

3. Okay, let's belabor them a little for Generations X and Y and the Millennials, who may have missed these back when they were everywhere, but may also pick up this book. Gordon Moore, a founder of Intel, was fond of comparing the progress in computer technology to progress in automobiles. He used measures like mileage and cruising speed as analogous to memory size and CPU cycles per second. Every year, the hypothetical "car" corresponding to a current computer got more fabulous— traveling at 100,000 miles per hour, getting 100,000 miles per gallon, and the like. Auto industry people felt dissed by all this, and said, "Yes, but it would crash 12 times a day." It's tough to mix metaphors.

4. Hans Moravec, *Mind Children: The Future of Human and Robot Intelligence* (Cambridge, MA: Harvard University Press, 1988).

5. Steve Snider, Fidelity Pyramis quantitative portfolio manager, personal communication.

6. Emanuel Derman, *My Life as a Quant: Reflections on Physics and Finance* (Hoboken, NJ: John Wiley & Sons, 2007). This excellent book's primary focus is on the use of quantitative methods applied to fixed income securities, but many of the insights have wider applicability.

7. "America's Top 300 Money Managers," *Institutional Investor*, July 2008.

8. Robert Schwartz and David Whitcomb, *Transaction Costs and Institutional Investor Trading Strategies*, Monograph 1988-23 (New York: New York University Stern School of Business, 1988).

9. Jonathan Stempel, "Citigroup Buys Automated Trading Desk," Reuters, July 2, 2007.

10. Try the Wayback Machine for yourself at www.archive.org. Type in a URL and a date, and spin the dial. The live music archive, at the same URL, is also quite a find, especially for fans of the Grateful Dead.

11. For current information and a perspective on the evolution of electronic markets, see the Tabb Group at www.tabbgroup.com.

12. A live version is available at http://marketrac.nyse.com/.

13. There is a huge collection of past and current HCIL work at the lab's site: www.cs.umd.edu/hcil/.

14. The tree map is still enormously useful for its original purpose—tracking down those files that suddenly take over your disk. A free utility along these lines is Sequoia View, from the computer science department at Eindhove Technical University in the Netherlands (www.win.tue.nl/sequoiaview/).

15. For more on this remarkable story, see *Paving Wall Street: Experimental Economics and the Quest for the Perfect Market* by Ross Miller (John Wiley & Sons, 2002).

16. See "Delving Deeper" by David Leinweber, *Bloomberg Wealth Manager*, October 2003.

17. The Harvard Business School e-Information project at www.people.hbs.edu/ptufano/einfo/ has a nice online collection of these studies.

18. Ser-Huang Poon and Clive Granger, "Practical Issues in Forecasting Volatility," *Financial Analysts Journal* 61, no. 1 (2005): 45–55.

19. Bill Alpert, "Can Computerized Language Analysis Predict the Market?" Barron's at WSJ.com, November 19, 2001, http://online.wsj.com/article/SB1005962163718064080.html.

20. See sites www.sec.gov, www.newsml.org, and www.rixml.org for the latest details on XML use at the SEC, in news, and in investment research.

Chapter 3

Algorithm Wars

"How about a nice game of chess?"

— WOPR COMPUTER IN *WAR GAMES*

There used to be two market structures for U.S. equity traders to contend with: the NYSE (for listed stocks) and NASDAQ. Recent counts put the number at roughly 40. Many are sources of dark liquidity, which sounds like red wine, but actually refers to market systems that allow (or require) hidden interest.[1]

This chapter goes into more depth on the flowering of electronic market access. Programs that started out as simple electronic order pads so brokers wouldn't have to bother with their paper slips[2] for small orders are now complex software entities that game against each other in an ever more complex and fragmented equity market.

Here we look at how the meanest, smartest algorithms (aka algos) on the street got that way, and at the even meaner, smarter algorithms that will replace them. The Cold War is history, but there's an arms race underway in algo trading. It started in the 1980s, and shows no signs of slowing down.

Early Algos

Readers of a certain age and juvenile sensibility are no doubt familiar with *Mad* magazine's "Spy vs. Spy" cartoons, which have run continuously

---

This chapter is an expanded version of an article, "Algo vs. Algo," that appeared in Institutional Investor Alpha magazine (February 2007). Reprinted by permission.

since 1961 in the "Joke and Dagger" department. We see the spies, identical except for the color of their coats and hats, engage in an endless series of elaborate schemes to gain an advantage. *Mad*'s spies use an assortment of daggers, explosives, poisons, military hardware, and Rube Goldberg schemes in their war. The battle for supremacy in algorithmic execution uses an assortment of mathematics, programming, communications, computing hardware, and, yes, Rube Goldberg schemes.

It's worthwhile to understand the simpler beginnings of electronic trading to better appreciate today's elaborate systems, and the more elaborate systems that will replace them. When market systems involved chalkboards, shouting, hand signals, and large paper limit order books, there was no possibility of using a computer to execute trades.

This changed in 1976, when the NYSE introduced the Designated Order Turnaround (DOT) system, the first electronic execution system. It was designed to free specialists and traders from the nuisance of 100-share market orders. The NASDAQ market, started in 1971, used computers to display prices, but relied on telephones for actual transactions until 1983 with the introduction of the Computer Assisted Execution System (CAES), and the Small Order Execution System (SOES) in 1984.

Simultaneous improvements in market data dissemination allowed computers to be used to access quote and trade streams. The specialists at the NYSE had a major technology upgrade in 1980, when the specialist posts themselves, which had not changed since the 1920s, were made electronic for the first time, dramatically reducing the latencies in trading. A study[3] of trading before and after the upgrade found major improvements in market quality.

Early electronic execution channels were for only the smallest market orders. But the permitted sizes grew quickly. Support for limit orders was added. DOT became SuperDOT. And the tool was adapted for direct use by the buy side, first by the little guys—a joint venture between Dick Rosenblatt and a technology provider, Davidge Data (more on that later)—and later by the big boys, who gave the product away for clearing business. It and the automated NASDAQ systems accommodated ever larger orders. Orders exceeding the size limits for automation were routed to specialists and market makers.

This was algorithmic trading without algorithms, an early form of direct market access. The first user interfaces were for one stock at a time, electronic versions of simple, single paper buy and sell slips. This became tedious, and soon execution capabilities for a list of names followed. Everyone was happy to be able to produce and screen these lists using their new Lotus 1-2-3 spreadsheets, which totaled everything up nicely to avoid costly errors.

We were only a step away from algorithmic trading. Programmers at the order origination end grew more capable and confident in their abilities to generate and monitor an ever larger number of small orders. Aha! Algo trading had snuck up on us.

Algos for Alpha

Early adopters of these ideas were not looking to minimize market impact or match volume-weighted average price (VWAP). They were looking to make a boatload of cash, and willing to commit firm capital to do so.[4] Nunzio Tartaglia, a Jesuit-educated Ph.D. physicist with the vocabulary of a sailor, started an automated trading group at Morgan Stanley in the mid-1980s. He hired young Columbia computer science professor David Shaw. At first, a few papers about hooking Unix systems to market systems emerged. Then the former academics realized there was no alpha in publications. Shaw went on to found D.E. Shaw & Company, one of the largest and most consistently successful quantitative hedge funds. Fischer Black's Quantitative Strategies Group at Goldman Sachs were algo pioneers. They were perhaps the first to use computers for actual trading, as well as for identifying trades.

The early alpha seekers were the first combatants in the algo wars. Pairs trading, popular at the time, relied on statistical models. Finding stronger short-term correlations than the next guy had big rewards. Escalation beyond pairs to groups of related securities was inevitable. Parallel developments in futures markets opened the door to electronic index arbitrage trading.

Automated market making was a valuable early algorithm. In quiet, normal markets buying low and selling high across the spread was easy money. Real market makers have obligations to maintain a two-sided quote for their stocks, even in turbulent markets, which is often expensive. Electronic systems, without the obligations of market makers, not only were much faster at moving quotes, they could choose when *not* to make markets in a stock. David Whitcomb, founder of Automated Trading Desk (ATD),[5] another algo pioneer, describes his firm's activity as "playing NASDAQ like a piano." There were other piano players. Morgan Stanley's trading desk transformed into an automated market making system. Along with firms like Getco, Tradebot, and ATD, they came to dominate the inside quote and liquidity in the largest names today. Joe Gawronski, president of Rosenblatt Securities at the NYSE, sees a massive change in market structure brought about by these algo wars.

Faster data feeds and faster computation let you run ahead of the other kids in line. This was a time when the lag between one desktop data feed and another might be as much as 15 minutes. The path from market event to screen event had significant delays. Slow computers, sending information to slow humans over slow lines, were easy marks for early algo warriors willing to buy faster machinery and smart enough to code the programs to use it. This aspect of the arms race continues unabated today.

Algos for the Buy Side: Transaction Cost Control

It didn't take long to notice that these new electronic trading techniques had something to offer to the buy side. Financial journals offered a stream of opinion, theory, and analysis of transaction costs. Firms like Wayne Wagner's Plexus Group—now part of Investment Technology Group, Inc. (ITG)—made persuasive, well-supported arguments about the importance of transaction costs. Pension plan sponsors, sitting at the top of the financial food chain, were convinced in large numbers.

Index managers did not have to be convinced. With no alpha considerations in the picture, they observed that it was possible to run either a lousy index fund or a particularly good one. The difference was the cost of trading. Those passive managers, on their way to becoming trillion-dollar behemoths, were high-value clients to brokers.

In addition to giving their high-value clients what they wanted, brokers had an additional incentive to adopt electronic trading. The end of fixed equity commissions spawned new competitive pressures. Electronic trading had the potential to cut costs dramatically, while improving quality of service.

The largest firms developed their own electronic order entry systems. Others bought from niche vendors. One of these was Davidge Data, headquartered in a loft a short walk from the financial center. Nick Davidge had many clients to support, and used bicycles to dispatch service people, mostly himself. In the course of this activity, he made the important discovery that girls' bikes parked on New York streets have a half-life 10 times longer than boys' bikes.

From Order Pad to Algos

The first direct-access tools from the sell side were single-stock electronic order pads, followed shortly by lists. The next step was breaking those orders down into pieces small enough to execute electronically, and spreading them out in time. Innovative systems like ITG's QuantEx, discussed in Chapter 7, allowed traders without large software staffs to use and define analytics and rules to control electronic trading. This began to look like what we consider to be algorithmic trading today.

The big news in algorithmic trading in the late 1980s was that you could do it at all. The first algo strategies were based on simple rules, like "send this order out in 10 equal waves, spaced equally in time from open to close." But these were predictable and easy to game by manipulating the price on a thin name with a limit order placed just before the arrival of the next wave, getting bagged in classic "Spy vs. Spy" style. There was little or no mathematical underpinning, just rules of thumb and educated guesses.

A Scientific Approach: Mathematics, Behavior, and Discovery

The obvious shortcomings of these simple strategies motivated several generations of mathematically based algorithms, using increasing levels of mathematical and econometric sophistication to include models of market impact, risk, order books, and the actions of other traders. The idea of an efficient frontier of trade path strategies and the use of optimization established a conceptual foundation, analogous to the efficient frontier in portfolio theory.

Markets have become even more fragmented and complex, and with decimalization (trading in pennies instead of eighths or sixteenths), less information is conveyed by the best bid and offer (BBO).[6] The ability to rapidly cancel and replace limit orders has a similar information-reducing effect on the limit order book. New markets, electronic communication networks (ECNs), and others create a need to exploit new order types and to access dark liquidity. This has given rise to behavior-based algorithms, probing for liquidity, driven by procedural logic and stimulus-response principles and as well as mathematical models. These are often called "gaming algos," and many traders and liquidity providers are actively deploying anti-gaming measures.

Algorithms at the edge probe, learn, and adapt. They need to make effective use of analytic tools, and know how to recognize their limitations. Many use small probe orders, examining the fill and replenishment response in multiple trading venues. Algos at the edge seek to exploit information beyond the traditional data, including news, pre-news, and other forms of market color found on the Web. There has been an explosion of progress in tools for processing text. Think, for instance, of Google.

When it comes to millisecond-scale "cancel and replace" decisions, algorithms rule. No human can react as fast. The combination of quantitative methods and artificial intelligence (AI) methods is increasingly effective. But how can human traders work with algorithms, using intelligence amplification (IA) to form a partnership that enhances the skill of both? Finding the proper mix of human and machine skills is a challenge for traders. Rosenblatt Securities' Joe Gawronski observes, "Humans definitely cannot react faster, but they can react smarter in many instances; one thing algos do extremely well is allow for one to reflect what one anticipates they would want to do if a certain set of circumstances occurs—a human in a trading crowd or on a trading desk actually reacts in the true sense to new info and changes his plan based on that new info; an algo works differently, being forced to anticipate what will occur and then having a set plan dealing with those circumstances if they do in fact occur; in an automatic execution, millisecond world one has no choice but to use algos and play the anticipation game, as trading will go on without your participation if you simply try to react—see the Hybrid."[7]

Garry Kasparov (the world chess champion who lost to Deep Blue in 1997) suggested that chess tournaments be open to human-machine teams. Part of Kasparov's job in that situation is to keep an eye on the machine's decisions, just in case it misses some of his insights. Carrying on this analogy to trading, imagine if the game was not tournament chess, which allows up to seven hours for the game, but blitz chess, which allows a total of three minutes. Some chess masters will take this even further, playing a roomful of opponents simultaneously, with strict time limits. Given Moore's law, it's not long before the computer that beat Kasparov with seven hours to think could beat him with three minutes. Many facets of trading are more like blitz chess than high-level tournament chess play.

Job Insecurity for Traders

There is no shortage of paycheck anxiety among traders. Their numbers have been dropping. IBM's consulting arm published a report called "The Trader Is Dead, Long Live the Trader."[8] A Finextra headline, "City [of London] Trading Jobs to Fall by 90% as Banks Take Up Algorithmic Technology,"[9] no doubt contributed to trader stress. Even the *Economist* magazine, in a story headlined "The March of the Robo-Traders," observed that "programs that buy and sell shares are becoming ever more sophisticated. Might they replace human traders?"[10] Like global warming, this is a reality that can't be ignored. Gawronski comments, "Specialist firms have been cutting staff at an extremely rapid rate—30 percent here, 50 percent there—which is no surprise considering keystrokes are down more than 50 percent, I believe, and algos are being employed to do some of the routine heavy lifting of market making."

This kind of press makes for anxious career planning. Some traders have already been replaced by algorithms, and some more will be. The traders who stay will be the ones who play well with machines. Understanding algorithms is a survival skill. Someone makes the decisions algorithms can't make (yet). Here is a CliffsNotes study guide for Algo Trading 101 from a technology perspective, annotated along the way with features from algorithms at the edge.

Algorithms have *sensors* and *effectors*, analogous to the eyes and motors of real robots. In between the sensors and effectors, there is a computer program that provides *control*. Sensors include the data feed of market information, quotes, trades, order books, and indications of interest. Algos feed on market data, and their sophistication grows with its scope, timeliness, and accuracy. Effectors are order entry components, including cancels and modify and replace instructions. They result in an additional sensor stream of execution information. Control comes from a program based on a combination of mathematical market models, rules (as in an expert system), and procedures.

You are what you eat, and algos eat market data. Consequently, a basic algo wars tactic is to improve the timeliness, scope, and accuracy of market data. Anyone using more than one data service notices lags from one service to another, and they all lag the actual event. There is disintermediation, removing the intermediary, going on in these businesses as well as in brokerages. Companies like Wombat Financial Software[11] will sell you the docking adapter to sidle right up to the Securities Industry Automation Corporation mother ship[12] rather than rely on consolidators like Reuters and Bloomberg. Being able to do this disintermediates[13] the data vendors, at least for the raw material.

In the algo wars, as in real wars, it's a good idea to control your communications, avoiding those slow satellite links. Communication satellites are in geosynchronous equatorial orbits (GEOs), 22,240 miles over the equator. Light travels at 186,000 miles per second, so a satellite hop takes at least a quarter of a second. Two hundred fifty milliseconds are hardly noticeable while talking, but it's long enough for a crowd to get ahead of you in the market.

So Many Markets, So Little Time

You can rent a parking space for your execution computer right next to the market center computers, eliminating communication latency. This service is now offered by the NYSE, NASDAQ, CME, London, Euronext, Tokyo Stock Exchange, Globex, and a growing list of other market centers.

This colocation can do wonders for latencies in execution. As the algo wars proceed, we will see tools that combine fast broad market access with access to proprietary execution channels. Brokers willing to commit capital will be able to offer zero latency executions. Zero is low enough for lots of fast trading strategies that are subject to the vagaries of execution. Watch out—here comes a mob of new hedge funds.

Algos at the edge see a thousand points of light, each with its own alternative trading system and its own clientele (brokers allowed or buy side only). In many of these systems, order size is hidden. Finding liquidity may require being in multiple systems for a period of time. This can create a risk of overexecuting unless very conservative rules are followed. Larger firms, willing to risk some capital by incurring the risk of overbuying (or overselling), will be able to allow their clients to make use of more aggressive trading tactics.

Multiple market fragments can be seen as providing a service to different classes of traders seeking liquidity, thus making markets overall more efficient, resilient, and robust—all good things. But in a complex, multiple-fragment market it is possible to shift from effective trading to gaming in a mix of different market structures. Some market fragments have price discovery, whereas others use prices derived from other fragments. When an algo finds that a price can be set in one fragment using a small order to create advantage for a larger trade in another fragment, *that* is an example of gaming the system.

Patient Trading, Transitions, and Trade Path Risk Control

Future algos will have uniform access to a mix of securities and derivatives. This will allow for improved, patient execution of large transitions by controlling risk during the course of a large trade, which can extend to days or more. Nearly all current algo trades occur over the course of a single day. There's no fundamental reason for this. Without a one-day rule, future algos will better serve institutions using patient transition trading to make sizable adjustments in their portfolios.

Full-service brokers will be able to offer customized short-term derivatives for controlling risk exposures along the path of longer trades. Algos at the edge can act like skilled transition traders.

The Naive Strategy

The well-wired trader has spared no effort or expense in obtaining the finest kind in data and market access of all flavors. What to do with it? Do math.

The earliest algorithms used the "keep it simple, stupid" strategy of splitting up orders in n parts, every $1/n$ of a trading day; for example, an order for 10,000 shares would be sent out as 10 orders for 1,000 shares, at 10 times spaced equally over the trading day. This signaling made it easy for traders on the other side to spot these algorithms, and pick them off. Later, smarter authors, whom we will discuss soon, called this "the naive strategy," which is a kind assessment.

The next round of Algorithm vs. Algorithm/People was to get the algorithms to be less naive—to hide by randomizing times and sizes. (If you want to cite academic/practitioner work on this, check out the Quantitative Services Group LLC [QSG] study that showed how real the randomization benefits were—massive.) But randomization made some stupid decisions—placing small orders at the open and close, not reflecting urgency or tolerance for risk, and missing transient opportunities in liquidity.

In 1998, Dimitris Bertsimas and Andrew Lo[14] at MIT coauthored one of the first academic papers on scientific approaches to trading, "Optimal Control of Execution Costs." It may be deeper than Algos 101, but motivated readers find an excellent compact description of their work in the abstract:

> We derive dynamic optimal trading strategies that minimize the expected cost of trading a large block of equity over a fixed time horizon. Specifically, given a fixed block S of shares to be executed within a fixed finite number of periods T, and given a price-impact function that yields the execution price of an individual trade as a function of the shares traded and market conditions, we obtain the optimal sequence of trades as a function of market conditions . . . that minimizes the expected cost of executing S within T periods.

They start with an analysis of the merits of mindless naive strategies, asking what sort of environment it would take for them to actually be optimal. This turns out to be an unrealistically simple world. They then model a more realistic world, where the trading strategy incorporates ideas of market impact and an "information variable," and examine how optimal trading strategies depend on it. Their illustration, reproduced here (Figure 3.1), shows the number of shares traded in each period in the top half, and an abstract information variable for that period below.

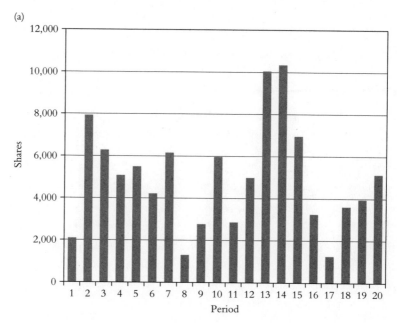

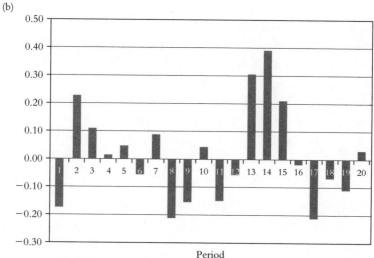

Figure 3.1   A complicated way of saying "use new information as you trade".
Best Execution Strategy (a) and Information Component (b)
Source: Reprinted from the Journal of Financial Markets, *Volume 1 (1998), Dimitris Bertsimas and Andrew W. Lo, "Optimal Control of Execution Costs," p. 50, with permission from Elsevier. Redrawn by* Institutional Investor Alpha, *February 2007.*

Notice that trading is strongly driven by the information component. This information variable is quite general and abstract; exactly how this is determined could include anything from micro-level empirical analysis to rumors heard on the bus.

Mix in Risk

Modeling market impact and information was a significant advance. But there was room for improvement. The next step was to incorporate the idea of risk aversion, and the distinction between passive and alpha-seeking trades.

Robert Almgren and Neil Chriss made that major step in their 2000 paper "Optimal Execution of Portfolio Transactions."[15] It explicitly included the risk aversion of traders, and introduced the idea of liquidity-adjusted value at risk as a metric for trading strategies. Okay, let's call this Algos 201, but again, the authors do a fine job explaining this for the mathematically inclined. This work has been very widely adopted in today's algo systems. From the abstract:

> We consider the execution of portfolio transactions with the aim of minimizing a combination of volatility risk and transaction costs arising from permanent and temporary market impact. For a simple linear cost model, we explicitly construct the efficient frontier in the space of time-dependent liquidation strategies, which have minimum expected cost for a given level of uncertainty. We may then select optimal strategies either by minimizing a quadratic utility function, or minimizing Value at Risk . . . , that explicitly considers the tradeoff between volatility risk and liquidation costs.

Figure 3.2 is worth many words in understanding this trading model, and the intuitively appealing implications of its results for traders of different risk tolerances. Trader A is realistically risk-averse, accelerating to reduce risk at the cost of higher impact. Trader B is patient and risk-neutral, executing only to reduce expected costs. Trader C is an unrealistic trader who likes risk and who slows down the execution to get more risk, also incurring more impact cost. The faster trading in path A, to reduce risk, is also what a trader who believed that he had short-term alpha would do to reduce opportunity cost.

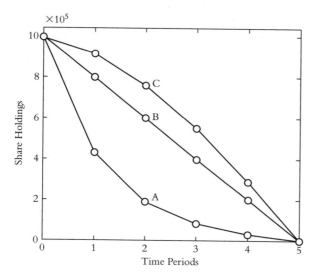

Figure 3.2 Optimal Trajectories. How fast is too fast? It depends how fast your information decays, and how willing you are to gamble that it will be known before you finish trading. *Source: Robert Almgren and Neil Chriss, "Optimal Execution of Portfolio Transactions,"* Journal of Risk *3, no. 2 (Winter 2000/2001).*

Mathematical models of markets can become very elaborate. Game theoretic approaches to other market participants, human and machine, in the spirit of the *Beautiful Mind* ideas of John Nash, bring another level of insight.

Known Unknowns and Unknown Unknowns

Almgren and Chriss close with an important point about the limitations of all model-driven strategies. As part of the Algos 201 track, here is what they say about connecting algorithms to real-world events:

> Finally, we note that any optimal execution strategy is vulnerable to unanticipated events. If such an event occurs during the course of trading and causes a material shift in the parameters of the price dynamics, then indeed a shift in the optimal trading strategy must also occur. However, if one makes the simplifying assumption that all events are either "scheduled" or "unanticipated," then one concludes that optimal execution is always a game of static trading punctuated by shifts in trading strategy that adapt to material changes in price dynamics. (p. 5)

This is a Ph.D.-ified version of the wisdom of two-time Secretary of Defense Donald Rumsfeld that there are "known unknowns and unknown unknowns."

Examples of known unknowns include scheduled announcements that affect particular stocks, like earnings releases or conference calls; announcements that affect groups of stocks, like housing starts; and announcements that affect broad markets, like macroeconomic data and interest rates.

There are many sources of this type of information. Thomson's StreetEvents offers a wide selection. Econoday is a calendar book for information on the latter two types of events just mentioned. Found in calendar form in every trading room since the 1950s, it's now a Web service. Some algorithms use this information, and some don't. Guess which ones are better.

Unknown unknowns include news, discussion, rumor, market color*, government agency actions, and research results. Computers are pretty good at finding this kind of thing—often too good, in fact, as there is a vast amount of hay for every needle.

This is another front in the algo wars: figuring out what to do with news and pre-news events. Determining when an unknown unknown that will change the trading strategy is a place where humans with machines have an edge on either of them working alone.

The microstructure tactics based on these cost-minimizing trading models are also deployed in VWAP and similar applications. These anticipate volume, and try to participate throughout the day (or time period), optimizing to those targets.

Models Aren't Markets

Even the most elegant models are abstractions of real markets. The real thing is a rapidly changing mélange of market fragments, continuous and call markets, ECNs, innovative matching systems, indications, and dark liquidity pools.

Limit order books just aren't what they used to be. In the days of eighths and of orders being modified by people, the inside quote

---

*Market color can be defined as the mood and general sense among traders. Back when floors were primary, it was something people got a sense of from talking to each other. While there is still some of that going on, with more electronic non-floor activity, people substitute calculations using volatility, buy/sell imbalance and the like.

conveyed actionable information. Now the average life of a limit order is measured in milliseconds, so the quote is a fast-moving target. With decimalization, the old total size at the inside spread became distributed over six or more price levels, so the BBO conveyed much less information. So ECNs and the exchanges exposed more of the book. Just when you could see the book, the algo battlefield shifted with dark liquidity, hidden preprogrammed orders to execute when others are filled, anonymous indication, and matching systems. These take the liquidity that, back in the day, would be in the light (visible in the open book), and conceal it in the dark of less transparent markets and real-time programs.

Here we need to look at the control part of algorithms. With models, we can write formulas to tell us what to do. Edge algorithms can use models as a basis for action, but they have a wider vocabulary of rule and procedural tools to execute across all market segments. As markets change, people will need to monitor and adjust algo and electronic strategies. Markets change rapidly, so humans will be critically important here.

Robots, RoboTraders, and Traders

Often, the best model of something is the thing itself. This is a key concept in robotics. Building a robot that explores a digital model of Mars is very different from building one that explores the actual planet of Mars.

An ever-growing collection of impressive robots have done well in complex dynamic environments.[16] Looking into how these robots "think" is looking at the future of algorithms. Looking at how humans and physical robots interact is a look at how humans and trading robots will coexist.

There are always multiple approaches to robotic tasks. Structuring and coordinating these approaches is the goal of multi-agent systems,[17] a unified approach to controlling complex systems. They are programs that cooperate, coordinate, and negotiate with each other. The list of key features of multi-agent systems reads like a description of key features of algorithmic trading:

- *Embedded in the real world*. The world in general and markets in particular are not static. Things change; information is incomplete.

Everything is dynamic. A reactive agent responds to events rapidly enough for the response to be useful.

- *Partial, imperfect models.* Models of financial market behavior never have the precision of engineering models. They are statistical, with wide error bands. This is particularly true for equities. Financial models never capture every aspect of market participants' motivations.
- *Varied outcomes likely.* Simple games like tic-tac-toe can be modeled exactly. One action always leads to another. This is clearly not the case in trading.
- *Performance feedback and reinforcement.* Performance measurement is natural for trading agents. For alpha-seeking algos, metrics like the Sharpe ratio* fit. Pure execution algos use implementation cost or VWAP shortfall.
- *Layered behaviors.* Agents should have default behaviors that complete their tasks and avoid errors. Basic behavior is at the lower layers, more sophisticated behavior above.

Some of these agents will be programs, and some will be people. We can call these people "the employed traders of 2015."

Markets in 2015, Focus on Risk

Two recent prognostications on markets in 2015 are remarkably similar. One is from BearingPoint, "Shifting from Defense to Offense: A Model for the 21st Century Capital Markets Firm."[18] The other is "Profiting Today by Positioning for Tomorrow: A Field Guide to the Financial Markets of 2015," from IBM Global Business Services.[19] They describe a shift from a product paradigm to a risk paradigm. Prognostications here include: an increase in the complexity of derivative and structured products driven by the demands of alpha-seeking strategies; some products' requirement of willingness to commit capital in innovative ways; and increased trading interest in risk classes, over individual securities.

---

*The Sharpe ratio is a measure of management skill that adjusts pure alpha (value added) by the variability of that value added. Details of the Sharpe ratio can be found at http://en.wikipedia.org/wiki/Sharpe_ratio.

Both articles forecast an increasingly risk-centric view of trading. IBM opines, "As the industry matures, many traditional activities will come under increasing pressure and new value engines will emerge. Activities under pressure are unnecessary bundles and transaction businesses. Value engines will be risk assumption and risk mitigation." (p. 1)

How will these trends be reflected in algorithmic trading systems? If the shifts described occur as predicted, we can anticipate that clients will want to control trade path risk, and sell-side firms will want to accommodate them.

Controlling risk exposures during the course of a complex trade using custom derivatives plays to one of the strengths (and profit generators) for large firms. Agents will have to be able to price these derivatives using quantitative measures and the firm's risk profile.

Playing Well with Robots and Algorithms

People will have to find their place in these multi-asset, risk-mitigated, fragmented, algorithm-infested markets of 2015 and beyond. With this in mind, it's informative to ask how people work with other algorithms, such as physical robots.

Some of the real robots work largely on their own. They have stimulus/response rules and internal representations of their tasks. There are two million iRobot Roomba vacuums sucking up dirt solo. The Mars rovers—*Spirit* and *Opportunity*—have significant control over their actions. They have an autonomous mobility system.[20] Humans set the goals; the rover takes care of the rest.

Other robots are on an extremely short leash. The iRobot PackBot Explosive Ordinance Disposal robot[21] comes with a substantial remote control. These are impressive items to see, and worth a visit to the web site. This is made by the same company that makes the Roomba vacuum cleaners. Robot surgeons, like the Da Vinci Surgical Robots,[22] are on the shortest possible leash. Every move is controlled by a human surgeon. This is really a teleoperated system, with very little autonomy other than safety stops.

These robots and the people they work with have a great advantage in being able to see what they are doing using cameras, well-armored ones for PackBot and little tiny ones in tubes for Dr. Da Vinci. Force feedback and texture sensors let the user feel what it's like to be there. In the real world of bombs and gallbladders, looking around is great way to work with robots. But where are the cameras for trading?

Seeing the Big Picture in Markets

How can traders get the equivalent of a robot camera view into the markets? The employed trader of the future will have learned to amplify his intelligence by working shrewdly with computers. How will this look?

Ideas about how to do this have evolved from simple to sublime, as we saw with algorithms. Human access to market data has moved from ticker tapes to green screens to windowed graphics. This is progress, no doubt, but not of the scale seen in other fields, like meteorology and molecular biology, where visual tools have truly created new insights. The reason for this is that, unlike weather and molecules, markets don't have a natural physical representation to use as a model for the visual representation. They are abstract entities. An excellent review of the issues in moving from visual representations of physical phenomena to abstract entities like markets is found in a 2004 MIT Sloan School master's thesis by Pasha Roberts, whose adviser was the prolific Andrew Lo.[23]

Let's revisit the microstructure display shown in Chapter 2, where it was shown as a generic example of a modern visualization. What you see on the printed page with these examples is about as close to actually using them as looking at the photos in *Bon Appétit* is to eating the tasty-looking concoctions themselves. (Do note the tasteful choice of magazine here; there are many other publications one could choose to make this point.) You get an idea of what these are about, but the black-and-white pictures in this book are nothing like the real thing. Almost all of these examples are not just animated; they are interactive, so you can control the view and drill down to details at will. Try that on the printed version.

The ability to see the market in the appropriate dimensions and detail is a key technology in electronic markets. Figure 3.3, also seen in Chapter 2, is a current example of a high-end viewer for trades, quotes, and the visible part of the limit order book. This is a snapshot, but activity by algorithms makes continuous display of the book an

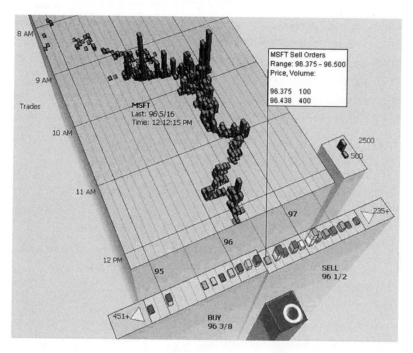

Figure 3.3   Dynamic Market View: Oculus Info's Visible Marketplace. Don't miss the movie version.
Courtesy of Oculus Info Inc. © 2001 Oculus Info Inc. All rights reserved.

incomprehensible blur. Rates of cancels and replacement of limit orders can be overlaid to turn the flood of data into useful information.

Layers on the limit order book show grouped sizes at each price. Customized versions of the Visible Marketplace display can include multiple market fragments, but only one is shown in this example. As with all of these graphics, the dynamics and drill-down-to-details ability are content-rich aspects that don't translate well to the printed page.[24]

If you are skillful and lucky, these market analytics will help you catch events before they are over. Textual and news systems, like Google and its automated cousins, help traders find the kind of unanticipated events that modify algo strategies. These decisions of when and how to steer the algo ship are where people make the decisions that the algorithms can't make.

There are two somewhat distinct benefits to visualization: The first is an interactive control panel display alerting the user to what the algo is actually doing, which with all the liquidity pools available and complex tactics an algo is employing is generally unknown to the trader in almost all cases, making it very difficult to work with the algo and add value as a human trader (the partnership that should exist with the algo).

Second, visualization may be able to display patterns that a computer may be unable to use to make a decision in the context of a broader market environment, but which a person could use.

Agents for News and Pre-News

A salient feature of the relationship between news and markets is that many news events lag the market, but some lead it. Examples of lagging news would include any story that says, "XYZ was up 30 percent today because. . . . " In the old, strong-form efficient market hypothesis days, academics would argue that there was no news worth trading on since all information, public and private, was immediately reflected in prices. The new so-called adaptive market hypothesis and a certain degree of common sense allow that some news (but not all) is news to everyone at the same time, and that someone can be the first to profit from it. This opens yet another front in the algo wars.

In the past year, we have seen the major news providers, Dow Jones[25] and Reuters,[26] offering costly high-end, low-latency news feeds designed for machines. In addition to being faster, they include extensive XML tagging for a variety of stories. These semantic Web approaches allow clever algo warriors to extract the salient facts with much greater accuracy than they could achieve writing code to parse plaintext feeds designed for human readers.

What kind of tags are they talking about? The Dow Jones product is described as over 150 macroeconomic indicators, in developed markets, and a wide range of news on publicly traded U.S. and Canadian firms, as well as some in the United Kingdom. Sample tag categories include earnings, mergers, analyst reports and opinions, executive changes, bankruptcies, splits, and accounting changes. Measures of sentiment and surprise are included. Reuters acquired a firm with roots in the Israeli military intelligence-gathering world, and uses its technology in Reuters' offering to identify entities (people, firms, places, etc.), events, and relationships. These textual systems are designed to integrate with the more established market data. Some of the tools (but not the fast tagged feed) have been made available as free Web resources for developers and experimenters.[27] Aspiring nerds on Wall Street (NOWS) will also find a variety of other open tools available to them.[28]

This is an active front in the algo wars, with new developments coming rapidly. One recurring observation is that it is much easier to find smoke (something of possible interest) than fire (something to act on immediately). Another way of saying this is that it is easier to provide intelligence amplification to help people overwhelmed by news than artificial intelligence to take over those tasks. Some categories of news are much easier to interpret than others; think of earnings revisions compared to membership changes on the board of directors.

A wide range of promising technologies are just being brought into play in this area. So far, English is the language for almost all of these systems. Machine translation, in general, has been difficult,[29] but for literal, as opposed to artistic, content, as is found in most business and financial stories, it can do a passable job. Systran offers a translation system that you can experiment with online.[30] The "as the world turns" time zone effect means that many stories will appear first in international sources in languages other than English. The proliferation of cross-listed or economically equivalent securities means there are often trading opportunities in countries that will be learning the news, via translation, later on in the news cycle.

We have seen how disintermediation (eliminating the middlemen) cut the ranks of sell-side traders as their clients turned to direct market access and algorithmic trading. The same effect can be observed in the news business. Reporters were necessary intermediaries in an era when (for example) press releases were sent to a few thousand fax machines and assigned to reporters by editors, and when SEC filings were found on a shelf in the Commission's reading rooms in major cities. Press releases go to everyone over the Web. SEC filings are completely electronic. The reading rooms are closed.

There is a great deal of effort to develop persistent specialized information-retrieval software agents for these sorts of routine news-gathering activities, which in turn creates incentives for reporters to move up from moving information around to interpretation and analysis. Examples and more in-depth discussion on these "new research" topics are forthcoming in Chapters 9 and 10.

Innovative algo systems will facilitate the use of news, in processed and raw forms. No dominant paradigm has emerged. There is no spreadsheet for language. In addition to financial users, the strongest interest in this area seems to be from the intelligence community. A number of interesting start-ups in this area are funded by In-Q-Tel, the CIA's venture capital firm.[31] Beware though. Don't ask too many questions, unless you look good in an orange jumpsuit.

Algorithms at the Edge

Algos are pushed in all directions that will improve their performance. The minute-to-minute market games people used to play are now millisecond-to-millisecond games for computers, soon to be microsecond-to-microsecond. If you want the impress the fast algo crowd, mention femtoseconds. Light travels about one ten-thousandth of an inch in one of those. Even the fastest algo traders will never have to worry about them.

Mathematical models will become more complex. Markets will proliferate and become even more complex, rapidly. Adaptive probing strategies will adapt and probe complex markets. Quantitative information expressed as numbers will be combined with qualitative information expressed as text. Latencies will go to zero, and information will go to the sky.

Get used to it.

Notes

1. Rosenblatt Securities, at www.rblt.com, maintains one of the most complete public sites for information on the fast-changing world of dark liquidity.

2. White slips were used for buy orders, pink for sells. Index arbitrage, a strategy that would buy or sell a basket of index (e.g., S&P 500) stocks and a simultaneous opposite position in the index futures, was just getting started at this time. Index arbitrageurs would bring their hundreds of order slips to the floor in wheelbarrows. So as not to signal whether they were buyers or sellers, they would have pairs of wheelbarrows, one with white slips and one with pink, ready at the edge of the trading floor. This got old fast, and the index arbs were eager early adopters of electronic trading.

3. "The Impact of Trading Technology: Evidence from the 1980 Post Upgrades," December 2006 working paper by D. Easley (Cornell), T. Hendershott (Berkeley), and T. Ramadori (Oxford), http://faculty.haas.berkeley.edu/hender/TradingTech.pdf.

4. This is a form of alpha, profits from trading and investing. In this case, the holding periods were extremely short. A long-term investment might be an hour. Contrast this with agency trading, which is a pure fee-for-service activity, with revenue coming in the form of commissions. Alpha comes in many forms, and is the subject of Part Two of this book.

5. Automated Trading Desk has an appropriately snazzy web site: www.atdesk.com.

6. Best bid and offer, the inside quote. It consists of four numbers: bid price, bid size, ask price, and ask size.

7. "The Hybrid" refers to the NYSE's ongoing effort to find a way to accommodate human and machine traders in the same market. It is something of a moving target, as various approaches are tried and modified. The handheld electronic device seen on the floor of late is part of this.

8. IBM Business Consulting Services, "The Trader Is Dead, Long Live the Trader" (2006).

9. www.finextra.com/fullstory.asp?id=15955. Finextra is a great bargain, a zero-cost, high-quality news update on global electronic markets with no spam and with good reporting.

10. www.economist.com/displaystory.cfm?story_id=E1_QPGRNTQ. This is the source for the cover of this book.

11. Wombat Financial Software (www.wombatfs.com) is a big arms dealer in the algo wars, sort of the Adnan Khashoggi of low-latency finance. The firm was purchased by the NYSE in 2008.

12. The Securities Industry Automation Corporation is the place where the consolidated tape gets consolidated. Once the mother of all market data, it has a long history as the market data arm of the New York exchanges, back to the New York Quotation Company, formed in 1889. The current firm was formed in 1972. NYSE Group acquired the part it didn't already own in 2006.

13. From the skepticism displayed by the spell-checker, *disintermediate* is not universally regarded as a word in English. It should be; it is a key idea in many aspects of Internet commerce.

14. Dimitris Bertsimas and Andrew W. Lo, "Optimal Control of Execution Costs," *Journal of Financial Markets* 1 (1998): 1–50, http://web.mit.edu/alo/www/papers/bertlo98.html.

15. Robert Almgren and Neil Chriss, "Optimal Execution of Portfolio Transactions," *Journal of Risk* 3, no. 2 (Winter 2000/2001). Almgren calls this "the most cited, least read paper in algo trading" (www.courant.nyu.edu/~almgren/papers/optliq.pdf).

16. Elizabeth Corcoran is the author of an excellent series of photo articles on robotics in *Forbes* (September 4, 2006).

17. Michael Wooldridge, *An Introduction to MultiAgent Systems* (Hoboken, NJ: John Wiley & Sons, 2002), www.csc.liv.ac.uk/~mjw/pubs/imas/.

18. Peter Horowitz, "Shifting from Defense to Offense: A Model for the 21st Century Capital Markets Firm," www.bearingpoint.com.

19. Sarah Diamond, "Profiting Today by Positioning for Tomorrow: A Field Guide to the Financial Markets of 2015," www.sia.com/ops2006/pdf/SarahDiamond.pdf.

20. http://marsrovers.nasa.gov/technology/is_autonomous_mobility.html. If you are looking for quality Internet entertainment, check the surprising video there. Those guys at the Jet Propulsion Laboratory are such a bunch of cutups.

21. www.irobot.com/sp.cfm?pageid=138.

22. www.ohioheartsurgery.com/robot.htm.

23. Pasha Roberts, "Information Visualization for Stock Market Ticks: Toward a New Trading Interface" (master's thesis, MIT Sloan School, February 2004). This can be found at MIT, or with video supplements at the visualization company Roberts founded, Lineplot (www.lineplot.com/expertise/thesis.html).

24. An animated version of the Visible Marketplace can be seen at www.oculusinfo.com.

25. Dow Jones Elementized News Feed, www.djnewswires.com/us/djenf.htm.

26. Reuters Newscope algorithmic offerings, http://about.reuters.com/productinfo/newsscoperealtime/index.aspx?user=1&.

27. These tools are called Open Calais (www.opencalais.com/).

28. For the technically ambitious reader, Lucene (http://lucene.apache.org/), Lingpipe (http://alias-i.com/lingpipe/), and Lemur (www.lemurproject.org/) are popular open source language and information retrieval tools.

29. Anthony Oettinger, a pioneer in machine translation at Harvard going back to the 1950s, told a story of an early English-Russian-English system sponsored by U.S. intelligence agencies. The English "The spirit is willing but the flesh is weak" went in, was translated to Russian, which was then sent in again to be translated back into English. The result: "The vodka is ready but the meat is rotten." Tony got out of the machine translation business.

30. This modern translator is found at www.systransoft.com. I tried Oettinger's example again, 50 years later. The retranslation of the Russian back to English this time was "The spirit is of willing of but of the flesh is of weak."

31. The CIA In-Q-Tel venture capitalists are found here: www.inqtel.org/.

Part Two

Alpha as Life

ndex funds are passive investments; their goal is to deliver a return that matches a benchmark index. The Old Testament of indexing is Burton Malkiel's classic *A Random Walk Down Wall Street*, first published in 1973 by W.W. Norton and now in its ninth edition. For typical individual investors, without special access to information, it offers what is likely the best financial advice they will ever get: It is hard to consistently beat the market, especially after fees. A passive strategy will do better in the long run.

Of course, no one thinks of oneself as a typical individual investor. That might be your brother-in-law or the guy across the hall. And index funds are just not as much fun as picking stocks. It's called passive investing for a reason. Alpha, outperforming a passive benchmark, is the goal of active investing. Even Malkiel has admitted to actively managing some his own money.* Recent additions to the Forbes 400 list include more than a few people who seem unusually adept at finding alpha, and keeping a piece of it.

---

*This surprising admission came in a dinner speech at the Investment Management Network "Superbowl of Indexing" Conference (December 1996, Palm Springs, California). No performance figures were disclosed.

The basic fee structure in the hedge fund world is "2 and 20." Managers are paid 2 percent of assets and 20 percent of alpha. Similar arrangements are also used for performance paid to institutional managers, blurring the distinction between these types of buy-side firms. To see how this works, consider a $100 million portfolio, benchmarked against Treasury bills. If the manager produced a return equal to the T-bills, the alpha would be zero, and the manager's fee would be $2 million, all from the asset-based portion. Unless the firm gave really good parties or had a great story, it would probably be replaced, since the client would end up earning the T-bill rate minus 2 percent, or something like a passbook savings account.

With a skilled, lucky, or skilled and lucky manager, the situation could be quite different. If the T-bills returned 3 percent that year and the hedge portfolio returned 28 percent, then the manager's alpha is 25 percent, $25 million on the original investment. Under the 2-and-20 plan the firm would get to keep 20 percent of that, another $5 million on top of the $2 million in asset-based fees. The client keeps $18 million, substantially more than the meager few percent the client would have gotten in Treasuries.

A $100 million portfolio is small as hedge funds go. It costs money to do the research or proprietary trading to produce that 25 percent alpha, so by the time all the bills are paid, that $7 million the manager takes is seriously pared down. But when the fund gets larger, the economies of scale kick in in a major way. Investment strategies don't scale to the sky, but it is (approximately) true that the cost to run a $1 billion portfolio is not that much more than for $100 million. In that case, the manager on the 2-and-20 plan takes home $70 million with performance as in the example. On $10 billion, the manager takes home $700 million, which begins to look like serious coin—even on the right side of the tracks in Greenwich, Connecticut. Deliver this kind of performance consistently, and you can raise the rates to 4 percent of assets and 40 percent of alpha, which would pay the $10 billion manager $1.4 billion with the same performance scenario. This is where those billion-dollar paydays for hedge fund managers we read about in *Institutional Investor* and *Parade* magazine come from, and why people with what seem like good, solid $5 million annual paychecks at places like Goldman Sachs leave to start their own hedge funds.

The whole alpha ecosystem depends on, and is a creature of, technology. Before computers, it was sufficiently tedious to compute the alpha of a portfolio that no one did it. Comparing one stock to another is easy. Real portfolios are much messier. They have cash flows in from additional investments, and cash flows out from payments or withdrawals. There are dividends paid in from long positions, and dividends paid out from shorts. Stocks split, companies merge, symbols change. International investments' returns are subject to currency variations to the extent that they are not hedged, and if they are, there are costs associated with those hedge positions.

Bill Fouse, who started the world's first index fund, tells a story about the early days of performance measurement. In the 1950s and 1960s the reporting from investment managers to clients was almost anecdotal. The manager would invite the clients up to the lavishly decorated dark wood-paneled office and show them a list of stocks in their portfolio, with the prices paid and the recent prices. Nothing would be said about cash flows, holding periods, or dividends, and nothing about closed positions. It was easy to pretty up the report by cleaning out the losers. Everyone would sit around the conference table to review the list of holdings, and enjoy a fine n-martini lunch.

In 1968 A.G. Becker, a brokerage firm, changed the game by using computers to keep accurate annualized scores for clients' accounts, and by comparing the results with index benchmarks. This was possible only because the firm had acquired one of the early mainframe computers, a room-filling behemoth like the IBM System 360. The news wasn't pretty. Any asset managers were much better at telling a good story and coming up with a good lunch than they were at managing assets. As Fouse tells it, managers resisted the idea of quantitative performance measurement. They sent out the word, "Hire them, and you can't hire us." Some of their objections were valid; a simple performance measurement doesn't consider the risks that a manager is allowed to take. Other measures—like the Sharpe, Jensen, and Treynor ratios*—refined the idea, but the alpha industry was born and has been growing ever since.

Finance students and Wall Street sorts around the world yearn for knowledge that will let them find ever more alpha. This raises the simple question: "Where does alpha come from?" That question is the title of Chapter 4, which opens this part of the book. The chapter explains why the search for alpha is more than just a snipe hunt, and why the people who find it may be more than just plain lucky.

Chapter 5, "A Gentle Introduction to Computerized Investing," starts out with a description of indexing, the great granddaddy of all quant equity strategies, and how it is transformed into active quant strategies by adding information beyond knowledge of an index's constituent stocks.

In Chapter 6, the last of this part, "Stupid Data Miner Tricks," we see how with the right mix of hubris, stupidity, and CPU cycles, it is possible to do some real damage to your financial health. In investing, as in the bomb squad, knowing what not to do is extremely worthwhile.

---

*The Sharpe ratio is a measure of management skill that adjusts pure alpha (value added) by the variability of that value added. The others (Jensen & Treynor) are refinements based on characteristics of the portfolio, such as beta. They are less commonly used. Details are here http://en.wikipedia.org/wiki/Sharpe_ratio.

ALPHA
likeStocks
INFORMATION
market
million
Figure
Information
performance just
based efficient Investment
hedge web
Two Markets
companies funds Chapter trading
Managers used
Surprises
innovation
arbitrage one
strategies
earnings
stock
Index prices new
financial
first make example
great investors
people
research
traders Barr
portfolio time return
indexing
BARRA
look come
Back
Bill good
institutional
browsers
another
book
Internet now
group active quant
keep
beta
manager
quantitative
Street industry
house billion
also long world
might factors returns technology
assets investor paid positions
Source news
early fund portfolios
may different came
fast ever days ide
bonds less
Real
computer
dollar
see

Chapter 4

Where Does Alpha Come From?

Life Is Alpha. The Rest Is Details.
—Popular T-shirt at hedge fund events

There was a time not too long ago when, if you posed the question "Where does alpha come from?" to a roomful of academic financial economists, most of them would complain: "It's a trick question! There is no alpha! Markets are strong-form efficient and you are a heathen!" Those complaints are rarer now, even among economists. Two of their own, Sanford Grossman and Joseph Stiglitz, crystallized the contradiction of strongly efficient markets in their eponymous paradox. It is summarized in Stiglitz's 2001 Nobel Prize citation:

> If a market were informationally efficient, i.e., all relevant information is reflected in market prices, then no single agent would have sufficient incentive to acquire the information on which prices are based.[1]

If there is no profit to be had from trading on information, traders with information will not trade, so prices will not reflect information and will not be efficient. The joke based on this paradox has an economist and his friend walking down the street, and the economist walks right over a $100 bill on the sidewalk. The friend asks why, and the economist replies, "If it was real, someone would have already picked it up." (See Figure 4.1.)

Figure 4.1   How Alfred E. Neuman might illustrate the Grossman–Stiglitz paradox. *If markets are efficient*, they reflect all information, and there is no profit to be had from trading on information. If there is no profit to be had, traders with information won't trade, so markets won't reflect it, and *will not be efficient*.

Warren Buffett expressed his appreciation to proponents of the efficient markets hypothesis (EMH) in the 1985 Berkshire Hathaway annual report:

> In the 1970s . . . institutions were . . . under the spell of academics at prestigious business schools who were preaching a newly fashioned investment theory: the stock market was totally efficient, and therefore calculations of business value—and even thought itself—were of no importance in investment activities.

We are enormously indebted to those academics. What could be more advantageous in an intellectual contest—whether it be bridge, chess, or stock selection—than to have opponents who have been taught that thinking is a waste of energy?[2]

Some academics crossed the road as well. Fischer Black, after leaving MIT for Goldman Sachs, said, "Markets look a lot more efficient from the banks of the Charles than from the banks of the Hudson."[3] Someone gets to pick up that $100 bill.

Back on the banks of the Charles in Boston 25 years later, Andy Lo wrote, "Profits may be viewed as the economic rents which accrue to [the] competitive advantage of . . . superior information, superior technology, financial innovation. . . ."[4] If this conjures up images of ever faster, better, larger computing engines at giant quantitative hedge funds, you are getting the message. But this idea is not suddenly true today; it has been true forever. Innovations used to use less electricity, though. In 1790, the technology that produced vast alpha for innovative traders was boats. After the American Revolution, war bonds were trading for less than a nickel on the dollar. There was a general expectation that the new country and the states would default on the substantial debt. George Washington thought this would be a bad rap for a new country, so the Funding Act of 1790 guaranteed, dollar for dollar, all debts of the new Union and the states. Word spread from the first Congress, in New York, by land messengers.

Technologically innovative traders chartered every fast-moving boat in the city, front-running the messengers and buying up bonds for pennies on the dollar.

Alpha from Innovation

In the early days of electronic market data feeds, the 1970s and 1980s, traders who noticed that the crusty slow centralized systems lagged the fast broadcast streams by up to 20 minutes played the same game—without boats.

In 1815, technological information advantage came from birds. In June of that year, there was a general panic in London that the empire would be routed by Napoleon. Financial markets crashed, and dealers frantically unloaded government bonds. Nathan Meyer Rothschild knew the outcome before the British press, by virtue of his use of fast carrier

Figure 4.2   Indexing pioneer Bill Fouse with the Prime minicomputer used
to run the first index fund. This machine has less computational power than
a mid-range high-end digital watch of 2008.
Source: Anise Wallace, "How Did Wells Fargo Get to the Top?" Institutional Investor,
June 1976.

pigeons to bring him the news of Napoleon's surprising defeat before
the rest of the market knew. He quietly bought everything British he
could get his hands on, and a few days later, when news of Napoleon's
catastrophic defeat at Waterloo arrived for the non-bird owning traders,
prices soared, and Rothschild became one of Europe's wealthiest men.

We see an important part of the beginnings of financial information
technology innovation in the form of the blinking, humming refrigerator-
sized computers of the 1970s. Bill Fouse, at Wells Fargo, bought a Prime
computer and used it to run the first index fund,[5] the granddaddy of
quantitative equity investing and the vast systematic investment industry.[6]
John C. Bogle founded Vanguard in 1974, doing the same thing for retail
mutual fund investors. Alas, I can't find a picture of Bogle and his first
computer, so Figure 4.2 shows Fouse with his.

Further innovation came in the form of factor models, notably
"Barr's better betas," a fundamental multifactor model developed by
Barr Rosenberg at Berkeley. The beta that Barr had better versions of
was the one in the capital asset pricing model (CAPM). The conventional wisdom in writing a book popularizing a technical topic is that
each equation included cuts book sales in half. So with great trepidation, here is a simplified version of main equation used in the CAPM:

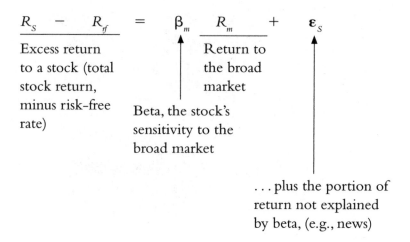

$$\underbrace{R_S \quad - \quad R_{rf}}_{} \quad = \quad \beta_m \quad R_m \quad + \quad \varepsilon_S$$

Excess return
to a stock (total
stock return,
minus risk-free
rate)

Return to
the broad
market

Beta, the stock's
sensitivity to the
broad market

... plus the portion of
return not explained
by beta, (e.g., news)

Bill Sharpe shared the Nobel Prize in economics for the capital asset pricing model. This is a simple representation of the key idea that the return to a stock is explained by the return to the broad market (e.g., the S&P 500) times the stock's sensitivity to the market (beta) plus stock-specific returns (e.g., from news). This is a simple idea. Think of it as "a rising tide lifts all boats" and you're pretty close. Some stocks, like utilities, are less sensitive to market returns than others (like tech or finance); they have lower betas. The average beta over all stocks is 1.0. Of course, the rising tide doesn't explain everything; there are stock-specific components of return—things like news and earnings events—that are added on, the epsilon on the right side of the equation. I hope that didn't cause you to put the book away.

Barr Rosenberg extended the CAPM based on the observation that there are more factors that explain stock returns than just the broad market, and these apply in different strengths to different stocks.

Some of these "better betas" are for industry groups, based on the insight that we do notice that, for example, financials or airlines or other similar companies tend to move as group. Others are things like exchange rates, which affect companies that have international income or bills to pay in foreign currencies in predictable ways. Those are the "better betas"— industry groups and common factors, about 60 of them in all. Instead of one lonely beta summarizing the stock's sensitivity to the entire market, we have a group of them that give a more fine-grained view of the market:

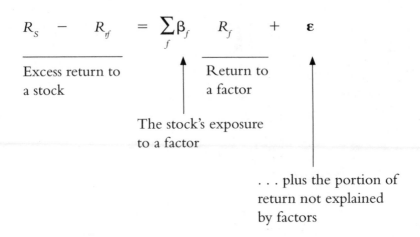

$$R_S \quad - \quad R_{rf} \quad = \quad \sum_f \beta_f \quad R_f \quad + \quad \varepsilon$$

Excess return to
a stock

Return to
a factor

The stock's exposure
to a factor

. . . plus the portion of
return not explained
by factors

Once that Greek summation symbol snuck in, people started to get lost. There weren't as many nerds on Wall Street back then, and it was more socially acceptable to make fun of guys like Barr who wrote equations like this. A prime example is found on the cover of the May 1978 *Institutional Investor*, which asked: "Who is Barr Rosenberg? And what the hell is he talking about?" (See Figure 4.3.)

Rosenberg's multifactor model was originally designed for risk control, to allow you to balance your portfolio's exposures to industry groups and common factors. It was embodied in the analysis and optimization tools from Barra, the company Rosenberg founded in 1977.

It turned out that these models were also particularly amenable to alpha strategies. Forecasting returns to hundreds or thousands of different stocks was an onerous task, particularly with the computers of the era. But with only 60 factors, the task was greatly simplified, and those forecasts could be used to construct active, alpha-seeking portfolios. Barr himself left Barra to found an active management firm in 1985, where his innovation produced, yes, a great deal of alpha. Quite a few of the early quant firms founded in the 1980s used similar approaches. After a great deal of success with this approach, Barr Rosenberg and his Barra colleagues were unable to resist the academic urge to publish. Andrew Rudd published a paper titled "Market Efficiency Revisited."[7] Rosenberg along with Barra veterans Kenneth Reid and Ron Lanstein published a paper presenting what they called "Persuasive Evidence of Market Inefficiency"[8] based on a fundamental-based multifactor analysis of stock market returns.[9]

Figure 4.3 Who is Barr Rosenberg? Inventor of the better betas.
Source: Institutional Investor, *May 1978.*

For these factor-based quant alpha strategies, the Barra models were updated monthly, and the portfolios generally adjusted on the same schedule. Chapter 3, "Algo Wars," included a discussion about market-making algorithms as a source of profit (i.e., alpha) by moving faster than specialists and human market makers, being able to choose which stocks to use, and avoiding the obligations to maintain a two-sided quote at all times. These strategies were alpha machines, producing just a little at a time, thousands of times a day.

Another group of fast alpha strategies relied on forms of arbitrage, finding mispriced identical, nearly identical, or highly correlated securities, then simultaneously buying the one that appeared underpriced and selling the one that seemed overpriced, then waiting for the markets to bring them back in line. You can think of this as "buying a 4.9-cent nickel." An example would be the same stock trading on two different markets, such as the NYSE and a regional exchange. When people were the main participants in a market, it could take seconds or minutes for things to line up, and the computers had a natural speed advantage.

Figure 4.4 Pure arbitrage, in the school supplies store.

Once, when shopping in an educational supplies store, I came across an item that illustrated the arbitrage idea so well that I had to explain why I was laughing in the elementary school supplies aisle and taking photos of the fairly dull-looking merchandise. The picture is shown in Figure 4.4.

Selling 100 pennies for $4.75 is a deal anyone would want to make. In the real world, you would never find a mispricing of 475 percent. In fact, these aren't real pennies going for that price; they are plastic imitations, used to teach grade-schoolers how to make change. The fact that this product exists and is sold to schools is a sorry statement about the state of the education world.

Examples of this type of riskless structural pure arbitrage include the cross-listed stocks mentioned earlier, convertible bonds that may be mispriced temporarily so a stock can be had for less than its market price by buying the bond and converting, and stocks trading in multiple countries that are mispriced when the exchange rates fluctuate but the stock prices have not yet reflected that. There is also a wide variety of arbitrage strategies involving options. The math on those can get complicated, and with two equations already cutting into sales in this chapter, the details will be left as a research project for technically inclined readers. Try looking for "options arbitrage" on Amazon, and you will find more than you probably want to know.

Another family of arbitrage strategies is statistically based, rather than structural. Think of a stock in a purely financial holding company,

A, that holds only one asset, stock in company B. These stocks should move in lockstep, though not necessarily at the exact same price, since there may be different numbers of shares outstanding. Fast traders, now all computerized, can exploit these mispricings to produce alpha. It also works for closely related companies (e.g., a supplier firm with one large customer firm).

Quant arbitrage traders sometimes used knowledge of these relationships to monitor the related pairs. Given that there are over a million pairs of stocks in the S&P 1500 (1,124,250 = 1,500*1,499/2, to be exact), this can require a lot of research on the relationships between companies. Instead of doing all that heavy lifting, it is reasonable just to look at the correlations between stocks to screen for promising pairs. This would be a 1500-by-1500 table showing those correlations over time. If a pair of stocks is correlated at 95 percent over a period of months, it is not a bad guess to say they are somehow related. Again, the arbitrageur takes two positions: long the underpriced security, and short the overpriced one. Eventually, usually quickly, they come back into line, the positions are closed out, and the arbitrage profit pocketed.[10]

Possible problems are changes in the economic relationship between the pairs. For example, the holding company could change its holdings, or tax changes might make one security more valuable than another for some investors.

Alpha, the ARPANET, and the Internet

There is another place to look besides the speed race and arbitrage strategies. There is a huge amount of information in prices and quantitatively derived measures, but that is not all the information we have about stocks. Some is in the form of news, research, and other textual sources. Having tomorrow's newspaper, even without the stock pages, would be valuable to investors.

We've seen how innovation on quantitative information can produce alpha. How about innovation in textual information? If innovation leads to alpha, it might be a good idea to follow innovation. And where is there more innovation than on the Internet? The basic components have been in place for some time. The ARPANET, which became the

Internet, was first operational two days before Halloween in 1969. The first web site did not appear until 1991 at the CERN nuclear research center. This technology could not be tapped by investors until the availability of Web browsers for the PC.

The first Web browser, Mosaic, was released by the University of Illinois in 1993. Then it was quickly commercialized as Netscape Navigator in 1994, Microsoft Internet Explorer, and other browsers. In the space of a year, the relationship between markets and information was transformed. Figures 4.5 and 4.6 illustrate the effect dramatically.

An *earnings surprise* is a very pure form of market-moving information event. You know exactly when it happens—when the company announces its earnings—and there is no ambiguity about interpretation. Positive surprises result in positive returns. Figure 4.5 shows event studies illustrating the market's response to earnings surprises in a period before the PC browsers were around to spread the news in real time. People read it the next day in the *Wall Street Journal*. Some read it in *Barron's*, over the weekend. Investment committees met weekly to adjust portfolios. Lunches were long. Both positive and negative surprises took over 10 trading days to be fully impounded in price. Prior to the event, on the left side of the chart in Figure 4.5, we see information leakage before the announcement, for negative surprises.

This picture changes dramatically after PC browsers appear, seen in the chart shown in Figure 4.6, which overlays the market response

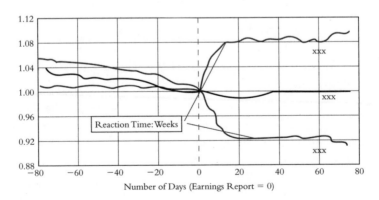

Figure 4.5 Earnings surprises before the Web, 1983–1989. Take your time. Skip a week, have a beer.
Source: Bob Butman, DAIS Group (1999).

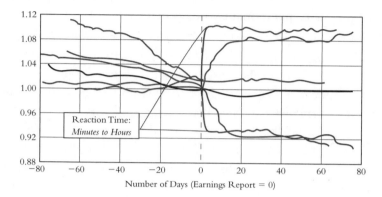

Figure 4.6 Earnings surprises after the Web, 1995–1998. Move it or lose it. *Source: Bob Butman, DAIS Group (1999).*

to earnings surprises when people could learn of them from the Web instead of the newspaper or the mail carrier. The information is now impounded in prices in less than one day (i.e., minutes to hours), and the leakage is even larger for negative surprises.

This is an early example of the democratization of information brought about by the Web. The Internet is a threat to people who make their living as intermediaries. Direct market access has disintermediated brokers, many of whom are now in other lines of work. Direct access to primary sources of financially relevant information is disintermediating reporters, who now have to provide more than just a conduit to earn their keep.

We would be hard-pressed to find more innovation than we see today on the Web. Google Finance, Yahoo! Finance, and their brethren have made more advanced information retrieval and analysis tools available for free than could be purchased for any amount in the not-so-distant past.

Other new technologies enable a new level of human-machine collaboration in investment research, such as XML (extensible markup language), discussed in Chapter 2. One of this technology's most vocal proponents is Christopher Cox, former chairman of the SEC, who has taken the lead in encouraging the adoption of XBRL (extensible Business Reporting Language) to keep U.S. markets, exchanges, companies, and investors ahead of the curve.

We constantly hear about information overload, information glut, information anxiety, data smog, and the like. Herb Simon's observation that an abundance of information causes a deficit of attention becomes more of a reality with every passing day. It is also becoming more obvious that a modern alpha-seeking research team will include automated assistants. We will delegate repetitive tasks to computers, rather than manipulating them. This will include persistent search, metaknowledge of linkages between entities and events, and natural language capabilities far beyond keywords. "This is interesting" can be a signal as useful as "buy" or "sell," in a process that includes intelligent humans. While true artificial intelligence remains elusive, intelligence amplification is something well-wired alpha seekers do today.

Summary

This chapter offered examples of how technology, often purely by speed, could produce alpha, and why this is in keeping with the new view of adaptive markets—efficient, but not perfectly and instantaneously efficient.

Quant managers started out running only index funds, but realized there was more to be made than the few basis points on assets that indexers can charge. The next chapter describes that evolution.

Notes

1. The Royal Swedish Academy of Sciences, "The Prize in Economics 2001: Joseph Stiglitz," Nobelprize.org, http://nobelprize.org/nobel_prizes/economics/laureates/2001/public.html.

2. Warren Buffett, "Chairman's Letter," Berkshire Hathaway Inc. Annual Report 1985, www.berkshirehathaway.com/letters/1985.html.

3. Fischer Black, quoted in *Against the Gods: The Remarkable Story of Risk* by Peter L. Bernstein (New York: John Wiley & Sons, 1996), p. 7.

4. Andrew Lo, *Market Efficiency: Stock Market Behavior in Theory and Practice* (Lyme, NH: Edward Elgar Publishing, 1997).

5. Of course, there is no alpha in an index fund, unless you are doing something wrong. That came later, in enhanced index and more aggressive quant strategies.

6. For an excellent text on this, try *Active Portfolio Management: A Quantitative Approach for Producing Superior Returns and Controlling Risk* by Richard Grinold and Ron Kahn (New York: McGraw-Hill; 2nd edition, 1999).

7. Andrew Rudd, "Market Efficiency Revisited," *Journal of Accounting, Auditing and Finance* (Spring 1984): 279–288.

8. Barr Rosenberg, Kenneth Reid, and Ron Lanstein, "Persuasive Evidence of Market Inefficiency," *Journal of Portfolio Management* (Spring 1985): 9–16.

9. Barr Rosenberg and Andrew Rudd, "Factor Related and Specific Returns of Common Stocks: Serial Correlation and Market Inefficiency," *Journal of Finance* (May 1982): 543–554. For a look at where these ideas have gone in the many intervening years, visit www.barra.com.

10. For the complete math, see *Pairs Trading: Quantitative Methods and Analysis* by Ganapathy Vidyamurthy (John Wiley & Sons, 2004).

Chapter 5

A Gentle Introduction to Computerized Investing

"Life would be so much easier if we only had the source code."
— HACKER PROVERB

The beginning of index investing in the 1970s was the result of a convergence of events, one of those ripe apple moments. Institutional investors began to use firms like A.G. Becker to actually compare the total performance of their hired managers with index benchmarks, and found that many of them fell short, especially after the substantial fees the investors were paying.

Yale professor Burton Malkiel popularized the academic efficient market arguments in *A Random Walk Down Wall Street*, writing in 1973, "[We need] a new investment instrument: a no-load, minimum-management-fee mutual fund that simply buys the hundreds of stocks making up the market averages and does no trading [of securities]. . . . Fund spokesmen are quick to point out, 'you can't buy the averages.' It's about time the public could."

Computers had gotten to the point where one could be put in an office setting without having to tear out walls and bring in industrial-strength air-conditioning, raised floors for the cables, and special power systems. It was slightly easier to install a computer in an office building than a particle accelerator, but not by much. I recall visiting an insurance company in Hartford one winter where they were using their IBM System 360 to heat several floors of a large building. Minicomputers, like the Digital Equipment Corporation (DEC) systems described in the Introduction, the Data General Nova, and the Prime, all from companies in the first Silicon Valley, Boston's Route 128 (the same crowd that came to the TX-2 going-away party), were manageable enough to fit in a normal office setting. You needed to crank the AC and have a high tolerance for noise, but they didn't break the bank, or the floor.

The idea, the desire, and the means to achieve it all came together in the early 1970s for index funds. But this is a chapter about alpha strategies, the anti-index funds—so why are we talking about them at all? Because they are a starting point for all active quantitative computerized equity strategies.

Indexing 101

Calculating an index is fairly simple. Multiply the prices of the stocks in the index by their weights (usually their share of the total capitalization of the index constituents), add them up, and there's your index. Charles Dow, a journalist, started doing it with a pencil and paper in 1896. You need to make adjustments for mergers, splits, and the like, and can get fancy, including dividends for total return.

Running an index fund is less simple. You have to figure out how many of hundreds or thousands of different stocks to buy (or sell) each time cash moves in or out of the portfolio in the form of investments, withdrawals, and dividends. For the most common S&P 500 there are 500 stocks to deal with. For a total market index like the Russell 3000, there are 3,000. For the Wilshire 5000, there are about 6,700.

The measure of how well you are doing in an index fund is clearly not alpha; that should be zero. It is tracking error, a measure of the difference between the calculated index and the actual portfolio. An ideal index fund has a tracking error of zero. Real-world index funds have tracking errors around 0.1 percent. If it gets much larger than that, someone is confused.

Index Funds: The Godfather of Quantitative Investing

Index funds have an interesting history. Prior to the 1960s, most institutional equity portfolios were managed by bank trust departments, and performance reporting was not the refined art that it has become today.

Bill Fouse, one of the founders of the world's first indexing group at Wells Fargo in the 1970s, tells stories of when performance reporting by a bank trust department consisted of a table listing all stocks held, the acquisition price of each, the current price, and the size of the position. This introduced some unusual biases into the perception of these reports. Looking at stocks just by price and ignoring dividends tends to favor stocks that don't pay dividends. Simply listing acquisition price and current price ignores the aspect of time, and not comparing it to any well-defined benchmark (like the S&P 500 index) leaves the meaning of even a well-studied report unclear.

A.G. Becker was the first firm to compare the total return of a stock portfolio to an index. Since an S&P 500 index fund is just a passive investment consisting of a capitalization-weighted portfolio of the 500 stocks in the index, it will do no better than the index—and if managed effectively, no worse.

An index fund can't just be started up and left alone to run itself forever. The stocks in the index change; dividends need to be reinvested, and most significantly, there are cash flows in and out of the portfolio from new funding or payment requirements. All of these events result in a need to trade, and it costs money to trade, not just in the explicit commissions, but in the market impact incurred when large volumes of stock are bought or sold. Managing an index fund effectively means keeping control of trading costs. These costs can drag the index portfolio's performance down from the theoretically calculated index we see reported all the time. The reported index levels don't include any real or simulated trading costs. They incur no commission costs and no market impact.

For smaller index portfolios, under $20 million or so, the trading costs can become a significant problem. The lower-weighted stocks in the index will be held in very small quantities, and the cost associated with trading 100 shares is much more than one-tenth of the cost of trading 1,000, or one-hundredth the cost of trading 10,000.

For large index portfolios, the sheer size of trades can impose another trading cost in the form of market impact. Even so, there are economies of scale to be had in managing large index funds. This is reflected by the current business situation in which there are a small number of large index fund providers around the world, such as State Street and Barclays Global Investments. Estimates of total assets managed using this sort of passive approach, in a variety of markets, now exceed $4 trillion.

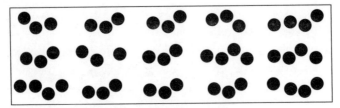

Imagine 500 stocks in this box,
one for each company in the S&P 500 index.

Figure 5.1   Full Replication Index Fund. All the stocks, all the time.

Setting aside considerations of trading costs for now, the idea of an index fund is a very simple one. Nevertheless, it is a quantitative concept, and running an index fund requires the use of a computer. The most straightforward way to manage an index fund is simply to hold all of the stocks in the index: every single one of them, each in its index weight. This is illustrated in Figure 5.1, which represents all of the stocks in the S&P 500 put into a portfolio. This is simple and will, in fact, ignoring trading costs, replicate the index exactly. This type of index fund is called a full replication fund.

Even with full replication funds, the trading costs and fixed 100-share increments for holdings will cause the portfolio to have a performance somewhat different from that of the index.

Stratified Sampling

Fortunately, it's not necessary to hold all 500 stocks to track the index very closely. Keeping the portfolio tightly constrained within each industry group, while perhaps leaving out the more illiquid names, will often simplify management of the index portfolio and lower trading costs.

The way this works is shown in Figure 5.2. We have taken the same box of 500 stocks and separated them into groups by industry and by size. These are the most commonly used classifications of stocks traded around the world. Notice that now, instead of one box, we now have 15 little ones in this example (three size categories and five hypothetical industry groups, since the 55 actual S&P industries make for a busy chart). Within each little box we find the stocks, for example, of a big automaker, or a medium-sized shoe company, or a small implements of destruction firm. These are called stratified samples. We keep the total

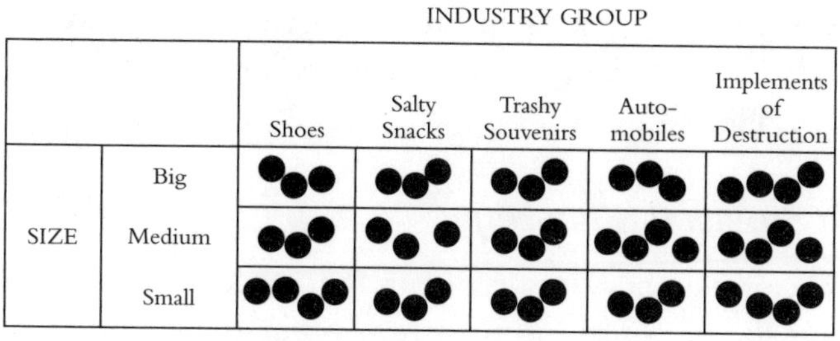

INDUSTRY GROUP

		Shoes	Salty Snacks	Trashy Souvenirs	Auto-mobiles	Implements of Destruction
SIZE	Big	●●●	●●●	●●●	●●●	●●●
	Medium	●●●	●●●	●●●	●●●	●●●
	Small	●●●●	●●●	●●●	●●●	●●●●

Stocks are grouped by industry and size.

Figure 5.2   Stratified Sampling Categories

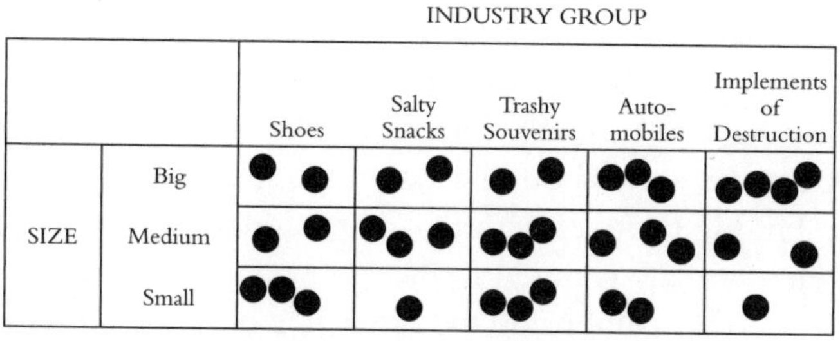

INDUSTRY GROUP

		Shoes	Salty Snacks	Trashy Souvenirs	Auto-mobiles	Implements of Destruction
SIZE	Big	● ●	● ●	● ●	●●●	●●●●
	Medium	● ●	●●●	●●	● ●●	● ●
	Small	●●●	●	●●●	●●	●

Adjust for stocks that are costly to trade, but you keep industry group
weights as they are in the index.
You *don't* hold all 500 stocks anymore.

Figure 5.3   Liquidity-Adjusted Stratified Sample Index Fund. We're still not
playing favorites, just accepting the realities of thinly traded names.

weight in each box (i.e., the total percentage of our portfolio in each
box) the same as it is for the index. Now we can adjust our holdings by
eliminating some of the more illiquid (i.e., more costly to trade) stocks
in each box, and track the S&P 500 very closely without owning each
and every stock in the index. Professional indexers use *portfolio optimization*, a more mathematical approach to sampling, based on factors like
Barr's better betas from the previous chapter.

On any given day, roughly one-third of the stocks in the United
States don't trade at all. Buying or selling these can be costly. Others
trade in small quantities and are also costly to trade.

Figure 5.3 illustrates how these illiquid stocks are avoided by holding others in larger proportions than their index weight. This approach
is used in many index fund portfolio management programs, such
as those from Wilshire Associates. Once systems are in place, this process
is not that complicated, so the fees commanded by index fund managers

tend to be very low. For U.S. institutional-size index funds, the fees are only a few hundredths of a percent of assets, around $30,000 for a $100 million portfolio.

Informed Stratified Sampling

Now let's consider the stratified sampling process again, only this time we're going to use a little information other than trading costs about the companies as we decide what to put in each sample box.

Suppose we decide we want to hold less than the full number of stocks in the category of "Implements of Destruction." We look and we see that there are several stocks. Two catch our eye: Commander Dave's Enforcers Plus and Colonel Curt's Assault Weapon Hut. Now suppose we just happen to know something about Commander Dave and Colonel Curt, since they both live down the street. Commander Dave is in trouble. His big contract with that subnational entity just fell through and the pins are all falling off the grenade launchers. By contrast, Colonel Curt, our neighbor on the other side of the street, appears quite prosperous. He just landed a big deal for the international merchandising tie-ins to a smash hit action film, *World War X—The Sequel*, paid for in advance with cash, and has been boasting about the company's new and improved robot artillery makers. It would be very tempting in managing a fund like this when we consider Commander Dave's wretched prospects and Colonel Curt's rosy outlook not to hold any of Dave's Enforcers Plus, but instead put the money in extra investment in Colonel Curt's Assault Weapon Hut, as seen in Figure 5.4.

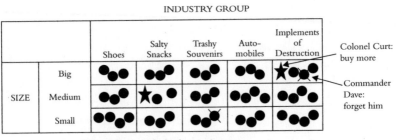

Pick what stays and what leaves using your
judgment about how particular stocks will perform.

Figure 5.4   Informed Sampling. Now we play favorites.

Our positive bets are marked with stars. Stocks we do not hold or hold in reduced proportions are marked with X's.

If this seems like a good idea to you, congratulations. You are now an active manager. It's time to raise your fees. This general notion of looking within each category or industry is in fact how many active equity portfolios are run.

Active Management

Institutional equity managers often operate in exactly this way. Unlike individual investors, they will not typically plunge into a very small number of concentrated positions in the stocks they favor. They do not want to stray very far from the S&P 500 and risk major differences in performance relative to the index. Consistent, if modest, value-added performance is typically the goal. The reason for this reluctance is that many institutional sponsors are themselves held to a performance standard based on the S&P 500, and they want their portfolios managed this way.

A traditional firm doing this sort of portfolio management would have a person or a group of people assigned to each industry group. Some might separate out large companies from small and medium-sized companies as well. Traditional fund analysts will specialize in an industrial area. They will sit down and have the same sort of discussion we had about Colonel Curt and Commander Dave for each group of companies in their sector. They may not be neighbors of the CEOs, but they've probably visited the plant, seen the products, read the literature, and talked to competitors and customers.

The analysts try to synthesize their pieces of information into a decision whether to include the stock in the portfolio, and at what weight, or not to include it or to underweight it relative to its index component. The reason for this underweighting, rather than eliminating an unattractive stock completely, is because of index tracking risk. Totally eliminating a company increases the risk of the portfolio return differing substantially from the index if these forecasts are wrong and the stock moves in an opposite direction. The sizes of these decisions, called "active bets," are constrained by the willingness to risk returns that stray from the index in either direction, in the hope of adding value by straying in a positive direction.

Constraints on Active Managers

These constraints require active managers to keep a certain portion of their assets in an indexlike subportfolio, either by replication or by sampling, and to use the rest of the portfolio to make active bets trying to outperform the index. For a portfolio designed to have very little risk relative to the index, the percentage of the portfolio available for bets outside of the index subportfolio might be 10 percent. For a looser portfolio willing to incur a little more risk, this might be 20 percent. These types of portfolios are called "active long equity portfolios." Even when active stock selection is based on purely subjective judgments, the process can be viewed as mildly quantitative in that the risk control bounds are set by quantitative analysis.

An investment committee meeting at a traditional management firm to decide the portfolio allocations would be the group of people, each assigned to an industry, sitting around a table. They apply their judgment to set the active bets in the portfolio. A quantitative management meeting might be a group of people sitting around the same table, also trying to apply their judgment, but they are using computers. They will be able to look at many more stocks than the people who have to go visit the companies. They can spread their risk and make many small bets, thus lowering the risk for a comparable level of value added (i.e., the return above a passive S&P 500 index fund). Dividing the value added by the variation in value added is a number called the information ratio. This is useful in measuring the reward of an investment strategy relative to its risk.

Risk is measured as the year-to-year variation of the value added. A manager who was way up one year, down the next, flat in the third, and showed generally erratic performance would be considered riskier than a steady (if much less exciting) performer. For example, a manager who outperformed the S&P index by between 2 percent and 3 percent year in and year out, with very little variation from year to year, would have a much better information ratio than another manager with the same average +2.5 percent performance, but with large differences from year to year. The diversification provided by the larger numbers of stocks in the portfolios of quantitatively managed funds often results in a higher information ratio than their traditionally managed counterparts.

What Do Quantitative Managers Do?

What are these people with the computers doing if they haven't gone and kicked the tires and had lunch with the CEO? This is a good question. We all know of many factors that one can consider when making an investment decision. For example, if there was a sudden increase in the price of oil, one would be more likely to invest in oil companies than airlines. If there was a sudden increase in interest rates, one would be more disposed to invest in companies with less floating debt than those with a substantial amount. If the dollar weakens against foreign currencies, one would be less inclined to invest in firms with a substantial amount of income from foreign sources, or supplies from foreign sources. These are general characteristics that one could apply across many industries. There are also specific industries that one would favor in response to say, a change in housing standards or oil price. A quick scan of the investment section in any large bookstore would yield a wide variety of other theories on how to pick strong stocks and avoid weak ones. Quantitative methods provide a means to verify and combine many of these theories.

Earnings are probably the most important single factor affecting stock prices. When the analysts make their forecasts to indicate their expectations of better earnings, it can often move a stock price up. A surprise announcement of better (or worse) than expected earnings is typically followed by a corresponding jump in the stock price (up or down).

Academics and practitioners have found many such market anomalies that allow excess returns to be made in the stock market.

A wide variety of *corporate actions* have been found to have predictable effects on stock prices. Companies often issue new stock in the form of *secondary equity offerings.* Others do the opposite and to buy back their own stock in the market. These *buybacks* are done for a reason, and those firms tend to outperform others. An opposite effect is often observed for companies selling additional shares.[1]

Stock splits are another effect. Stocks that split tend to do much better for a period extending over two years than stocks that don't split, and far better than stocks that do reverse splits.

Yet another example is the financial indigestion suffered by companies that acquire other companies that are of substantial size relative to themselves. Such acquirers tend to underperform relative to companies that don't make these acquisitions.

Insider trading is another source of stock-specific information. These trades must be reported to the Securities and Exchange Commission (SEC), and the reports are available directly from the SEC or from commercial sources that get them from the SEC. Many investors report that insider trading is a valuable source of information when selecting stocks.[2] The occasional buy or sell by an insider in the amount of a boat payment or a college tuition check doesn't mean much of anything. When insiders consistently, and as a group, become major buyers or sellers, this may tell you something about the company's future. Some insiders in particular seem more willing to test the limits of regulations governing insider trading. Finding those persons and following their actions is one of the most valuable ways to use insider trading information.

Valuation methods range from sophisticated Graham and Dodd* techniques to simple price-earnings (P/E) tilts. The P/E ratios vary often within an industry group. The lower-P/E stocks often tend to do better than the higher-P/E stocks. This kind of simple filter can be (and often is) used to choose the dogs (the ones to make active negative bets against) and stars (the stocks to make positive bets on) in the previous example with Commander Dave and Colonel Curt.

The list of candidate market anomalies can be quite long. Of course, not all of these rules work all the time. Some work for a while and gradually stop working when they become widely known. Certain stocks are more predictable than others by these methods.

Quantitative analysis tries to bring a great deal of this information into one place, assess which ideas apply, and determine how to combine them most effectively. Simply adding up the individual effects observed from splits or stock buybacks and so on does not give a very accurate answer. Many of these signals are strongly related to each other. When combined in a simple fashion, they can overstate a stock's prospects in a major way.

For example, we may find that stocks that have unexpected earnings growth outperform the market by 1 percent per month. Similarly,

---

*Based on their book *Security Analysis,* which inspired generations of investors including Warren Buffett.

we may find that stocks that split outperform by 1 percent per month, and stocks in companies that buy back their own shares also outperform by 1 percent per month. For a company that had good earnings news, did a stock split, and bought back some of its own stock, we could add all these together and conclude that the company's stock would outperform the market by 3 percent per month. But that would be wrong. These morsels of good news tend to come in clusters, they are correlated, and the total effect is less than the sum of the parts. Similarly, a company with bad marks on several scores will typically not crash and burn with the severity indicated by combining the separately analyzed effects.

In a quantitative equity portfolio, sophisticated mathematical analyses combine all these factors to pick the stars and the dogs, bringing a systematic and scientific tilt to the use of a broad set of investing ideas.

Comparing Quantitative and Traditional Management: Where Does Judgment Apply?

Many of the same ideas used by quantitative managers are also used by traditional managers and vice versa. The difference is that the quantitative manager sets strict methods and criteria for gauging the effect of each indicator, whereas traditional managers combine indicators with each other and other factors for each stock using subjective judgment.

People often think these indicators require little or no subjective judgment in quantitative investing. This is true *only* at the very back end of the process. The rule for quant managers regarding the models they use is "trust it or trash it." Many models are trashed in the process before an acceptable one is found. The subjective judgment is at the model level, in the design of a disciplined investment strategy. Judgment is not used to second-guess the outputs of the process.

This does not mean that managers will blindly follow the recommendations of their models. In special situations such as takeovers, nationalizations, or a speculative bubble in the market, such as Internet stocks, there may be reason to ignore the model's suggestions in these areas, and this is often done.

Quantitative equity portfolios managed in this way can outperform the index on a remarkably consistent basis.

Active Management on Steroids: Market Neutral Portfolios

In the previous section, we mentioned that the consistent requirement not to stray too far from the index requires institutional equity managers to hold what amounts to a hidden index subportfolio. This is designed to minimize the risk of large differences in performance between the portfolio and the index. In effect, only a portion of the total invested capital is available for implementing the investment decisions, whether they are made by quantitative or traditional means. It is the classic trade-off of risk and return. The maximum return you can realistically expect goes up as the risk you are willing to tolerate (in terms of deviation from the index) increases. If no deviation is tolerated, the portfolio becomes an index fund and no excess return is possible.

There is a way around this. You can put all the invested capital to work in an attempt to add value with a market neutral long-short portfolio. A $100 million long-short, market neutral portfolio consists of $100 million in long positions and $100 million in short positions. Notice that since you get $100 million from the short sale, spend $100 million on the long side, and had $100 million to start, you still have $100 million in cash. There's no net capital required to put on a position such as this. This cash will earn roughly a T-bill return from the brokers. If this cash is left earning short-term interest, the value added by the long and short positions will be on top of this interest rate.

Notice the important fact that an investor doing this would forgo the market return.[3] In recent years, few investors would have been happy to do this. There's an easy way to bring back the returns from the stock market and let the value added go on top of the market return. The cash in the portfolio can be used to finance an unleveraged futures position, essentially $100 million worth of exposure to the index return. An ongoing S&P 500 index futures position, reinvested at the contract expiration dates, will very closely track the index return. When a long-short portfolio and an index futures position are put together, what you get is a total return equal to the return on the index plus whatever you make from the long and short portfolios. This is called an "equitized" portfolio. You make money from the long

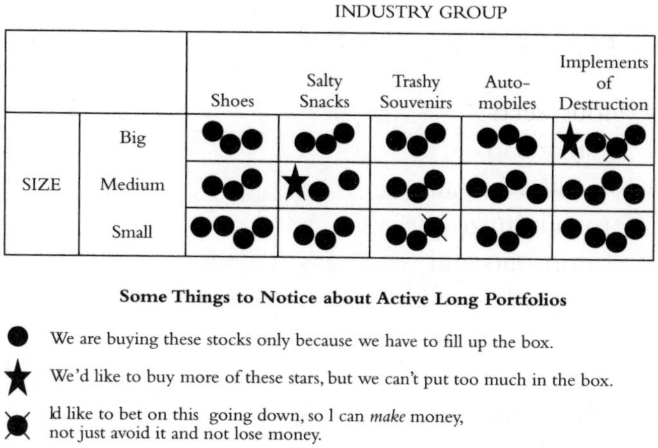

INDUSTRY GROUP

		Shoes	Salty Snacks	Trashy Souvenirs	Auto-mobiles	Implements of Destruction
SIZE	Big	●●●	●●●	●●●	●●●	★●●
	Medium	●●●	★●●	●●●	●●●●	●●●
	Small	●●●●	●●●	●●✖	●●●	●●●

Some Things to Notice about Active Long Portfolios

● We are buying these stocks only because we have to fill up the box.

★ We'd like to buy more of these stars, but we can't put too much in the box.

✖ Id like to bet on this going down, so l can *make* money, not just avoid it and not lose money.

Figure 5.5 Active long portfolio (if you think this looks just like informed sampling, you're right).

portfolios when your stocks outperform the market. You make money from the short portfolios when your stocks underperform.

We can use our stars and dogs picture to illustrate the idea of a market neutral portfolio and its relationship to a traditional long-only portfolio.

Figure 5.5 shows an actively managed long portfolio. We selected the dogs and the stars to underweight or overweight to produce alpha. Other stocks not designated as dogs or stars are there for the index subportfolio, to keep exposure to the benchmark.

In Figure 5.6, we have separated the active bets out into the long and short sides of the market neutral portfolio. The long portfolio contains *only* the stars, and the short portfolio contains *only* the dogs, sold short so we profit when they go down. We have a lot of money left because we no longer have to hold the hidden index stocks. We can pick *more* stars and *more* dogs, or increase the positions we have in the ones we have already selected. All of the money is working *twice*: once on the long side of the portfolio and once on the short side, to add value for the investor. This is the James Brown of quant stock strategies, the hardest-working portfolio in the equity business.

There's another advantage to market neutral investing, which comes on the short side. In a long portfolio, even if we have incredibly adverse opinions regarding a stock, the strongest negative statement we

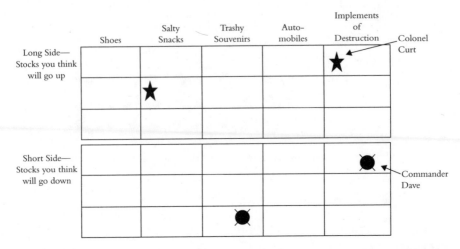

Figure 5.6 A "stars and dogs" view of market neutral investing. Playing favorites to the max, without bothering to own the rest.

can make is not to hold it at all. And, if it was a significant portion of the index, doing so would introduce a high level of risk. The active bet that one could make in a long portfolio is limited by the weight of the stock in the index; you can't go below a zero holding. In contrast, on the short side of a market neutral portfolio, you can sell as much stock short as you believe you can trade efficiently. For these reasons, the Stanford professor and Nobel laureate Bill Sharpe said of market neutral investing, "It's the only way to invest if you believe in active management." All the money works twice, and it can work harder. To summarize, the advantages of market neutral investing are:

- Capital is put to work twice (long and short).
- Value added can be overlaid with simple equity index futures to capture market return.
- Negative information can be fully exploited.

What kind of performance would one expect from a market neutral portfolio? When market exposure is restored using index futures, it should do at least as well as twice the long portfolio, in relation to the index. This is true if the investor is as good at picking stocks that will go down as he is at picking those that will go up. In theory, one would expect the value added to be more than double, since the negative active bets can be larger than the index weight.

What does all this tell us? First, in many ways quantitative investing really is not that much different from traditional investing. If you look inside the process, the quantitative strategies are really just mathematical expressions of fundamental investing ideas. Quantitative methodology allows many disparate concepts to come together in a single forecast. Because the process is automated, it can be applied to many more stocks—not only the S&P 500, but the Russell 1000, Russell 2500, and other broad indexes. Risk can be limited by spreading bets over more active positions.

Finally, we talked about one of the more interesting financially engineered strategies, market neutral portfolios. Market neutral portfolios work twice as hard to deliver extra performance, because they do not contain hidden index components and allow the fullest exploitation of stock selection skill.

The general plan of these strategies is no mystery. Investors who are wary of quantitative ideas may be more comfortable in investing the way many large institutions do once they understand how these systematic approaches work. This is a sound, sensible, and scientific approach to investing.

There are all sorts of investment legerdemain that can be done with market neutral portfolios. If the investor wants to get the stock market return while still using all capital for active bets, the manager hold futures contracts on the index, using the funds already in the account as collateral. This is called equitizing the portfolio—using a futures overlay as a synthetic index fund, which effectively puts back the market exposure for investors who want it, including most pension funds. A recent variation is to use asymmetric long-short portfolios, such as "130-30" strategies.*

An even snappier trick is to use futures from a market other than the U.S. stock market. Many large pension investors need to keep assets in stock markets all over the world, in order to pay future obligations all over the world. And of course, they'd like some alpha with that. So,

---

*The 130-30 strategy is a strategy that uses financial leverage by shorting poor performing stocks and purchasing stocks expected to have high returns. A 130-30 ratio implies shorting up to 30% of the portfolio value and then using the funds to take a long position in stocks projected to outperform the market.

a pension that had a strong U.S. market-neutral manager, and wanted to invest for payments to German pensioners, could equitize with German stock futures. This is called *portable alpha*. It sounds complicated, and is. The futures expire, so you have to roll the contracts over at the right times; and you can really screw up if you change the size of the portfolio and neglect to simultaneously adjust the futures. A big adverse market move during the mismatched period has led to more than one career change.

Finding Information and Inefficiencies to Produce Alpha

With the market neutral investment plan laid out, the quant investor is ready to start looking through financial databases, prices, ticks, SEC filings, and anything electronic to discover patterns or events that can be used to forecast returns.

How do we recognize market inefficiencies? There are, of course, many complicated answers, but first it's worthwhile to take a look at a golden oldie—an apparently simple market inefficiency: excess returns observed following stock splits. Don't run out just yet to make the down payment on that boat. This is not a perfect and inexhaustible source of four-cent nickels, and is not common enough to be used as the sole basis for an institutional investing strategy. Also note that the data for the nice-looking bar chart in Figure 5.7 ended in 1995, so further study is warranted.

A stock split is a perfect example of a fully public information event. In an efficient market, such a public event would convey no useful information. But for a long time in the U.S. stock market, a stock split did appear to convey information, and may still. The average listed stock over the past two decades has sold for about $50 in very round numbers. When the stock price gets too high, the company splits the stock two or three shares for one to keep the price affordable for employees and individuals without forcing them into odd lot purchases. Similarly, when a stock gets very low in price, companies do a reverse split to get the price back up into a more respectable-sounding range, and to meet listing requirements.

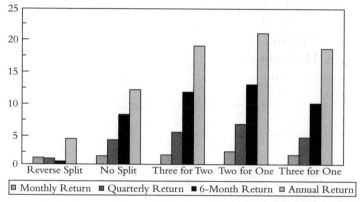

Stock splits appear to have a persistent and consistent effect on stock returns.

Figure 5.7   A Simple Inefficiency: U.S. Equity Splits and Subsequent Returns, 1980–1995. Everyone knows when stocks split, so why should this matter? Maybe people like a "two for one" sale. Call your neighborhood behavioral economist.

A stock split is a textbook example of public information, and even under the weaker forms of the efficient markets hypothesis, we should not expect to see any difference in the returns to stocks that split in comparison to those that don't. Two nickels make a dime, and, in an efficient market, two $50 shares in a company should be no better or worse than one $100 share in the same company with half as many shares outstanding. What really happens is shown in Figure 5.7.

Each group of four bars shows the returns to U.S. stocks for the one-, three-, six-, and 12-month periods following a split. The control group of stocks is the stocks that don't split; their returns are shown in the second group of bars from the left. The returns following "good news" positive splits are seen in the three groups to the right.

Returns to stocks with "bad news" reverse splits are seen in the leftmost set of bars. If the market were efficient, then all the bars corresponding to the same time period would be the same. We would expect all the 12-month return bars to be pretty much at the height shown by horizontal line on the 12-month "no split" bar. This is clearly not the case, and it is not true for any of the shorter time periods. All of the groups with positive splits have done better than the no-split group on each time scale. The reverse split group (on the left) has been truly dismal in comparison. This is not a picture of an efficient market.

The split events themselves may be conveying information. They may be drawing additional attention from analysts, who then find additional information that underscores the reason for the original split.[4] However, if the market were perfectly efficient, this information shouldn't matter, either.

Remember, there aren't enough stock splits for this information to be useful as the sole basis for a large institutional equity strategy. The portfolio would also tend to be undiversified. Also, as mentioned, note the data for the nice-looking bar chart ends in 1995.

More Market Inefficiencies

Look at the shelves in almost any bookstore and you'll find one labeled "Stock Market." It will be filled with books about market inefficiencies and techniques for forecast returns. Investing publications and web sites thrive on producing these in industrial quantities. These range from the ridiculous (investing based on stocks' horoscopes) to the sublime (detailed security analysis, along the lines of Graham and Dodd, exemplified by Warren Buffett's approach).

Here is a partial list of just a few of the hall of fame market inefficiencies that are popular with quants in the quest for alpha:

- *Earnings forecast analysis.* Earnings are a primary driving force behind stock price movements. Analysts spend a great deal of time forecasting future earnings, but all forecasts are not created equal. Many analysts' forecasts are colored by underwriting and investment banking relationships between the firms they analyze and the firms they work for. There are many more buy recommendations than sells. There are thousands of companies to cover. It is easy for an analyst to fall into a me-too style, particularly for small regional firms, leaving the real work to the locals. All forecast revisions are not equal. Careful and ongoing analysis of analyst forecasts and subsequent returns can separate the leaders from the followers.

- *Earnings surprises.* Even the best analysts are not always right. When a company announces actual earnings that are a surprise relative to the consensus forecast, the stock price often responds dramatically. The pace of this response has accelerated greatly in recent years.

Adjustments which used to occur over a period of weeks now occur in minutes or hours.[5]

- *Insider trading.* Insiders are often an excellent source of information about a company's future returns. Their trading and option activity is a matter of public record. Some trading by insiders is simply to pay tuition or buy boats, but when all the insiders sell all at once it may be a sign that something is awry. Like analysts, certain insiders may prove to be more reliable indicators of future stock returns than others.

- *Secondary equity offerings and stock buybacks.* These are the corporate equivalents of insider trading as indicators. When a company buys back its own stock, it sends the signal that it believes this is the best use for its own capital. When a company issues additional equity, it sends a different signal. Companies buying back stock outperform, in aggregate, relative to new issuers and companies taking no actions.

- *Mergers and acquisitions.* These make for catchy stories, but more often than not they result in financial indigestion for the acquiring firm, particularly when the acquiree is large relative to the acquirer, and debt is used to fund the acquisition. Analysis of the growing history of these transactions and their subsequent effects on stock prices provides a basis for estimating the return consequences of current deals.

- *Sector analysis.* Industries tend to respond in predictable and economically sensible ways to market events. Rising oil prices are better for oil companies than they are for airlines and other oil consumers. Rising copper prices are good for copper companies. These ideas are not new, but the effects can be quantified by detailed examination of past events and ensuing price changes.

- *"Common factor" analysis.* Industries are not the only meaningful way to group companies for analysis. Some simple examples: firms with floating-rate debt tend to respond in much different ways to rising interest rates than firms that issue debt. Firms with large foreign currency income or costs respond differently to exchange rate moves than purely domestic companies. Value and growth stocks tend to do well in different parts of the business cycle.[6]

This list could go on endlessly; it doesn't include the huge industries of technical analysis (looking for patterns in prices) and fundamental analysis (looking in detail at a firm's business). Every investment book, newsletter, web site, and magazine will bring you yet another flavor of how to exploit a market inefficiency.

All the Stocks, All the Time

The previous section had a lengthy list of possible sources of information that can be used to detect market inefficiencies that could potentially add value in an active portfolio. Much of time, any one of these potential sources of value added is likely not to be large enough to cover the cost of trading. When enough of them stack up to indicate a good stock to hold or bad one to avoid, the combined signals can be used to make investment decisions in a very disciplined way.

There are many thousands of stocks to choose from. The broad Wilshire index in the United States includes 6,700 names. Globally, there may be 40,000 investable stocks. The use of a computer-driven process allows an investor to analyze *all the stocks, all the time.*

The combined contributions of the various inefficiencies can stack up to provide *potential* value added, if the investor can trade fast enough to capture the value of the signals, and effectively enough not to lose their value in turning ideas into portfolios.

Jumping the Trading Cost Hurdle

The next step is to turn the raw material of *potential* value added into *real* value added. Lots of investment ideas look great on paper, but don't work out very well in practice. There are a variety of reasons why this is true. In the next chapter, we see the dangers of data mining, a leading cause of disappointment. But even for carefully designed strategies, the cost of trading often eats whatever theoretical alpha might be there. Simple simulations often assume that you can buy or sell all the stock you might want to at your decision price, which is far from accurate. Many stocks trade in very low volumes. I saw one astonishing simulated strategy, disclosed only after tedious legal work, that involved simulated trading of billions of shares of stock in a single firm that traded only a few hundred thousand shares a day in the real world. One consequence of basic supply and demand is that it often costs more to trade in size than the idea is worth. Trading costs, in institutional-size portfolios, are not just the broker's commission. The biggest piece of the real cost of trading is in the market impact, the price movement caused by the trade itself.

Here's how market impact works. A typical market quote will be along lines of "1,000 shares offered to buy at $50, 1,000 shares to sell at $50.25." Anyone can buy or sell at those prices in the advertised quantities. This is how specialists and market makers make a living: buy low, sell high.

Market impact comes into play when you want to trade in quantities larger than the quoted size. By the inexorable laws of supply and demand, larger buy orders will generally happen at higher prices, and larger sells at lower prices. For our example, a skilled (or lucky) trader trying to buy 50,000 shares would buy the first 1,000 at the quoted $50, and might be able to find the next 49,000 at the same price, or close to it. A less skilled trader might be paying up at $50.50 for the next 5,000 shares, 50.75 for the next 5,000, and so on up to 52 or more for the last piece.

A poorly executed trade in an illiquid stock can easily have a market impact of 5 percent or more. A two-cent commission on a $50 stock is only 0.04 percent. The market impact could easily be 100 times larger than the commission alone. Paying a higher commission to reduce the market impact might be a good idea.

The market impact demon whacks you again on the way out, when you go to sell the stock. Lower selling prices received on the exit can erode the potential profitability of the transaction still further. Oftentimes, there's nothing left. Investors who trade without considering the cost will often be disappointed with the results. In making future trading decisions cost control can be applied at all phases of the process: in deciding what to trade; in deciding how, when, and where to trade; and in carefully analyzing the results of trades already made.

In the real world, potential alpha is reduced, and sometimes eliminated, by transaction costs. The goal of traders in active management is to keep the real value added as large as possible by trading effectively and efficiently, in the appropriate size and manner. Trading is the implementation of investment ideas, and poor implementation can negate the potential value of any idea.[7]

Putting the Pieces Together

This business of analyzing all the stocks all the time and controlling trading costs produces a lot of information, including investment signals, trading costs, and liquidity constraints. We need to put them all together in a portfolio of balanced, prudent bets to enhance the index return, and to adjust the portfolio periodically.

This is where the idea of portfolio optimization comes in. Behind the math and the Nobel Prizes,[8] portfolio optimization is about trading off risk and reward to produce a diversified portfolio. Thirty years ago, this was considered a crackpot idea. In *Capital Ideas* (Free Press, 1993), Peter L. Bernstein includes a story of young Bill Sharpe wandering Wall Street in the 1960s, trying to shake loose enough computer time to run a small optimization. Most people thought he was a crackpot. In 1990 Crackpot Bill shared the Nobel Prize in economics, and optimization is used in the management of trillions of dollars in assets around the world.[9]

If someone utterly and completely believed in a forecast that a stock would spike up, that investor would hold a one-stock portfolio. But forecasts are rarely perfect. In order to spread the risk around, an intelligent investor intuitively diversifies away from such concentrated bets. The optimizer does the same thing in a very systematic way. The goal of the optimizer is to find the portfolio with the highest expected return at the risk level desired. A low risk corresponds to enhanced index strategies, a higher one to active management.[10]

The portfolios that emerge from this process tend to have more stocks than conventionally managed portfolios, since the much broader analysis allows it, and it is good for risk control.

Does This Really Work?

It takes forever to distinguish luck from skill with 100 percent certainty, so definitive claims in this regard must be viewed with caution. But these approaches are not weird black-box ideas. They are based on a few very fundamental ideas:

- *Market inefficiencies are out there.* Use the scientific method to systematically evaluate potential market inefficiencies on an ongoing basis. Look at stocks individually and in groups.
- *All the stocks, all the time.* Search for these inefficiencies in all the stocks, all the time. The progress in computer technology is one of the wonders of history. IBM's Deep Blue used an analogous relentless approach to chess.
- *Keep what you find.* Don't lose potential value added in poor implementation. Avoid overly costly trades entirely. Trade effectively to make balanced, diversified bets to add value at the chosen level of risk.

A computerized, quantitative investment process is emotion-free, is without distractions, and is willing to take contrarian positions when they are warranted. All you need is skill, luck, or both in forecasting returns. There is no limit to the amount of information available to you for this, and almost no limit to how many times you can pore over it looking for exploitable inefficiencies. The goal is maximizing predictability. A useful view of maximizing predictability, popularized by Andy Lo at MIT, is illustrated in Figure 5.8.

You really have three things to consider when you are setting out to be a predictor: What are you going to predict? What information are you going to use to predict it with? And how are you going to use the latter to predict the former?

In a financial setting, an obvious choice of what to predict is individual stock returns, but over what time horizon? Tomorrow? Next month? Next quarter? Next year? That will have you making a large

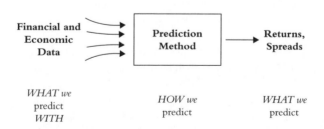

Figure 5.8   Maximizing Predictability: Three Places to Look

number of predictions, since there are so many stocks. Maybe forecasting returns for industry groups will be easier, and less subject to noise. Or even broader groups may be used, like value stocks versus growth stocks.[11] Spreads, or differences between stocks or industry groups, may be easier to predict.

What to predict with? Past returns are always popular. Trading in related securities or commodities ranks high. Macroeconomic indicators like inflation, interest rates, housing starts, and oil reserves all seem reasonable in the right context.

For an idea of the many ways to predict, look for books on regression analysis, times series methods, classification and regression trees (CARTs), neural nets, and wavelets, to name a few. This doesn't touch ideas like collective intelligence and prediction markets, which bring people into the mix.

Doing this correctly can put you on the fast track to that hockey rink in the yard or the Forbes 400, or both. Doing this incorrectly will keep you off the streets for a while, but will prove detrimental to your financial health if you follow your own advice. In the next chapter, "Stupid Data Miner Tricks," we explore the dark side of maximizing predictability.

Notes

1. Tim Loughran and Jay R. Ritter, "The New Issues Puzzle," *Journal of Finance* 50, no. 1 (March 1995): 23–51.

2. Vanessa O'Connell, "Some Stock Funds Beat Rivals by Following Insiders'Trades," *Wall Street Journal*, January 29, 1997.

3. This is true when the long and short portfolios have equal betas, or sensitivity to broad market moves. For long-short portfolios where this is not the case, a portion of the overall return may be due to exposure to the overall market.

4. Jia Ye, "Excess Returns, Stock Splits, and Analyst Earnings Forecasts," *Journal of Portfolio Management* 25, no. 2 (1999): 70–76.

5. See www.starmine.com for a world of information on this subject.

6. David Leinweber, "Uses and Views of Equity Style," in *Handbook of Equity Style Management*, ed. T. Daniel Coggin and Frank J. Fabozzi (New Hope, PA: Fabozzi Associates, 1997).

7. The all-time classic paper on trading costs is "Implementation Shortfall" by Andre Perold, published in the *Journal of Portfolio Management* (Spring 1988). It is a hot

topic in algo trading, so a search may be overwhelming. Perold was the first to demonstrate the significance of trading costs in such a persuasive manner. The transaction cost measurement industry, which followed, was really originated by one firm, Plexus Group, founded by Wayne Wagner and now part of Investment Technology Group, Inc. (ITG). Wayne's personal perspective is found in "The Incredible Story of Transaction Cost Management: A Personal Recollection," *Journal of Trading* 3, no. 3 (Summer 2008).

8. See "Founders of Modern Finance" ((c) 1991, Research Foundation of the Institute of Chartered Financial Analysts, www.aimr.org) for the goods from the founders themselves, or *Capital Ideas* by Peter Bernstein for the salient points, intellectual history, and best stories.

9. Visit www-sharpe.stanford.edu for the word from the Crackpot himself. He has an extensive web site on quantitative finance.

10. The difference between index enhancement and active management is a matter of degree. Enhanced index and fully active portfolios each have two components: one piece to provide the benchmark index return and another to provide additional return on top of the benchmark. The difference between enhanced index strategies and active management is really just a matter of the relative sizes of the two pieces.

    Use just a little bit of active management, and you are enhancing the index. Use some more and you have an active strategy. Make really large active, often leveraged, bets and you have a hedge fund. It's like the progression from 3.2-proof beer to 151-proof rum. The active ingredient is the same; the difference is a matter of degree.

    The distinction can be quantified by specifying a target *tracking error* for the portfolio, analogous to the proof content for bar beverages. The tracking error is just the standard deviation of the difference between the portfolio return and the benchmark index return. A perfect index fund would have a tracking error of zero. An enhanced index fund is usually designed to have a tracking error of less than 2 percent, meaning that the returns are expected to be within 2 percent of the index return 68 percent of the time.

11. Value and growth are called "equity styles." When all stocks are ranked by book-to-price ratio, value stocks are in the top half and growth stocks are in the bottom half. Value stocks tend to have lots of real assets, like land and plants. Extreme examples are utilities. Growth stocks are generally the more exciting, newer firms, with ideas and products that get on the covers of magazines. Historically, value stocks have outperformed growth stocks, though this changed for a while in the late 1990s when the tech stocks, all growth stocks, did so well. Now we have returned to the old pattern.

Chapter 6

Stupid Data Miner Tricks

To Err Is Human. To Really Screw Up,
You Need a Computer.
—POPULAR CAMPUS T-SHIRT, CA. 1980

his chapter started out over 10 years ago as a set of joke slides showing silly, spurious correlations. Originally, my quant equity research
group planned on deliberately abusing the genetic algorithm (see
Chapter 8 on evolutionary computation) to find the wackiest relationships, but as it turned out, we didn't need to get that fancy. Just looking
at enough data using plain-vanilla regression would more than suffice.

We uncovered utterly meaningless but statistically appealing relationships between the stock market and third world dairy products and
livestock populations which have been cited often—in *BusinessWeek*,
the *Wall Street Journal*, the book *A Mathematician Plays the Stock Market*,[1]
and many others. Students from Bill Sharpe's classes at Stanford seem to
be familiar with them. This was expanded, to have some actual content
about data mining, and reissued as an academic working paper in 2001.
Occasional requests for this arrive from distant corners of the world.
An updated version appeared in the *Journal of Investing* in 2007.*

---

*This article originally appeared in the Spring 2007 issue of the *Journal of Investing* ("Stupid
Data Miner Tricks: Overfitting the S&P 500"). It is reprinted with permission. To view the
original article, please go to iijoi.com.

Without taking too much of a hatchet to the original, the advice here is still valuable—perhaps more so now that there is so much more data to mine. Monthly data arrives as one data point, once a month. It's hard to avoid data mining sins if you look twice. Ticks, quotes, and executions arrive in millions per minute, and many of the practices that fail the statistical sniff tests for low-frequency data can now be used responsibly. New frontiers in data mining have been opened up by the availability of vast amounts of textual information. Whatever raw material you choose, fooling yourself remains an occupational hazard in quantitative investing. The market has only one past, and constantly revisiting it until you find that magic formula for untold wealth will eventually produce something that looks great, in the past. A fine longer exposition of these ideas is found in Nassim Taleb's book, *Fooled by Randomness: The Hidden Role of Chance in Markets and Life* (W.W. Norton, 2001).

"Your Mama Is a Data Miner"

It wasn't too long ago that calling someone a data miner was a very bad thing. You could start a fistfight at a convention of statisticians with this kind of talk. It meant that you were finding the analytical equivalent of the bunnies in the clouds, poring over data until you found something. Everyone knew that if you did enough poring, you were bound to find that bunny sooner or later, but it was no more real than the one that blows over the horizon.

Data mining is a small industry, with entire companies and academic conferences devoted to it. The phrase no longer elicits as many invitations to step into the parking lot as it used to. What's going on? These new data mining people are not fools. Sometimes data mining makes sense, and sometimes it doesn't.

The new data miners pore over large, diffuse sets of raw data trying to discern patterns that would otherwise go undetected. This can be a good thing. Suppose a big copier company has thousands of service locations all over the world. It wouldn't be unusual for any one of them to see a particular broken component from any particular copier. These gadgets do fail. But if all of a sudden the same type of part starts showing up in the repair shops at 10 times its usual rate, that would be an indication of a manufacturing problem that could be corrected at the factory. This is a good (and real) example of how data mining can work well, when it is applied to extracting a simple pattern from a large data set. That's the positive side of data mining. But there's an evil twin.

The dark side of data mining is to pick and choose from a large set of data to try to explain a small one. Evil data miners often specialized in "explaining" financial data, especially the U.S. stock market. Here's a nice example: We often hear that the results of the Super Bowl in January will predict whether the stock market will go up or down for that year. If the National Football Conference (NFC) wins, the market goes up; otherwise, it takes a dive. What has happened over the past 30 years? Most of the time, the NFC has won the Super Bowl and the market has gone up. Does it mean anything? Nope. We see similar claims for hemlines, and even the phases of the moon.[2]

When data mining techniques are used to scour a vast selection of data to explain a small piece of financial market history, the results are often ridiculous. These ridiculous results fall into two categories: those that are taken seriously, and those that are regarded as totally bogus. Human nature being what it is, people often differ on what falls into which category.

The example in this paper is intended as a blatant instance of totally bogus application of data mining in finance. My quant equity research group first did this several years ago to make the point about the need to be aware of the risks of data mining in quantitative investing. In total disregard of common sense, we showed the strong statistical association between the annual changes in the S&P 500 index and butter production in Bangladesh, along with other farm products. Reporters picked up on it, and it has found its way into the curriculum at the Stanford Business School and elsewhere. We never published it, since it was supposed to be a joke. With all the requests for the nonexistent publication, and the graying out of many generations of copies of copies of the charts, it seemed to be time to write it up for real. So here it is. Mark Twain (or Disraeli, or both) spoke of "lies, damn lies, and statistics." In this paper, we offer all three.

Strip Mining the S&P 500

Regression is the main statistical technique used to quantify the relationship between two or more variables.[3] It was invented by Adrien-Marie

Legendre in 1805.[4] A regression analysis would show a positive relationship between height and weight, for example. If we threw in waistline along with height, we'd get an even better regression to predict weight.

The measure of the accuracy of a regression is called R-squared. A perfect relationship, with no error, would have an R-squared of 1.00 or 100 percent. Strong relationships, like height and weight, would have an R-squared of around 70 percent. A meaningless relationship, like zip code and weight, would have an R-squared of zero.

With this background, we can get down to some serious data mining. First, we need some data to mine. We'll use the annual closing price of the S&P 500 index for the 10 years from 1983 to 1993, shown in Figure 6.1.

This is the raw data, the S&P 500 for the period, what we are going to predict in terms of the idea of "maximizing predictability" discussed at the end of the previous chapter. Now, we want to go into the data mine and find some data to use to predict the stock index. If we included other U.S. stock market indexes such as the Dow Jones Industrial Average or the Russell 1000, we would see very good fits, with R-squared numbers close to 1.00. That would be an uninspired choice, though—and useless at making the point about the hazards of data mining.

Now we need some more data to mine in which to fit the S&P data; that is, make a correlation. Let's go find some on a CD-ROM published by the United Nations. There are all kinds of data series from 140 member countries. If we were trying to do this S&P 500 fit for real, we might look at things like changes in interest rates, economic growth,

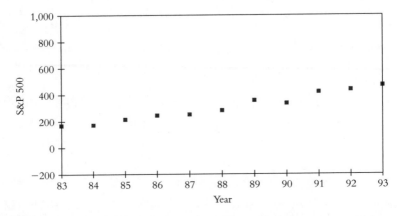

Figure 6.1   The S&P 500, 1983–1993: The Unmined Raw Data

unemployment, and the like, but we'll stay away from those. Let's use something even better: butter production in Bangladesh. Yes, there it is: a simple, single dairy product that explains 75 percent of the variation in the S&P 500 over 10 years. R^2 is 0.75; not bad at all. (See Figure 6.2.)

Why stop here? Maybe we can do better. Let's go global on this and expand our selection of dairy products. We'll put in cheese and include U.S. production as well. This works remarkably well. We're up to 95 percent accuracy here. (See Figure 6.3.) How much better can we do?

How about 99 percent with our third variable: sheep population? This is an awesome fit. (See Figure 6.4.) It seems too good to be true, and it is. That is the point. It is utterly useless for anything outside the

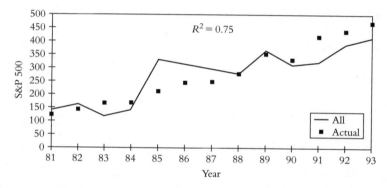

Figure 6.2   Overfitting the S&P 500: butter production in Bangladesh—a single variable that "explains" 75 percent of the S&P's returns.

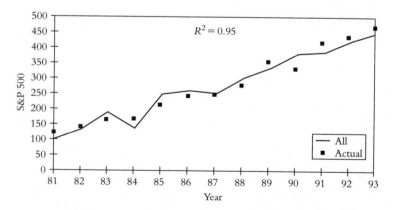

Figure 6.3   Overfitting the S&P 500: butter in Bangladesh and United States, plus U.S. cheese production—two more dairy variables that take us to 95 percent.

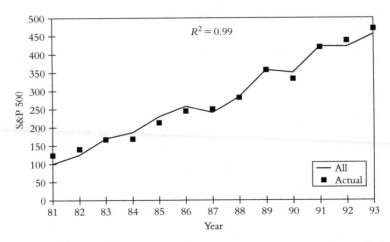

Figure 6.4 Overfitting the S&P 500: butter in Bangladesh and United States, plus U.S. cheese production, as well as sheep population in Bangladesh and United States. Now we're at 99 percent. You can do this as long as you can find data not perfectly correlated with butter, cheese, sheep, and so on. There is no shortage of that.

fitted period, a total crock before 1983 or after 1993. This is just a chance association that would inevitably show up if you look at enough data series. The butter fit was the result of a lucky fishing expedition. The rest comes from throwing in a few other series that were uncorrelated to the first one. Pretty much anything would have worked, but we liked sheep. They are more photogenic than dairy products, and make for a great slide when this stuff is shown to an audience at one of those open-bar financial conference dinners.

If someone showed up in your office with a model relating stock prices to interest rates, gross domestic product (GDP), trade, housing starts, and the like, it might have statistics that looked as good as this nonsense, and it might make as much sense (i.e., none), even though it sounded much more plausible.

Enough Regression Tricks

To hammer a little harder on this point about the dangers of data mining, look at another equally bogus example. Who wants to go count pregnant

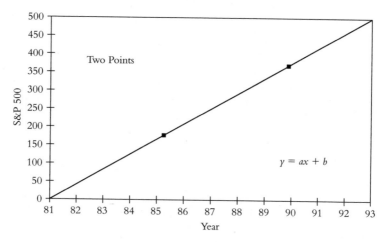

Figure 6.5 First-degree polynomial fit: just a plain old line.

sheep in Bangladesh to figure out next year's sheep population? We'll get away from ordinary linear regressions and show how we can fit a *perfect* model, with $R^2 = 100$ percent, using only one variable: the year's digits.

This has to be about the most accessible data on the planet. There is no need to go counting sheep. Instead of regression, we'll use a different prediction method to make this work, a polynomial fit. Everyone with a recollection of junior high school math knows that there is a line (a first-degree polynomial) through any two points, as shown in Figure 6.5.

Put in a third point and you can fit a parabola, or second-degree polynomial, through all three points, as shown in Figure 6.6.

We have 10 points in the S&P 500 annual series from 1983 to 1992, so we fit a ninth-degree polynomial. However, as Mr. Wizard says, "Don't try this at home," unless you have some sort of infinite precision math tool like Mathematica or Maple. The ordinary floating point arithmetic in a spreadsheet or regular programming language isn't accurate enough for this to work. That said, our ninth-degree polynomial hits every annual close *exactly*. We have a 100 percent in-sample accuracy with only one variable, as shown in Figure 6.7.

$$.25 \star 10^{16} - .26 \star 10^{13}y + .12 \star 10^{10}y^2 - 320000.y^3$$
$$+ 56.y^4 - .0064y^5 + .49 \star 10^{-6}y^6 - .24 \star 10^{-10}y^7$$
$$+ .69 \star 10^{-15}y^8 - .88 \star 10^{-20}y^9$$

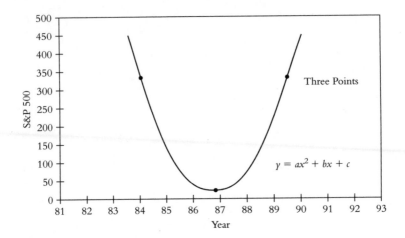

Figure 6.6 Second–degree polynomial fit: a plain old parabola.

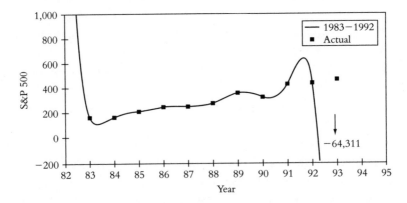

Figure 6.7 Polynomial fit to the S&P 500: big mistake or bad Idea? That minus 64,311 looks like trouble.

Notice that the fitted curve in the chart is suddenly heading south very rapidly. What closing value for the S&P did this method predict for the end of 1993? Minus 64,311. Fortunately for the global economy, it actually turned out to be positive, +445. We seem to have a problem with our model's out-of-sample performance, as shown in Figure 6.8.

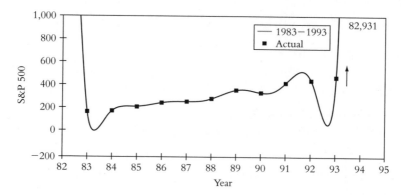

Figure 6.8   Polynomial fit to the S&P 500: big mistake or bad idea? Add a new data point. An S&P 500 at 82,931 is nice think about, but ridiculous.

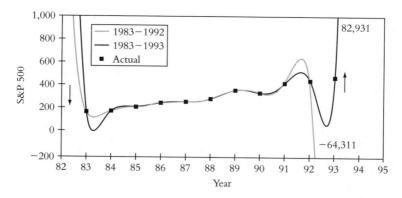

Figure 6.9   Polynomial fit to the S&P 500: big mistake or bad idea? It is both. If only all bad investment ideas were as easy to spot.

Don't panic! The year 1993 ends, we get another data point, and we restore our 100 percent in-sample accuracy, this time with a tenth-degree polynomial using the 11 data points in the sample. What did this new fit predict for the S&P close in 1994? Plus 82,931!

$$.77 \star 10^{17} - .88 \star 10^{14}y + .45 \star 10^{11}y^2 - .14 \star 10^8y^3$$
$$+ 2700.y^4 - .37y^5 + .000035y^6 - .23 \star 10^{-8}y^7$$
$$+ .99 \star 10^{-13}y^8 - .25 \star 10^{-17}y^9 + .28 \star 10^{-22}y^{10}$$

So in Figure 6.9, we have two models—each 100 percent accurate in-sample, and each 100 percent nonsense out-of-sample.

Is There Any Hope for Data Miners?

The central problem in mining financial data like this is that the market has only one past. This will not go away. Some forecasters just ignore this fact, dive in, and hope for the best. This makes about as much sense as the "butter in Bangladesh" story. It would be a healthy idea to take measures to mitigate the risk of data mining. Here are a few suggestions:

- *Avoid the other pitfalls of investment simulations.* These include survivor bias, look-ahead bias, use of revised data not available at the time of the forecasts, ignoring transaction costs, and liquidity constraints. There are many ways to fool yourself, even before you set foot in the data mine.[5]
- *Use holdback samples, temporal and cross-sectional.* Reserve some of the data for out-of-sample testing. This can be hard to do when the history is short, or the frequency is low as is the case for monthly data. Be cautious about going to the holdback set, since with each new visit, you are mining that as well. This approach to temporal holdback samples is easier with higher-frequency data, such as daily information or ticks. In these cases, a three-level holdback protocol using in-sample, out-of-sample, and in-the-vault out-of-sample can be (and is) used.

   When there are multiple securities to analyze, you can also hold back a cross-sectional sample. As an example, if you were developing a model to forecast individual stock returns, keeping back all the stocks with symbols in the second half of the alphabet, or even Committee on Uniform Securities Identification Procedures (CUSIP) numbers, would retain half of the data for out-of-sample testing. Temporal and cross-sectional holdbacks can be combined in data-rich situations.
- *Apply statistical measures of data mining and snooping.* Econometricians have performed explicit analyses of the problem of data mining in forecasting models. These techniques are based on the idea of testing the hypothesis that a new model has predictive superiority over a previous benchmark model. The new model is clearly data-mined to some extent, given that the benchmark model was developed beforehand.[6]
- *Use truly bogus test models.* You can calibrate the model-building process using a model based on random data. There is a ferocious

amount of technology that can be brought to bear on forecasting problems. One neural net product advertised in *Technical Analysis of Stocks & Commodities* magazine claims to be able to "forecast any market, using any data."[7] This is no doubt true, subject to the usual caveats. Throw in enough genetic algorithms, wavelets, and the like, and you are certain to come up with a model. But is it any good? A useful indicator in answering this question is to take the same model-building process and use it to build a test model for the same forecast target, but using a completely random set of data.[8] This test model has to be truly bogus. If your actual model has performance statistics similar to the bogus test version, you know it's time to visit the data miner's rehabilitation clinic.

Summary (and Sermonette)

These dairy product and calendar examples are obviously contrived. They are not far removed from many ill-conceived quantitative investment and trading ideas. It is just as easy to fool yourself with ideas that are plausible-sounding and no more valid.

Just because something appears plausible, that doesn't mean that it is. The wide availability of machine-readable data, and the tools to analyze it, easily means that there are a lot more regressions going on than Legendre could ever have imagined back in 1805. If you look at 100 regressions that are significant at a level of 95 percent, five of them are there just by chance. Look at 100,000 models at 95 percent significance, and 5,000 are false positives. Data mining, good or bad, is next to impossible to do without a computer.

When doing this kind of analysis, it is important to be very careful of what you ask for, because you will get it. Holding back part of your data is the first line of a defense against data mining. Leaving some of the data out of the sample used to build the model is a good idea as is holding back some data to use in testing the model. This holdback sample can be a period of time or a cross section of data. The cross-sectional holdback works where there is enough data to do this, as in the analysis of individual stocks. You can use stocks with symbols starting with A through L for model building and save M through Z for verification purposes.

It is possible to mine these holdback samples as well. Every time you visit the out-of-sample period for verification purposes, you do a little more data mining. Testing the process to see if you can produce models of similar quality using purely random data is often a sobering experience. An unlimited amount of computational resources is like dynamite: If used properly, it can move mountains. Used improperly, it can blow up your garage or your portfolio.

If someone knocks on your door with a new strategy that beat the market by 5 percent a year for the past 50 years in the back tests, wait. Someone else will put some money into it. If it tanks by 10 percent in the year after the real cash showed up, you just met a data miner. There are plenty of them, and some have really nice suits.

Counting the Kiddies

Despite warnings like this one, the temptation to data mine remains strong. Fidelity's Steve Snider sent me a 2007 paper called "Exact Prediction of S&P 500 Returns."[9] The authors demonstrate a near-perfect method of predicting index returns based on the U.S. population of nine-year-olds—not eight, not ten, just nine.

> A linear link between *S&P 500* return and the change rate of the number of nine-year-olds in the USA has been found. The return is represented by a sum of monthly returns during previous twelve months. The change rate of the specific age population is represented by moving averages. The period between January 1990 and December 2003 is described by monthly population intercensal estimates as provided by the US Census Bureau. Four years before 1990 are described using the estimates of the number of 17-year-olds shifted 8 years back. The *prediction* of *S&P 500* returns for the months after 2003, including those beyond 2007, are obtained using the number of 3-year-olds between 1990 and 2003 shifted by 6 years ahead and quarterly estimates of real GDP per capita.

The authors do some pretty fancy econometrics, but find that the near-exact fit breaks down after 2003. Their conclusion? "Therefore, it is reasonable to assume that the 9-year-old population was not well estimated by the U.S. Census Bureau after 2003." Children are our future and all that, but, please, think before testing cointegration.

A computer lets you make more mistakes faster than any invention in human history—with the possible exceptions of handguns and tequila. The easy access to data and tools to mine it gives new meaning to the admonition about "lies, damn lies, and statistics." The old adage *caveat emptor*, buyer beware, is still excellent advice. If it seems too good to be true, it is.

Notes

1. John Allen Paulos, *A Mathematician Plays the Stock Market* (New York: Basic Books, 2003).

2. It gets much wackier than this. A man named Norman Bloom, no doubt a champion of all data miners, went beyond trying to predict the stock market. Instead, he used the stock market, along with baseball scores, particularly those involving the New York Yankees, to "read the mind of God." I offer a small sample of Bloom, in the original punctuation and spelling, here: "The instrument God has shaped to brig proof he has the power to shape the physical actions of mankind—is organized athletics, and particularly baseball. the second instrument shaped by the one God, as the means to bring proof he is the one God concerned with the mental and business aspects of mankind and his civilization is the stock market—and particularly the greatest and most famous of all these—i.e., the New York Stock Exchange." Mr. Bloom's work was brought to my attention by Ron Kahn of Barclays Global Investing. Bloom himself did not publish in any of the usual channels, but seekers of secondary truth can consult "God and Norman Bloom" by Carl Sagan, in *American Scholar* (Autumn 1977), p. 462.

3. There are many good texts covering the subject. For a less technical explanation, see *The Cartoon Guide to Statistics* by Larry Gonnick and Woolcott Smith (New York: HarperCollins, 1993).

4. Stephen M. Stigler, *The History of Statistics: The Measure of Uncertainty before 1900* (Cambridge, MA: Belknap Press, 1986). This invention is also often attributed to Francis Galton, never to Disraeli or Mark Twain.

5. See John Freeman, "Behind the Smoke and Mirrors: Gauging the Integrity of Investment Simulations," *Financial Analysts Journal* 48, no. 6 (November–December 1992): 26–31.

6. This question is addressed in "A Reality Check for Data Snooping" by Hal White, UCSD Econometrics working paper, University of California at San Diego, May 1997.

7. This was the actual ad copy for a neural net system, InvestN-32, from Race Com., which was promoted heavily in *Technical Analysis of Stocks & Commodities* magazine, often a hotbed of data mining.

8. There are several alternatives in forming random data to be used for forecasting. A shuffling in time of the real data preserves the distribution of the original data, but loses many time series properties. A series of good old machine-generated random numbers,

matched to the mean, standard deviation, and higher moments of the original data will do the same thing. A more elaborate random data generator is needed if you want to preserve time series properties such as serial correlation and mean reversion.

9. Ivan Kitov and Oleg Kitov, "Exact Prediction of S&P 500 Returns," Russian Academy of Sciences—Institute for the Geospheres Dynamics and University of Warwick, December 2007, http://papers.ssrn.com/sol3/papers.cfm?abstract_id=1045281.

Part Three

Artificial Intelligence and Intelligence Amplification

Markets are machinery now. This raises the question of how to best participate in the world's new wired markets. People who use information technology most effectively will be rewarded.

Artificial intelligence (AI) as an academic discipline began at the famous 1955 Dartmouth conference organized by John McCarthy from Stanford University and Marvin Minsky from MIT. The goal of the AI pioneers was to create a mind, a human in silicon. One key idea was that the brain was a biological computer so all the researchers had to do was figure out what the brain was doing and put it into an actual computer and they'd be done. This was something that people thought in the 1950s might take 10 years to accomplish, maybe 15 with long lunches.

So far, it hasn't exactly worked out. In fiction we have the example of HAL, from *2001: A Space Odyssey*. Letting the computer do the thinking turned out badly in that case. HAL discovered the lie in the first reel, and quickly moved on to become a paranoid serial killer.*

In financial circles there was a lot of sort of irrational technology exuberance as well. As seen in Chapter 2, there were some inspired magazine covers from the magazine *Wall Street Computer Review*† that showed the unrealistic expectations for AI. One, from 1987, depicts Socrates on the steps of the stock exchange surrounded by a horde of PCs, and touts: "Teaching Computers to Emulate Great Thinkers."

---

*Sci-fi buffs have a rich amount of material to consider in this context. Vernor Vinge, a computer scientist who has also won five Hugo awards, deals with the topic in much of his work, including his latest novel, *Rainbow's End*. If we construct an artificial superintelligent entity, what will it think of us?

†Since renamed *Wall Street & Technology*, and a useful resource for nerds on Wall Street (NOWS) at www.wallstreetandtech.com.

Source: Wall Street Computer Review *(now* Wall Street & Technology*), June 1987.*

Other examples of the high expectations for AI in finance are also evident. The machine receives the spark of life on a cover from 1989, as Adam did from God on the ceiling of the Sistine Chapel.

Source: Wall Street Computer Review *(now* Wall Street & Technology*), June 1989.*

Notice the reference to neural networks, once a hot topic in financial forecasting, now largely seen as power tools for data mining. The circuitry has moved into the head of a somewhat clunky replica of Rodin's *Thinker* in 1990 with the title "Knowledge–Based Systems: Computers That Think Like Pros."

Source: Wall Street Computer Review *(now* Wall Street & Technology*), June 1990.*

Computers "thinking" like a person didn't really work out as well as people had hoped. In the academic AI world, the artificial sentients were persistent no-shows. Artificial intelligence got kind of a bad rep on Wall Street as well. To get into the game, you had to buy a LISP (list processing) machine, a $100,000 machine that ran the elegant but arcane AI language of choice, LISP, and related expert system tools with names like Automated Reasoning Tool (ART) and Knowledge Engineering Environment (KEE).

You could prove a theorem or two with this stuff right out of the box, but getting a price for IBM on the screen proved to be a prodigious amount of work.

As recounted in the Introduction to this book, I worked for one of the companies that made these machines—there were two, LISP Machines and Symbolics—and came to the realization that building from the high-concept top down was a poor idea. Here is a picture I used back then to show the user reaction to AI investment systems, showing a mix of fear and rage.

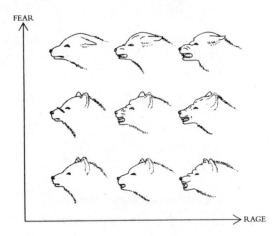

Note to dog owners, if your pet shows up in
the upper right, get a new dog.

Chapter 7, "A Little AI Goes a Long Way on Wall Street," describes a successful application, built in the early 1990's, which was much more modest in scope than bringing back the great thinkers. The goal was to get computers to be decent users of other computer systems, which were overloading their users. Recently, this idea has been called *intelligence amplification* (IA). The systems here were market data and execution systems, and the combination was an early version of algorithmic trading.

The AI/IA-flavored approach to algo trading and market surveillance used in QuantEx and MarketMind, described in Chapter 7, was very effective in many contexts—equity strategies, quant option trading, and monitoring liquidity—but, like spreadsheets, they were clever ways to get the computer to do what you said, and didn't have anything in the box that would let the machine *learn* what you *should* have said and adjust its behavior or models to better meet your needs.

One of the early enthusiasts for these technologies was Henry Lichstein, an MIT graduate then serving as technology adviser to John Reed, chairman of Citicorp. Henry was also on the board of the Santa Fe Institute (SFI),[*] a new high-powered research institute interested in complex interactions of complex entities. SFI did a great deal of computer experimentation in artificial life (ALife). The ALife people had much more modest goals than AI; all they wanted to do was build software entities that displayed lifelike behavior. And their efforts were met with early success. A bunch of random ALife birds might fly in random directions, and not act much like birds. But giving them a few simple rules, like "fly toward the closest bird," "go with the flow," and "don't hit other birds," could give rise to distinctly birdlike behavior.

The original ALife flock is Craig Reynolds' "Boids," done at Symbolics in 1986.[†] Simulated herding and flocking turn out to be of some commercial interest. Those massive stampedes in Disney cartoons, with thousands of <insert fast, large mammal of your choice>, and all those schools of talking fish are descendants of the Boids. Hollywood showed its appreciation by giving Reynolds an Academy Award in 1998.

---

[*]"The Santa Fe Institute is devoted to creating a new kind of scientific research community, one emphasizing multidisciplinary collaboration in pursuit of understanding the common themes that arise in natural, artificial, and social systems." It was founded in 1984 (www.santafe.edu/).

[†] . . . and still flocking after all these years at www.red3d.com/cwr/boids.

Like our early algos, the SFI artificial life was dumb, just obeying a few simple handwritten rules, without any ability to learn from mistakes. But the ALife researchers had a good answer—evolving intelligent behavior by mimicking natural evolution. Represent the programs as digital chromosomes, and simulate crossover and mutation, to breed better programs. The original version was called the *genetic algorithm* (GA), which later evolved into *evolutionary computation* (EC). Henry Lichstein suggested this approach for use in trading around 1990. The results for ALife had been striking. All sorts of tasks could be learned by the programs operating in an electronic world, which sure sounded like quant investment and trading. ALife programs evolved behavior to solve problems, avoid obstacles, find rewards, and cooperate. These are remarkable to watch.*

Chapter 8, "Perils and Promise of Evolutionary Computation on Wall Street," is one of the few detailed descriptions of the use of the GA and EC in finance. Actual chromosomes and fitness functions are included. If that last sentence made your eyes glaze over, skip to Chapter 9. It was satisfying research, and the power of evolutionary search truly teaches you to be careful what you ask for.

Evolutionary approaches could be given rules to avoid many sins of data mining, and had many appealing features. As much as I would like to see this work, we don't see a torrent of EC scientists flowing toward greater Wall Street. We don't even see a trickle. Olsen & Associates was a Zurich-based currency trading firm, founded in 1992, heavy with physicists from the Eidgenössische Technische Hochschule (ETH), Einstein's alma mater. They were keen

---

*Until they start barcoding these into books, printed URLs are annoying, but it is actually worth typing these in. Karl Sim's MIT video is here: www.youtube.com/watch?v=F0OHycypSG8.

on genetically adaptive strategies and well funded, but vanished, and few of the principals are still keen on genetic algorithms.

After sending the GA to the back of the breakthrough line in the previous chapter, in Chapter 9 we get to "The Text Frontier," using IA, natural language processing, and Web technologies to extract and make sense of qualitative written information from news and a variety of disintermediated sources.

In Chapter 6, "Stupid Data Miner Tricks," we saw how you could fool yourself with data. When you collect data that people have put on the Web, they can try to fool you as well. Chapter 10 on Collective Intelligence and Chapter 11 on market manipulations include some remarkable and egregious examples.

Chapter 7

A Little AI Goes a Long Way on Wall Street

"If you give someone a program, you will frustrate them for a day; if you teach them how to program, you will frustrate them for a lifetime."

This is a history and technical overview of one of the earliest artificial intelligence (AI) successes in securities trading. In the Introduction, I described the early experiences in the late 1980s at the MIT Artificial Intelligence Laboratory spin-offs LISP Machines and Inference to apply their tools and techniques on Wall Street. Once we stopped blowing air at the subject and tried doing something useful with real market data, it became obvious that the LISP world and Wall Street were far from compatible.

LISP was (and is) an elegant, mathematically pure approach to computation that made for some remarkable feats of programming. My very first exposure to anything from the AI world came in 1971, when I was a newbie at MIT. Up in the truly strange Technology Square AI Lab machine room, filled with humming PDP-10s programmed to push the boundaries of computer science (and to operate the vending machines in the hall), someone showed me Macsyma, the first symbolic math program, developed by Joel Moses. Computers had been doing math in the

This article originally appeared (coauthored by Yossi Beinart) in the Winter 1996 issue of the *Journal of Portfolio Management*. It is reprinted with permission.

sense of calculations from the beginning. ENIAC did ballistics. Big science machines did big numerical science problems from nuclear physics to meteorology.[1] In all cases, what was going on was that the formulas were in the program; then the machine read in all the numerical inputs and ran with it to produce numerical answers.

The difference in Macsyma was that the formula or equation itself was the input, and the machine produced transformations of formulas or solutions to equations in the same symbolic language used in abstract, nonnumerical math. It could take derivatives, do integrals, and do fancy matrix manipulations, all in terms of the x's, y's, integral signs, d/dx's, and all the rest. When you asked for the derivative of "$x^3 + x^2 + x$" you got "$3x^2 + 2x + 1$" and, unlike all the programs that preceded it, Macsyma didn't have to know the value of x to do this.

It was absolutely amazing to see. Macsyma utterly blew us away. The median math SAT score for MIT guys hanging in the AI Lab was 800. Everyone thought that, while they had a tough time getting a date and maybe were a little confused on personal hygiene, they were BSDs when it came to doing integrals and derivatives. And here is this machine solving problems in a second that would take any of us a week (likely with a mistake), and solving problems in 10 seconds that we couldn't touch. It was a humbling experience, and the first time I experienced awe at what clever people could do with computers.

When the Macsyma symbolic math system was first run, it found hundreds of errors in the *CRC Handbook* tables of integrals and derivatives. The *Handbook*, at the time, was in its 42nd edition, and on the bookshelf of every working engineer and scientist. Other programs proved theorems, solved logic problems, and played more than passable chess.

But all of this logical magic came with a great deal of baggage. The showstopper was the long pause LISP had to take periodically for "garbage collection" to recover the memory left behind as programs ran. The ability to change large, complex data structures on the fly allowed LISP to deal with the complexity of problems like symbolic integration, but the need to clean up after those changes created the need for garbage collection.[2]

When we ran our first, very simple LISP trading systems demonstrations (crossover rules, for the most part) using recorded data for our visitors from Wall Street, we saw their eyes glaze over when, in the middle of the simulated run, the machine would take a break for a few minutes and we would offer more coffee.

My colleague Dale Prouty, a brilliant Caltech Ph.D. physicist whose metabolism seemed to make his own caffeine, and I quickly realized there was no way LISP systems would fit in trading. Similar realizations, in other contexts, contributed to the AI winter, described in Chapter 2.

Dale had heard that PaineWebber's equity block desk was looking for proposals for an "intelligent hedging advisory system" for the desk. Ideally, the block traders would "go home flat," with no net long or short exposure to the market, to sectors, or to other common equity factors. This was not always possible, so the firm had more overnight risk exposure than it wanted. There were many ways to reduce that risk; portfolios of long or short positions in options, futures, and stocks could be constructed to offset the risk on the desk's book, and unwound as that risk changed. These differed in their effectiveness as a hedge (all those Greek letters dear to the quants) and in the implementation cost of putting them on and taking them off.

Prouty read everything he could find on hedging, shuffled in what he knew about expert systems, and after a competition with some of the bigger names in whiz-bang computer consulting (IBM, Coopers & Lybrand, and Arthur D. Little, as I recall), he walked off with a million-dollar contract to build an Intelligent Hedging Advisory System (IHAS) for PaineWebber. Dale and I had commiserated over our woeful situation of banging the square peg of LISP systems into the round hole of trading. His new contract let us do something about it. IHAS was pretty specialized, and there were only so many block trading desks on Wall Street, but pieces of the solution had much wider applicability. It would fund the development of software components with much broader appeal.

We decided to start a new company, Integrated Analytics Corporation (IAC), to use what made sense from the LISP world, but without LISP and LISP machines. Sun Microsystems was emerging as the platform of choice for serious computation. The DOS-based 640K PCs of the time were great for WordStar and Lotus 1-2-3, but not what you would choose to analyze the torrent of data on a market feed in real time.

Our product, which we called MarketMind (later incorporated into QuantEx), was written in the mainstream language C, and ran on Sun hardware. It included only as much AI as the financial user community could deal with, and integrated tightly with their electronic environment. Computational resources were used to make a simple, highly application-specific user interface. This combination of advanced technologies, appropriately applied, resulted in a system used by many of the largest institutional equity investors and money managers in the United States. The system was directly linked to the New York Stock Exchange (NYSE) and other electronic equity execution channels. This was not a prototype or a proposal. This was real and was in wide use for many years, often generating transaction volumes exceeding five million shares per day.

Traders used a special purpose rule-based language to describe a wide variety of market conditions. The system kept up with high-speed incoming market data in real time. Its displays told traders when, where, and how strongly their specified conditions matched the current state of the market. Trading recommendations were formulated based on those specified conditions. Finally, and most importantly, direct electronic execution channels allowed quick action on these recommendations.

Tight integration with both market data and electronic execution channels, combined with an appropriate, accessible user interface and a high level of support contributed to a major AI success story with MarketMind/QuantEx. The transactions flowing through these systems produced more revenue on a busy day than many other AI applications generated over their entire operational lifetimes.

Prehistory of Artificial Intelligence on Wall Street

Summer 1987. AI godfather Marvin Minsky warns American Association for Artificial Intelligence (AAAI) Conference attendees in Seattle that "the AI winter will soon be upon us." This isn't news to most of them. Many of the pioneer firms have been pared down to near invisibility. AI stocks have dropped so low that Ferraris are being traded in for Yugos in Palo Alto and Cambridge.

On Wall Street, the expert systems that were last year's breakthrough of the century are this year's R&D write-off. LISP[3] machines can be had in lower Manhattan for 10 cents on the dollar.

What went wrong? Minsky and many of the others in the AI community had it exactly right: Overblown expectations, awkward user interfaces, and a near total absence of any connection to the real world would send many promising applications into the bit bucket.

Wall Street was enamored of expert systems early on. The June 1987 cover of *Wall Street Computer Review* showed Socrates standing on the steps of the stock exchange, with the caption, "Teaching Computers to Emulate Great Thinkers." Actually, Socrates didn't have much of a reputation as a trader. The thinkers the financial world had in mind were the Jesse Livermores, J.P. Morgans, and Warren Buffetts, but they didn't look as good in a toga.

Wall Street firms were easy sells for the AI companies in the mid-1980s. They had money to spend, and traded in such volume that only a small improvement in performance would justify their investment many times over. What they found when they unpacked their $60,000 worth of LISP machine and loaded on their $40,000 worth of expert system shell was that they couldn't get the last price of IBM on the screen. They'd have to hire four hackers from MIT and give them six months to persuade the machine to digest a basic market data feed. Worse, the machine seemed to have six or eight extra shifts (control and alt were okay, but what was going on with hyper, meta, super, greek, triangle, circle, and square?). Worse still, the machine took a leisurely break now and then to do something called "garbage collection." Unfortunately, the stock exchanges kept going while the machine stood still. Things looked bleak, really bleak.

Bright young MBAs began to think about how to hide the whole project in the basement before bonus time came around.

AI People Can Use

Meanwhile, back at the AI ranch, the vendors who sold all these tools couldn't help noticing that their financial customers were less than happy. Some introspection was in order. Why was this happening? The answer was being repeated over and over again at the proliferation of AI conferences held around the country. These systems were too isolated and too hard to use. You might have three different flavors of truth maintenance to choose from, but simple communications and mathematical functions were hopelessly tedious and complex.

In mid-1987, Dale Prouty and I founded a small firm, Integrated Analytics, and tried to solve these problems by designing an expert system tool specialized for trading. This was called MarketMind. The top-level requirements for the design were:

- Detect the kinds of patterns and events in the market that traders look for themselves, but do this for hundreds or thousands of securities simultaneously.
- Be a record player, not a record; support a language that expresses a wide variety of trading techniques.
- Work right out of the box—connect to market data feed without any systems work.
- Support real-time calculations using real-time and historical market data.
- Use quantitative logic. Be able to distinguish between barely true and whoppingly true.
- Run on standard hardware, with no nasty waits for garbage collection.
- Provide a standard, simple user interface appropriate to trading problems.
- Use only as much AI as the users can digest. Hide it, if possible.
- "Keep it simple, stupid" (KISS). Allow users with Lotus 1-2-3 level of sophistication to function effectively.
- Be supportable and comprehensible. Be able to help the users and have them understand what was done.

All of these goals were realized in a commercially successful product. This design, unadulterated vaporware at the time, with hand-drawn graphics, was first described in an article published in an AI journal in 1988.[4]

Where's the AI?

Where can AI be applied in finance? Many early attempts fell into the trap of trying to build all-encompassing investment and trading systems, typically with horrendous results. The aims of these ill-fated systems fell into two categories:

1. *Make all the money in the universe, now.* These were typically the brainstorms of people who knew just enough about AI to be dangerous. They believed what the software vendors told them: AI would lead them to the holy grail.
2. *Use every conceivable esoteric AI technique, now.* These were typically the brainstorms of people without a clue about finance. They were entirely capable of convincing themselves that a program that could solve Rubik's Cube would be a great options trader. Unfortunately, they were often a little fuzzy on exactly what an option was.

In designing MarketMind (and later QuantEx), the goal was not to use AI for its own sake, but rather to apply AI techniques where they could be used appropriately and within their limits to provide an advantage over conventional technologies.

A clue to the question of how to apply AI in trading is found by looking at the many thousands of electronic trading support systems that were already in use. A new product must provide a readily perceptible advantage over those systems.

Real Charting

Soon after reliable machine-readable market data became available in the mid-1980s, there were many services available to traders that would let them put a chart on the screen. As desktop computers became more powerful, people would put more graphs on the screen, and go through them more rapidly. They would look for patterns or relationships and often take some action when they found them. But when a trader tried to do this for 2,000 stocks at a time, it became an awesomely tedious task.

There were (and are) thousands of users of market data and charting systems. Different users look for different types of relationships. Options traders look for mispriced options, out of the thousands of options traded. Buy-side equity traders look for indications that allow

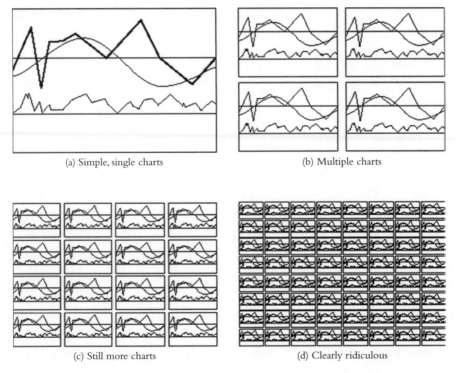

(a) Simple, single charts   (b) Multiple charts

(c) Still more charts   (d) Clearly ridiculous

Figure 7.1 Limits of the Conventional Approach

them to buy or sell the stocks assigned to them by portfolio managers at favorable prices. Market makers and specialists look for information that helps them set their quoted prices and sizes. Proprietary traders and arbitrageurs look for short-term mispricings among related securities. Market surveillance officers look for indications of illegal insider transactions.

In all cases, there are a lot of relationships to examine. There are over 7,000 stocks traded on the major U.S. markets, and over 3,000 options. Ignore fixed income securities for now since the market data still has a long way to go. Can anyone possibly digest all this information by paging through thousands of charts? No, as the illustration in Figure 7.1 shows; this road leads to madness, or at least a vicious headache.

Virtual Charting

The central idea behind MarketMind was to build an assistant to take over all this mind-numbing screening. All the underlying computations and so-called virtual charting go on in real time in a robust, reliable way. An application-specific rule-based language is used to describe events of interest in the virtual charts.

These programs are composed using an intelligent editor, driven directly from the underlying grammar that describes the rules of the language. It completely eliminates syntax errors (i.e., errors resulting from violating these rules), but the user can still make logical errors. The word-processor type of editing program typically used to create programs is replaced by what's called an "intelligent assistant," which knows all the rules and elements of the language. It helps the trader along at each step, presenting all the possible alternatives and rejecting incorrect choices on the spot.

Finally, a simple, natural, graphical method is used to indicate when these events occur, to prioritize among them, and to explain results in a way that is comprehensible to users.

These are all practical applications of AI technologies.

Descriptive Programming

Most programs are written in a procedural language. This means that the programmer tells the machine exactly what to do, one step at a time. Each step is executed in turn unless the previous step explicitly chooses a different order.

Descriptive programming is one of the quiet successes of the artificial intelligence community. Simply stated, in descriptive programming the programmer *describes* the solution sought, instead of specifying the exact steps to *find* it. The best examples of descriptive programming are spreadsheets, which came out of the visual programming tools developed in AI labs in the early 1970s. In a spreadsheet, the user describes the desired program by creating an example. Change the data, and the program runs painlessly. Without knowing it, millions of unsuspecting people have become programmers, using spreadsheets to write programs they couldn't begin to think of in a procedural language.

Other fancier forms of descriptive programming allow people to write programs to solve an impressive array of problems in a concise and logical manner. These include many serious and useful applications, such as fault medical diagnosis, configuring complex systems, and process control. They also include a number of less serious (but mathematically interesting) problems like how to arrange n queens on an n-by-n

square chessboard so no queen attacks another, many variations of the "missionaries and cannibals" and "monkeys and bananas" problems, and the aforementioned Rubik's Cube.

These clever programs used a very general symbolic pattern-matching technique, called Rete matching, which was a central element of the expert systems tools being promoted as "this year's breakthrough of the century" in the mid-1980s.

However, this sophisticated pattern matching is complex, requires an astonishing amount of computer power, and is only marginally relevant to the types of chart scanning real traders do. MarketMind uses a much simpler rule language. It won't play chess, but it does what it's supposed to do.

Information Flows and Displays in MarketMind and QuantEx

The purpose of MarketMind programs is to put alarm indications on the screen when the conditions described by the trader occur. The screen alarm indicator is just a group of upward- or downward-pointing green or red arrows. The more arrows that appear, the more strongly the conditions are indicated. For example, a highly overvalued option would show up with five green up arrows. A highly undervalued option would have five red down arrows next to its symbol.

But there are many more options to watch than there is room to display them on the computer screen. Traders aren't really interested in the options with no arrows at all or only a single up or down arrow. So out of the many thousands of listed options, MarketMind sorts out those with five arrows (in either direction) and puts them on top of the display window, followed by the four-arrow indications, then the threes, and so on.

All of this is updated continuously as the option prices, stock prices, and valuations change in real time. The machine effectively watches thousands of charts (of fair value versus price) at the same time and tells the trader which are worth looking at.

This is a single, simple example. MarketMind doesn't have to look at options. The alarms can deal with liquidity indications for traders and market makers, or anything else you can calculate using real-time

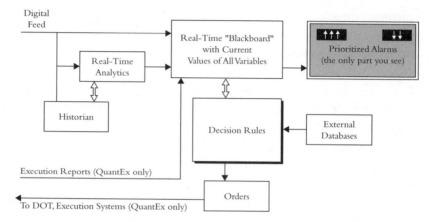

Figure 7.2 Information Flows in QuantEx. Market data in one end, orders out the other.
Source: Screenshots of QuantEx® are reproduced with the permission of Investment Technology Group, Inc.

and historical market data, in combination with any other data you choose to bring into the process. The language allows traders to express a wide variety of technical and quantitative concepts.

The basic information flows in MarketMind and QuantEx are illustrated in Figure 7.2. Real-time data passes through an error detection and correction process. It is combined with historical information as needed, and histories are updated as the system operates. This results in a unified data space containing all the relevant data, from all sources. Information going into MarketMind includes a real-time market data feed, historical market data, and data from fundamental or user-specific databases. There are no explicit flows out of MarketMind; all its results are shown on the screen. This is not the case with QuantEx. Orders (including cancellations and modifications) are explicitly sent out to various execution channels. This gives rise to another input stream and to the execution reports produced as those orders are executed.

The rule language allows descriptions of events of interest to be written in a way that contribute votes for or against alarm conditions. As explained earlier, these alarms are shown onscreen as a number (zero to five, in fractional steps) of up or down arrows. Several methods are available to determine the number of arrows from the alarm signals. These methods include explicit calculation, auto-ranging over a set of alarms (with the most strongly positively and negatively indicated conditions at any given time showing up with five arrows up and down, respectively), or automatically setting a range over time (with five arrows counting for the most strongly indicated condition observed over some period, such as an hour, a day, a week, a year, and so on).

An alarm window is shown in Figure 7.3. Each cell in the window has an alarm name (often a stock symbol) and a number of arrows indicating current alarm status. Each cell can also display the results of calculations that might be needed by the trader, such as a suggested order size or price. An alarm window can contain an unlimited number of cells, many more than will be visible on the screen at any given time. Automatic alarm sorting brings the trader's attention to the most strongly indicated alarms. The frequency of these sorts can be set anywhere from once per second on up to once a day.

This is a good example of the virtue of simplicity in a user interface. Nobody in the securities business has any problem in immediately understanding what five green arrows pointing up mean relative to five red pointing-down arrows. Alarms are prioritized within each window. Lower-priority alarms do not appear in the visible portion of the alarm window.

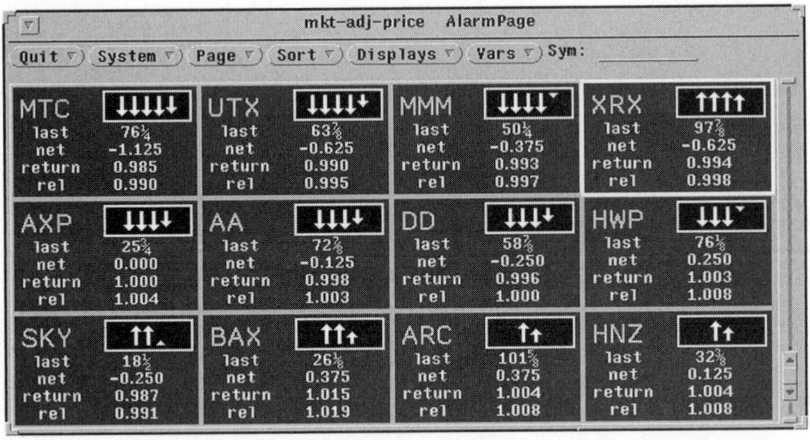

Figure 7.3 MarketMind Alarm Window. Cells for the most strongly indicated events of interest float to the top. Answers the questions "what's important? What's new?"

Source: Screenshots of QuantEx® are reproduced with the permission of Investment Technology Group, Inc.

The alarm windows are the tip of a constantly changing iceberg. It's reasonable to think of each alarm cell as representing a page on a conventional market data and charting system. This is called a "virtual chart." It exists only in the computer, not on the screen.

A MarketMind user can drill down to these pages using mouse clicks on the alarm cell (Figure 7.4a). One mouse action brings up an elaborate chart page, with multiple axes, zoom, direct numerical read-out, and so on (Figure 7.4c). Another action brings up tables containing

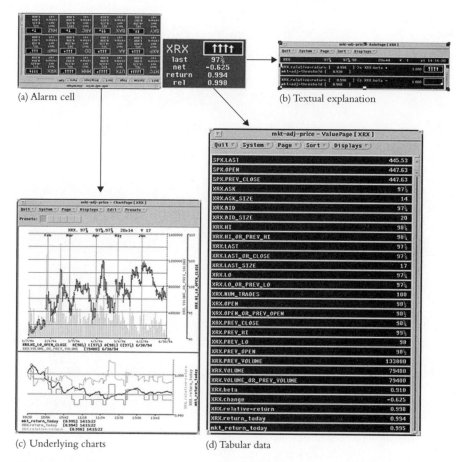

(a) Alarm cell

(b) Textual explanation

(c) Underlying charts

(d) Tabular data

Figure 7.4 "No GUI, no glory": MarketMind's hierarchical graphical user interface—the "overview and zoom down" mantra at work.
Source: Screenshots of QuantEx® are reproduced with the permission of Investment Technology Group, Inc.

live numerical values that go into the alarm calculation (Figure 7.4d). A third mouse action brings up an explanation page, showing which rules caused the alarm to appear in the first place (Figure 7.4b). With QuantEx, there is an additional choice, which is to pass order information directly to an automated equity execution system. On a busy day, over five million shares are traded in this manner.

This is a true KISS approach to intelligence amplification. All MarketMind programs have the same type of user interface: alarm pages with active cells allowing drill-down access to graphic, tabular, and textual explanations.

Multiple alarm pages, corresponding to different rule sets, strategies, or portfolios, can be active simultaneously, as shown in Figure 7.5. Traders using this tool have a cadre of tireless automated assistants.

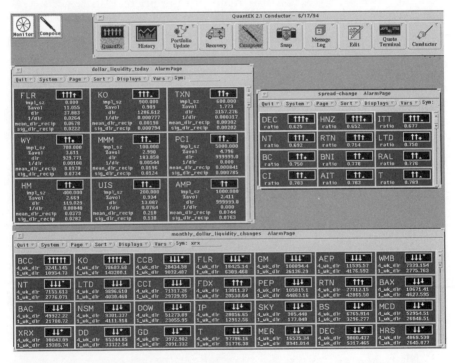

Figure 7.5 Multiple Alarm Windows. You could have as many of these as you wanted, and could add new ones as needed. Like having your own army of data monkeys.

Source: Screenshots of QuantEx® are reproduced with the permission of Investment Technology Group, Inc.

There is no restriction on the number of alarm pages under MarketMind/QuantEx. Traders can watch the same portfolio in any number of ways, watch multiple portfolios in the same way, or run completely unrelated strategies simultaneously.

This paradigm has proven to be a good fit for a wide set of real investment and trading applications. It is used for market surveillance, market making, options trading, equity transaction cost control, and proprietary trading.

Integration with Real-Time Feeds and Historical Databases

Trading analytics often involve many measurements made over many days. An example is a measurement of past volatility over 100 trading days as an input to an option valuation function. Without access to historical data, filling up this analytic would take 100 days, which is clearly unacceptable.

Many attempts to use general-purpose AI tools in finance assume away the nasty details that must be accommodated in a real system. Systems requiring a great deal of additional programming to access the data feeds and databases so pervasive in finance will not be accepted in the marketplace. When MarketMind programs are compiled, one output is a set of queries for historical data services. A single click on the appropriate icon (see Figure 7.5) retrieves the data, calculates any derived quantities, and initializes the MarketMind database.

Composing Syntactically Bulletproof Programs

Artificial intelligence systems can be difficult to program. One popular AI software tool was known within the company that sold it as "syntax relief for LISP."

Many AI programming concepts are totally alien to normal business users. Simplification of the language and provision of automated assistance in developing programs are needed to make AI tools useful commercially. An excellent example is found in the Gensym Corporation's G2 process control systems, which combine graphic layout, tight real-world integration, and "intelligent" grammatical support to facilitate the development of useful programs for process control. Gensym programs now run power, water, and chemical plants around the world, and the subways of Paris.[5]

There are no natural graphic standards for describing trading strategies, so MarketMind's assistance for program developers consists of a text-based grammar-driven real-time parser/editor, called the "Composer." Sophisticated real-time parsing based on the Earley parsing algorithm is used to present all grammatically valid alternatives as the program is written, and all valid alternatives when a program is being edited. This is illustrated in Figure 7.6. Syntax errors cannot be made using this approach. It provides a rich extensible language that can express a wide range of trading/investment ideas in a natural way.

The icon buttons, arranged in a bar called the Conductor (seen at the top of the screen), control all functions. The functionality of these buttons reflects the tight integration with the environment. "History" automatically accesses a dial-in database service to initialize all variables

Figure 7.6   The Conductor Control Panel and Composer. This was a very complex piece of software. It kept nonprogrammers from making mistakes. Programmers preferred text editors. (See the opening quote for this chapter.)
Source: Screenshots of QuantEx® are reproduced with the permission of Investment Technology Group, Inc.

used in the program. "Quote terminal" specifies the type of market data feed that will drive the system in real time. The larger panel is the Composer. This is the grammar-driven editor for MarketMind/ QuantEx programs that does not abide syntax errors. Notice how the insertion point in the definition for the variable "xx1.change" is positioned on OPEN, a data item found directly on the feed. The smaller right-hand panel shows all the grammatically acceptable alternatives to OPEN at this point in the program. These alternatives include feed data, historical information, and derived quantities defined within the program itself.

From Indications to Orders to Executions

The hardware for a MarketMind system consists of a Unix workstation with a wire coming in carrying market data. In virtually all cases (the exception being in market surveillance), the system makes buy and sell suggestions. These can be the investment decisions themselves, or trading suggestions on how to implement decisions made by other means. A MarketMind user decides which of these actions to follow and then picks up the telephone and calls a broker. A collection of MarketMind machines can thus become a high-volume generator of order flow to brokers.

This did not escape the notice of brokers, in particular Jefferies' Investment Technology Group (ITG), which purchased Integrated Analytics in 1992 and integrated MarketMind with its electronic execution technology.

The system, called QuantEx, now has two wires, one bringing in the data, as was the case with MarketMind, and one that can send out orders for electronic execution through a variety of channels. (See Figure 7.2.) These channels include the New York Stock Exchange/ American Stock Exchange (NYSE/AMEX) Designated Order Turnaround (DOT) system, the POSIT crossing network, and the call market on the Arizona Stock Exchange.

QuantEx users control their executions using the same information that was available in MarketMind, plus information from the partial fills (or lack thereof) for their orders. The software interface to perform these important functions is called the execution pad (seen in Figure 7.7). It is fully integrated with the rule language and analytic engines. A rule-based computation can deposit its suggested order size, type, and price directly on the execution pad and alert the user that it has done so. Most users still want to exercise final human control over the release of orders, since they are often valued well into the millions of dollars.

This panel is the last stop before orders are sent out for execution. It is fully integrated with the rule and analytic systems, which are used to control order parameters.

The connection to execution channels adds a rich dimension to the types of financial problems that can be addressed with the system. The return stream of executions—the actual prices and sizes at which orders are filled (or the lack of fills)—contains valuable information for controlling transaction costs using electronic order working strategies.

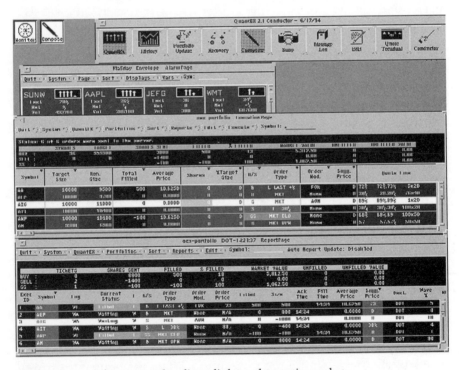

Figure 7.7   Execution pad: a direct link to electronic markets.
Source: Screenshots of QuantEx® are reproduced with the permission of Investment Technology Group, Inc.

The MarketMind/QuantEx rule and analytic language integrates these information flows just as it incorporated raw market data, historical information, external data, and analytics calculated from them.

Vapor No More

MarketMind was unadulterated vaporware in 1987. By 1992, as incorporated in QuantEx, all of the design goals were fully realized. Much of its success is due to a near-seamless integration with the information environment in which it works, from market data to execution channels.

There is only a little AI here. It is used to bury complexity and provide relief for the information overload produced by modern market systems. It provides technological leverage for more traditional and quantitative techniques. It is not used to "emulate great thinkers" or make momentous discoveries. It does, however, provide a real and substantial advantage over previous technologies. Traders using these systems can work in ways that were impossible without them. They have a new set of tools to use in the efficient implementation of investment ideas.

Jefferies' Investment Technology Group, which created the POSIT crossing network in 1987, developed QuantEx with Integrated Analytics in 1990–1991, and acquired the whole company in 1992. It has been a resounding business success. ITG went public in April 1994, with an initial market capitalization of $230 million, rising to over $2 billion today.

As in many acquisitions, particularly those combining companies of very different flavors, like a large, established New York brokerage made up of guys who wore suits to work and a small, scrappy West Coast start-up with nerds in Birkenstocks, there were cultural issues. Some of the Birkenstock guys refused to put up with the brokerage fingerprint and background checks and headed for the exits.

One cultural issue was: "What do the users of these systems really want?" Integrated Analytics Corporation (IAC) succeeded by being innovative and new. It was a hard lesson for many of us to learn that an established industry can digest only so much innovation at a time. Traders did not immediately begin clamoring for more sophisticated AI methods. The level of technology was about right. What they did want were additional execution channels, which increased the system's abilities by providing broader and more diverse market access. The open architecture and rich language of the system allowed traders to extend the basic engine to serve a wider variety of purposes than was ever envisioned. This kept QuantEx alive and thriving for a remarkable 12 years, an astonishingly long time for a technology product.

Future Plans for AI in Finance (in 1995)

Learning is an important aspect of both real and artificial intelligence. Many AI systems, however, do not learn; they merely mimic what we might consider intelligent behavior. MarketMind and QuantEx fall into this category.

Suppose, for example, you have *almost* found the holy grail of trading systems: the magic formula that makes money every time. But due to a programming error, your QuantEx system buys when it should sell and vice versa, and you go broke. QuantEx will never notice.

However, this is not true for all AI systems. There are techniques that *will* allow construction of systems that will notice this kind of error, and learn how to correct it. They can also notice much more subtle errors and deficiencies and make appropriate adjustments. They can also use the results of these adjustments to refine or restructure the process still further. When people do this, we call it "learning." These AI systems are much more modest than the grand AI ultimate goal of machine sentience. They are typically the extended applications of quantitative techniques, enhanced by machine learning.

Artificial learning systems are now being applied in finance and investment. Applications include asset allocation, quantitative equity portfolio management, market making, and currency trading.

That was 1995. To hear how some of this turned out, keep reading the next chapter.

Notes

1. One of those numerical meteorology problems led to the discovery of deterministic chaos, the strong dependence of a result on what was presumed to be meaninglessly small differences in the inputs. This was popularized as the so-called butterfly effect,

since the seemingly insignificant pressure changes caused by a fluttering butterfly, well within the limits of error of barometers used to measure them, could result in wildly different simulated future weather and climate outcomes. James Gleick's book, *Chaos* (New York: Viking Penguin, 1987), is the place to start for the story of chaos.

2. Garbage collection is just gathering up blocks of memory no longer needed by the program. It is part of most implementations of the LISP language. It is very useful to programmers, who then don't have to keep track of memory themselves. It is obviously not a good idea to use in a real-time application like trading unless it can be accomplished without stopping.

3. LISP is a computer language particularly suited to manipulation of symbols (as opposed to numbers). It is widely used in the academic AI community. LISP machines are workstations with specialized hardware to run LISP programs efficiently.

4. First described in "Knowledge-Based Systems for Financial Applications," D. Leinweber, *IEEE Expert* (Fall 1988).

5. The names "Gensym" and "G2" are subtle LISP jokes. LISP and other AI programming languages sometimes need to create variables, which need names. Gensym is the name of the "generate symbol" function that returns these names. The first time it's called, you get "G1," the second time, "G2," and so on. When Gensym's founders, including Ed Fredkin of MIT's AI Lab, needed names for both company and product, they did what LISP programmers do and called them "Gensym" and "G2." They are found here: www.gensym.com.

Chapter 8

Perils and Promise of Evolutionary Computation on Wall Street

Be careful what you ask for—you might get it.

M y enthusiasm for machine learning, described at the end of the previous chapter, led me to kiss many artificial intelligence (AI) frogs. This included many flavors of inductive and explanation-based learning, as well as connectionist ideas, such as neural nets, that were based on simulating simple nervous systems. There were some interesting notions, but nothing came close to reproducing that "Wow!" Macsyma moment, until I found artificial evolution and genetic algorithms (GAs).

These techniques used populations of solutions, and applied digital versions of the principles of evolution to select the fittest, and to combine the best of the bunch for successor generations of hybridized and mutated solutions. There were some remarkable examples—robots that started out wandering aimlessly and bumping into things evolved before your eyes into what looked like precision drill teams. Symbolic regressions "discovered" complex algebraic relationships instead of

This article originally appeared in the Winter 2003 issue of the *Journal of Investing*. It is reprinted with permission. To view the original article, please go to iijoi.com.

just calculating coefficients on an assumed model structure. There were very capable network controllers and logic circuits, all of which emerged from a clearly useless population of random initial solutions.[1]

I became a major cheerleader for learning in finance using artificial evolution. I attended academic conferences where I met the leading lights in the field and hired their grad students, and where I got to stay in college dorms. It was a refreshing change from all of the four-star hotels favored for investment management conferences. Actually, sharing a bathroom with 25 other people is not so refreshing, but it was a change.

One of the founding fathers was Dave Goldberg, the big dog of evolutionary computation (EC), at the University of Illinois in Champaign-Urbana (also home to *2001: A Space Odyssey*'s HAL 9000). In 1989 Dave wrote the classic and still best-selling text, *Genetic Algorithms in Search, Optimization and Machine Learning* (Addison-Wesley, 1989). I borrowed code from Dave for the experiments described in this paper, and got to speak at the GA and EC conferences. Eventually, Dave felt sorry for me getting in the bathroom line with all the grad students, and reserved one of the prime speaker slots at another conference, arranging to have me quartered in accommodations with my own plumbing at the spectacular Jumer's Bavarian Grotto in Champaign-Urbana.

Fans of the Madonna Inn in San Luis Obispo, California, which features the Cave Man Room, the Spanish Inquisition Room, and the Li'l Abner Suite, among too many others to mention, would feel right at home in Jumer's. I gather that Jumer's has gone more upscale and mainstream, but back in the mid-1990s it was one of the kitsch capitals of the United States. You should trust me on this—I have been to Gatorland, home of the Gator Jump-a-roo, nine times.

Jumer's had an all-medieval, all-Teutonic all the time theme going on: lots of stuffed actual bears; lots of weaponry on the walls, including in the guest rooms; battle axes, chain mail, and heavy purple draperies everywhere you looked; many, many suits of armor; and an actual stuffed horse, wearing more armor. All were well secured to the walls and floor to discourage University of Illinois students trolling for dorm decor items. I didn't want to leave for the GA and EC events down the road at the much duller university, but I did, and hired more grad students and borrowed more code.

My willingness to show up at Jumer's earned me an invitation to do a keynote talk on evolutionary computation and finance at the 2002 Genetic and Evolutionary Computation Conference (GECCO) in New York. GECCO was the major confab for this branch of the AI world, and there were more than a few fellow travelers on the EC-finance trail. I was willing to talk about it, since I'd begun to have some doubts and felt that maybe I'd learn more than I gave away. This chapter is based on that talk.

The AI Spring?

The AI winter was not just a write-off for the venture capitalists who had drunk too deeply of the Kool-Aid; it spawned many genuine innovations, which came from questioning in a scientific way what had gone wrong. The symbolic predicate calculus logic programming view of AI had its limitations. Learning how to solve problems in the really messy, noisy, dynamic world was different from theorem proving and chess.

Scientists looking for successful models of learning and adaptive behavior do not have to look far. Birds do it, bees do it, even monkeys in the trees do it. But they all do it using wetware that we understand well enough to appreciate the crucial lessons for the next generation of AI paradigms. There is massive parallelism. Computation is going on all over the place, not in one instruction stream. Brains do not have accumulators.

AI went parallel. Thinking Machines, founded by computational superstar Danny Hillis (son-in-law of Marvin Minsky, the pope of symbolic AI), gathered some of the leading lights to build and program massive machines with up to 64K (65,536) processors. That is a lot more than one, but still a lot less than the 100 billion neurons in the brain.

You don't need a machine with a billion processors to try out solutions that would use them. A simulator will do fine, if not as fast. For theory buffs, this is an example of the idea of a universal computation; a Turing machine or its equivalent can emulate anything you want. The Nintendo 64 emulators you can run on your PC to play Pac-Man are another.

The neural net movement exploited this idea, seeking to realize learning by mimicking structure and function. Another branch of the turn to biologically inspired approaches to learning used the intriguing idea of mimicking evolution. The mechanics of evolution at the chromosome level—the processes of mutation and crossover, dominant and recessive traits—are understood well. John Holland of the Santa Fe Institute proposed the idea of genetic algorithms, using computers to emulate evolution of solutions to problems, in order to use computer programs to evolve better programs.

Genetic algorithms are a tool for machine learning and discovery modeled on the time-tested process of Darwinian evolution. Potential forecasting models and trading rules are modeled as "chromosomes" containing all of their salient characteristics. A population of these solutions is allowed to "evolve," with the fittest solutions rewarded by inclusion in subsequent generations. Each individual's fitness is calculated explicitly as a payoff.

For example, fitness can be measured by predictive ability or alpha (excess return over the benchmark). Solutions with the lowest fitness become extinct in a few generations.

Variety is introduced into the population of solutions by mimicking the natural processes of crossover and mutation. Crossover effectively combines features of fit models to produce fitter models in subsequent generations. In crossover, we blend chromosomes (bit strings) defining two successful models in the hope of developing a still better model. Mutation stirs the pot and introduces variations that would not be produced by crossover. Here we randomly alter any bit in any chromosome to create a mutation. Most fail badly, but a few survive. As long as we are playing God, we can give the fittest members of the population a free pass into the next generation without participating in the breeding and selection cycle.

Genetic Algorithms

Genetic algorithms have been used successfully in many contexts, including meteorology, structural engineering, robotics, econometrics, and computer science. The genetic algorithm is particularly appealing for financial applications because of its robust nature and the importance of the payoff in guiding the process.

The genetic algorithm is robust in the sense that very few restrictions are placed on the form of the financial model to be optimized. It can include conventional models (e.g., time series regressions), but is not restricted to them (allowing, for example, heuristic decision rules). Almost any form of constraint can be applied, including self-referential constraints involving the form of the model, its complexity, and similarity to other known models.

Genetic algorithms are particularly well-suited for financial modeling applications for three reasons:

1. They are payoff driven. Payoffs can be improvements in predictive power or alpha. There is an excellent match between the tool and the problems to be addressed.
2. They are inherently quantitative, and well-suited to parameter optimization (unlike most symbolic machine learning techniques).
3. They are robust, allowing a wide variety of extensions and constraints that cannot be accommodated in traditional methods.

The key aspect of the genetic algorithm's appeal in trading is clearly made in Dave Goldberg's book: It is payoff driven. (See Figure 8.1.) Think of flipping the switches to maximize payoff. The switches are bits, binary digits; and in real problems, there are many more of them, representing complex solutions as binary chromosomes.

Start with an initial population, random for purists, with known good solutions included for engineers. Let the programs (phenotypes)

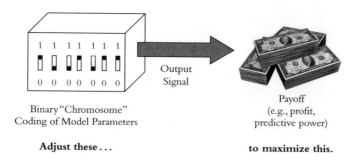

Figure 8.1 Payoff drives the genetic algorithm.
Source: Adapted from Genetic Algorithms in Search, Optimization and Machine Learning *by Dave Goldberg (Addison-Wesley, 1989), 8.*

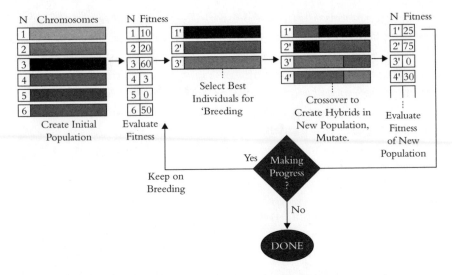

Figure 8.2   Simulated Evolution in the Genetic Algorithm

represented by the chromosomes (genotypes) do that thing they do, whatever it may be, and keep score. Favor the high scorers in the next generation, and mix things up by using crossover—taking complementary parts of each of two "parent programs" chromosomes—to evolve hybrids. Mix things up a little more with an occasional mutation. (See Figure 8.2.)

Evolving Financial Models

For all of the aforementioned reasons, I saw the genetic and evolutionary algorithms as a great idea, one that could take the use of AI in finance to another plane, where trading and investment programs would successfully adapt to changing environments. My quant equity research group tried these algorithms in a variety of contexts, from short-term trading to longer-term forecasting.

At the start of this chapter, I recounted my adventures as I became an avid booster of genetic computation and a guest at Jumer's Bavarian house of bears and armor for the Genetic and Evolutionary Computation Conference.

Dave Goldberg's opening address to the conference included an insightful assessment of the state of evolutionary computing, in theory and in practice. Somehow, he managed to work in a story involving his

Lithuanian grandmother's recipe for chicken soup, which began, "First, steal a chicken."

There was no Lithuanian chicken soup at that GECCO, but there were some amazing demonstrations of learning programs. Robot control strategies started out as random walks, and after a few hundred simulated generations, they were moving like R2D2 on a good day. There were novel circuit, network, and even protein designs produced by artificial genetic methods.[2]

The financial guys, many of whom I recognized from more Wall Street–oriented events, and I were trolling for ideas, people to hire, and software to take home. I found all three, and so, several years later, when the GECCO crowd came to New York to focus on financial applications (and maybe get some of these guys hired), I was invited to give one of the keynote talks on what we had been up to. The centerpiece of the talk is a declassified description of a real application of evolutionary computation in institutional asset management in the early 1990s. Real-world examples of these technologies in use on greater Wall Street are scarce. The passage of time and the intellectual generosity of the sponsoring firm allow publication at this time.

A second theme of the paper is to underscore the problems of applying techniques that rely on massive computation, such as evolutionary computation, neural networks, and knowledge discovery in financial settings. Much of the published work in these areas exhibits at least one of the sins of data mining. Statistical techniques developed in an era of manual or expensive machine computation can be fooled as we push the edges of Moore's law. Additional measures are needed to find financially and economically meaningful solutions.

It starts by relating the evolutionary ideas to the expert system ideas in the previous chapter.

An Early Lesson: Intelligence without Learning

When it comes to applications of evolutionary computation for trading and investment, it's possible to become a grizzled veteran in a relatively short time. This is fairly new territory, so 10 or 12 years qualifies as a long-term historical perspective. By that low standard, I qualify as a grizzled veteran, so let me start by telling how I ended up here.

If you were to look at a high-end trading room back in the early 1980s, you'd see rows and rows of people sitting in front of what appeared to be computer screens. It looked like mission control. It may have looked like computers, but it was really keyboard-controlled cable television, showing prices in text format. You'd type in what you were interested in, and a *picture of the data* would appear on the screen, fed in as video.

All you could do with the data was look at it. It wasn't until the mid-1980s that true machine-readable market data feeds appeared. At first, they were just used to show digital pictures of data. Then cheap, socially acceptable computer hardware (in the form of the IBM PC) appeared that allowed Wall Street people to put something in front of them that could actually do computation with the data. Of course, everyone's favorite computation was to make a graph. With Moore's law in high gear, soon there were graphs everywhere—more graphs than anyone knew what to do with. People were typing in symbols and paging through graphs with a vengeance. More and more graphs appeared on the screen together. This worked nicely for a while, but got out of hand when screens rapidly filled with dozens of charts, far too many moving targets for a human to track.

This clearly ridiculous situation gave me my first job on greater Wall Street (see Chapter 7, "A Little AI Goes a Long Way on Wall Street"). It was a nice application for a specialized expert system that could sort through all these hundreds, even thousands, of graphs, and tell you which ones were interesting by the standards of the trader or investor, who would otherwise be furiously typing and gazing at one chart after another.

In 1987, a group of people with AI backgrounds, including myself, founded a company called Integrated Analytics to solve this problem. We built a specialized expert system called MarketMind, which virtualized all sorts of charts and let people describe what made a particular chart interesting to them. It was an intelligent alerts system in the sense that people could say what they were interested in at a nice high descriptive level. The events of interest would sort up to the top; then the viewer could drill down to the detailed charts and tables below.

This system, which was kept going strong for 12 years in the form of Investment Technology Group (ITG)'s QuantEx, used AI techniques to allow people to build intelligent graph-watching assistants, but it didn't do any learning. There were all sorts of uses for it, ranging from market surveillance to proprietary trading, but it just did what you told it to do, no matter how stupid that might be. If you had actually found the holy grail of quantitative trading, but had made only one little mistake—you were buying when you should sell, and selling when you should buy—the system would never notice. But a genetic algorithm *would* notice this kind of sign error, along with a host of other mistakes and miscalibrations. It seemed to be an ideal tool for tuning, refining, and evolving quantitative investment and trading strategies.

In 1989, Henry Lichstein, of Citibank, who was also on the board of the Santa Fe Institute, introduced me to the genetic algorithm. Some people thought that it was a crackpot idea, but crackpot ideas have often been welcome in trading and investment. The sense that innovation is rewarded is well established.

Genetic algorithms seemed to be perfect tools for these applications. The technology was there in the form of networked Unix workstations to allow us to solve large problems in a reasonable time. (Now this is much easier to do, and GAs are natural uses for parallel computation on networks or clouds. The fitness evaluation of any individual in the population is independent of the others.) A number of features of the GA seemed to promise better solutions than we were likely to find using more conventional techniques.

Arbitrage and Predictive Strategies

Some quantitative strategies work by pure arbitrage, essentially finding the 4.9-cent nickels in the market before anyone else does. Examples are commodities, such as gold, that trade at the same time on multiple markets around the world. Arbitrageurs move in to equalize the disparities between markets when they arise, buying on the low-priced side and selling on the high-priced side. "Buy low, sell high" is what keeps markets together. Those participants with the lowest transaction costs jump in first, and the physics of supply and demand brings prices back in line.

Being an arbitrageur is nice work if you can get it, but it is largely a game for only the largest players. Another level of quantitative strategy involves making some kind of a prediction. Increasing predictability increases investment return. Improving the consistency and downside error of predictive models reduces risk.

Maximizing Predictability

Much of published material on the use of genetic and evolutionary methods in trading focuses on using the past history of prices to predict the future, as in technical analysis. This is an age-old approach. For much of the twentieth century, it was considered a legitimate area of academic investigation. Strategies based on daily stock prices alone were shown to be futile in the 1960s, and they fell into academic disrepute. This hasn't stopped people from using all sorts of tools and techniques for ever more complex forms of technical analysis. Neural nets are currently popular in this regard. This is simple in terms of the data needed, and popular among active individual investors and traders. This has resulted in a somewhat skewed perspective on the topic of financial prediction in the EC and GA literature.

In 1992, I had joined First Quadrant, an institutional investment management firm[3] that applied quantitative forecasting techniques to a variety of investment strategies. Figure 8.3 revisits the idea of maximizing predictability introduced in Chapter 5 and is a high-level perspective on maximizing predictability in finance.[4]

To expand on the previous discussion, the key point is that there are three central decisions to make in financial prediction:

1. *What to predict.* You can choose to predict the returns to an asset class, such as a broad market or industry group, an exchange rate, interest rates, or returns to individual securities of many types.

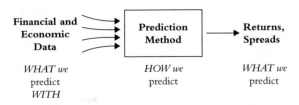

Figure 8.3   Maximizing Predictability: Three Places to Look

There is also money to be made by predicting the return differences (spreads) between individual securities or groups of securities. Options-based strategies can also use predictions of volatility.

2. *How to predict.* There are a wide variety of statistical and mathematical methods for prediction. Simple windowed regression methods are widely used for this purpose. Each period, data from the past to predict value in the next period, and the expanded data set is used to recalculate the coefficients of the model. There are many flavors of regression that can be used—moving or expanding windows, robust methods, kernel estimation. Autoregressive integrated moving average (ARIMA) time series models are used in many engineering forecasting applications, and in finance as well. Neural networks have also been popular in these applications. In many instances, one of these methods can be shown to be equivalent to another.

3. *What to predict with.* Simple technical analysis strategies use only past prices to predict the future. These are relatively rare as the driving force behind institutional trading. A variety of factors influence asset returns. In many cases, one set of returns will affect another. For example, rising copper prices tend to drive up the prices of stock in copper companies, and drive down the prices of stock in companies that have to buy large amounts of copper. The inverse relationship between oil prices and transportation stocks is another example. Shifts in foreign exchange rates affect companies doing business across national borders. A shift in analysts' opinions on a stock is often reflected in its price.

Choosing how to measure and transform predictive data are key elements of the "what to predict with" decision. The obvious choice of just using the current value of whatever is selected seems problematic on deeper inspection. People create market prices, and people are sensitive to new highs and new lows; whether an indicator is rising or falling; where it is compared to last month, last quarter, last year, and the same quarter a year ago; and so on. Application of simple mathematical transforms, such as rate, square root, and log, are useful in many contexts. The decision of what to predict with is vastly complicated by the decision on how to measure the indicators chosen.

Chromosomes for Forecasting Models

The preceding list suggests the design of a chromosome for a forecasting model to be developed using genetic and evolutionary techniques. It will consist of three segments, corresponding to the three main design components of the model: what it forecasts, how it forecasts, and a large and complex segment specifying the variables and transformations with which it forecasts.

Not all of the basic GA manipulations on these chromosomes will correspond to reasonable models. For example, a model that looked only at data from five years ago would not make much financial sense (even though it might have great statistical properties, it would be a fluke of data mining). These nonsensical chromosomes, such as those that don't look at the most recent data, can be weeded out in the mechanics of the GA itself by rejecting some products of crossover and mutation, or they can be penalized severely in their fitness function. It is a better use of computational resources to get rid of them early.

Variants on the chromosomes[5] used for the forecasting models, as seen in Figure 8.4, allowed for higher levels of flexibility. The simplest

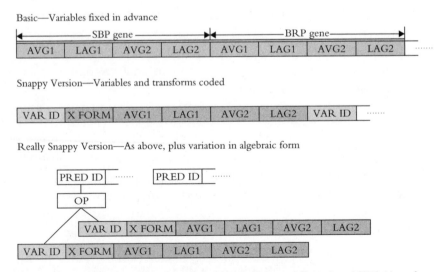

Figure 8.4 Chromosomes for Global Tactical Asset Allocation (GTAA) and Tactical Currency Allocation (TCA) Models

chromosomes assumed that the standard predictor variables used in the existing models were utilized, and only the transforms were adjusted. A more complex variant allowed the predictor variables to change as well as the transform. The most sophisticated chromosome allowed for variation in functional form, introducing ideas from genetic programming.

Fitness Functions for Forecasting Models

There are many aspects to what makes one forecasting model better than another. Ultimately, we don't really know what a model's true value will be, since only the future will tell. We use a variety of hold-back samples, statistical and financial measures, and heuristics to identify what we consider promising models. The ability of the GA to incorporate these diverse elements (in contrast to simpler statistical tools) is part of its appeal in this context.

- *Risk and return.* The obvious candidate for fitness in this context is financial return. This is used in most simple GA trading strategies, and certainly makes sense. In more complex strategies, there are other aspects to consider. Measures of risk–adjusted returns, such as the Sharpe ratio, are more appropriate.
- *Statistical fitness.* In many contexts, the performance of an investment strategy will depend on multiple models working together; there may not even be a sensible measure of the return to a single model in a complex strategy using combined forecasts and portfolio optimization. In these situations, a statistical measure of the fitness of the model is appropriate. A common choice is the information coefficient, simply the correlation of the predicted and actual outcomes. This is sensible, but hides some subtle errors. Correlations and other measures based on squared errors don't distinguish between a forecast that is in the right direction but wrong by the same amount as another forecast that is in the wrong direction, even though one makes money and the other loses it, as seen in Figure 8.5. The idea of directional consistency is helpful here.

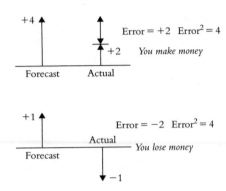

Figure 8.5 Squared error metrics lose valuable information. You can lose money with the same statistics that make money, if you use many common measures.

- *Plausibility and parsimony.* Data mining is a constant risk in financial fore-casting. All of these stories about hemlines or the outcome of the Super Bowl predicting the market do not come out of nowhere. If you look hard enough, you will always find something that looks great statisti-cally, but makes no sense. Believe it or not, there was a 10-year period when the annual change in the S&P 500 had a 75 percent correlation with butter production in Bangladesh. Favoring models with fewer var-iables and simpler transforms can be reflected in the fitness function.
- Simplicity and parsimony is also fostered by some deviations from the purist approach to GA and GP (genetic programming). A fully random initial population of models that can include many vari-ables is likely to have more needlessly complex individuals than a structured initial population of simpler models.
- *Novelty.* Finance is not physics. What we are looking for in these forecasting models are plausible empirical associations. There may be many such models. Elitism is used to keep the *n* most fit models in the population. A statistical measure of the differences between mod-els, such as the correlation of their errors, will allow the GA process to drive the solution to new areas. In practice, this has proved very useful.

Use of the GA for Coping with a Combinatoric Explosion of Models

After we have selected a chromosome that describes the class of models we are interested in, and a fitness function to rank models, we are ready to venture out into the truly vast space of possible models.

Let's simplify the problem by assuming the questions of *what* and *how* to predict have been decided. These were in fact the conditions that we faced at First Quadrant. The investment strategies in place called for forecasts of particular financial variables (broad market returns for the asset allocation, stock industry groups and common factors for equity strategies). The methodology of automated data collection and forecasting with expanding window time series regressions was already institutionalized. Much of the ongoing research therefore centered on questions of *what to predict with*, which by itself is a very large problem.

To get a feel for how large this is, consider a set of possible predictor variables and simple measurements and transforms along these lines:

Number of base variables (interest rates, exchange rates, etc.)	40
Number of plausible first-period measurement intervals (year, six months, quarter, month)	4
Number of plausible comparison period intervals (previous year, previous quarter, same period one year earlier, etc.)	4
Number of useful measurements (percent change, rate, difference, shock)	4
Number of useful statistical transforms (square, square root, log)	3

Just multiplying these numbers ($4 \times 4 \times 4 \times 3$) together gives 192 possible predictive variable based on *each* of the 40 base variables. The combinatoric explosion occurs when we start combining the possible predictive variables. If we are willing to allow up to eight predictor variables in a model, then we quickly find that we have a fearsome number of models to contend with,[6] as seen here:

Number of plausible models with 1 regressor	7,680
Number of plausible models with 2 regressors	28,753,920
Number of plausible models with 3 regressors	69,929,533,440
Number of plausible models with 4 regressors	1.24195 E+14
Number of plausible models with 5 regressors	1.71687 E+17
Number of plausible models with 6 regressors	1.92289 E+20
Number of plausible models with 7 regressors	1.79324 E+23
Number of plausible models with 8 regressors	1.42024 E+26
Total	*1.42204 E+26*

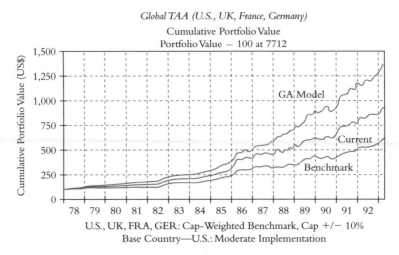

Figure 8.6 Performance of Genetically Optimized GTAA Models. Getting what you ask for.

Even if one of these models could be evaluated in a millisecond, it would still take more than 10^{15} years to evaluate all of them. Years of human directed iterative model specification research had been put into model development before the introduction of the GA into the process. We used the GA system to develop a wide variety of models, including asset allocation, forecasting returns to stock and bond markets, currencies, and equity factor models.

Our first results were clearly data mined, containing utterly implausible variables. However, when we introduced the measures discussed earlier to mitigate these effects, we were extremely pleased with the results, shown in Figure 8.6. Keep in mind that the base models that these were compared against had been the subjects of intensive research at four different investment firms, spanning a 10-year period.[7]

Genetic algorithm models' fitness was evaluated on an in-sample period that went from 1978 to 1988, so we would expect them to look very good over this period. The next four years, from 1989 to 1994, were held back as an out-of-sample test, visited only manually to see how the models performed and not used in the GA process. It was extremely satisfying that they performed well in this period as well, as seen in Figure 8.7.

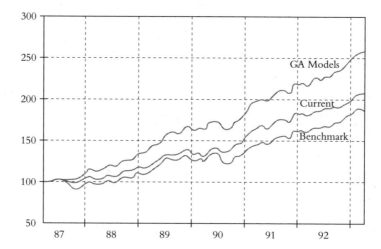

Figure 8.7   Four-Country GTAA Example: Out-of-Sample Performance. In hindsight, making more than one visit to the out-of-sample period makes it less than out-of-sample. We were more than occasional visitors.

Genetically Optimized Forecasting Models in Hindsight

Looking back on these models many years after we developed them is highly instructive. We did get what we wanted from the GA. It allowed us to produce much better models using the criteria we chose than other previous methods had. It produced simpler, more reasonable models with better statistical and financial performance in the test periods.

We tried to avoid data mining, but the market has only one past, and we knew what it was. The bias introduced by that knowledge cannot be removed.

After they were developed, these models made money in some countries, but not in others. Arguably, there were structural changes in the markets that ran contrary to what any rearview model based on the past would predict. Long Term Capital Management, a veritable who's who on Wall Street with multiple Nobel laureates as founders, had similar, though more spectacular, troubles.

No matter how much we want to think otherwise, financial markets are not physics experiments. They reflect a shifting combination of economic forces and human emotion. Like all other facets of human behavior, they are a mixture of the rational and the irrational, not necessarily the best target for the approach described here.

Some of the risks in modeling markets, with or without the aid of evolutionary computation, are unavoidable. Others are not. There is no guarantee of future wealth. There are some basic caveats one should follow to avoid the known pitfalls of financial forecasting, as amplified by a tool as powerful as evolutionary computation.

Genetic Algorithm Warning Label

A central danger in using the GA (and many other techniques) is that you may fall deep into the data mine. Recall that if you look at 100 statistical relationships that are significant at the 5 percent level, five of them are there only by chance. If you look at a million relationships, then 50,000 will be significant at that level. During the early stages of our use of the GA technology, a chromosome evolved encoding for a variable based on a 15-month average lagged 7 months minus a 7-month average lagged 15 months. It had a nice symmetry to it. It had high statistical significance. Was this data mining? You bet. Was the high predictive power spurious? A virtual certainty. It was ignominiously retired to the bit bucket.

With the GA, we know that we can dig down to the deepest region of the data mine and produce models with much better statistics and even wackier variables than the previous example. It is very easy to generate models with near-perfect predictive power, and coefficients significant at the 0.1 percent level on randomly generated data. It is important to be very careful not to fool ourselves. Here are some of the ways we achieve this:

- *Wetware before software.* Wetware is the gray matter between your ears. The brain needs to be engaged before the GA is put into gear. The starting population always includes models developed using established econometric and quantitative methods. They make sense economically. Often, the result of the GA is only a slight refinement or adjustment of the initial solution.
- *Immortality for the stars.* The best few solutions in each generation survive unchanged into the next. This is also called elitism. It keeps

good results from being submerged by random events. It is a technique that is regrettably unavailable to Mother Nature.

- *Keeping nonsensical variables out.* We design our own genetic code. It does not permit the type of nonsense variable described earlier, or many other equally specious varieties.

- *Good fitness functions.* Predictive ability measured by information coefficient is just one part of fitness. Total squared error, consistency and correctness of direction, stability, and plausibility are also important measures of model quality.

- *Judicious use of out-of-sample periods.* To be absolutely 100 percent not guilty of any data mining sins, each financial researcher would be allowed only one look at the out-of-sample period, and not be allowed to read any books or papers on the subject. Ideally, all researchers would not have seen the *Wall Street Journal* or each other for the prior five years. These people are hard to find. We all have lived through the out-of-sample period. The next best thing is to be extremely careful about human looks into the out-of-sample period, and never to let the GA look at it at all.

- *Cross-sectional and cross-country validations.* It is easier to have faith in similar models that produce similar results for different securities and different countries than those that do not travel well across borders.

- *Calibrate new and improved tools carefully.* If a new process can produce fabulous results using random inputs, there is something wrong with the process. *As always, if it seems too good to be true, it is.*

Notes

1. A good starting point for genetic algorithms is ILLIGAL, the GA lab at the University of Illinois (www.illigal.uiuc.edu/web/). For genetic programming, John Koza's work is found here: www.genetic-programming.org/. The Santa Fe Institute, where many of these ideas first got started, is still in the game: www.santafe.edu/research/topics-innovation-evolutionary-systems.php.

2. There are videos of some these early examples accompanying John Koza's books, *Genetic Computation I* and *II* (Cambridge, MA: MIT Press). A search for "genetic algorithm demonstrations" turns up hundreds.

3. First Quadrant (www.firstquadrant.com), in Pasadena, California. Assets under management were in excess of $20 billion; clients were primarily pension funds.

4. Thanks to Andy Lo of MIT for this clear view of the central issues, discussed in many other contexts in his fine text *Econometrics of Financial Markets* (written with John Y. Campbell and A. Craig MacKinlay; Princeton University Press, 1996) and popular work *A Non-Random Walk Down Wall Street* (written with A. Craig MacKinlay; Princeton University Press, 1999).

5. Actually, just the variable specification portion; as will be discussed later, the first two segments were fixed.

6. Using the formula $n!/[(n - r)!r!]$ and recognizing that there are 192 variations on each variable.

7. For information on these models, see "A Disciplined Approach to Global Asset Allocation," by Robert D. Arnott and Robert M. Lovell, Jr., *Financial Analysts Journal* (January/February 1989).

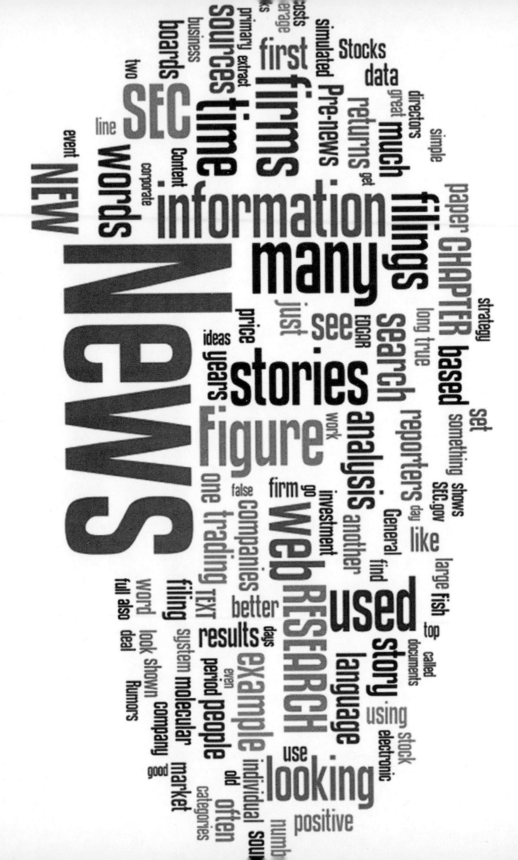

Chapter 9

The Text Frontier

AI, IA, and the New Research

Alpha hunters are always looking for new territory. When a strategy becomes known and used by too many players, the collective market impact of getting in and getting out will squeeze out all the profit juice, and only the lowest-cost transactors (large sell-side firms and hedge funds) will be able to use it. The pack needs to move on.

The Web is promising new territory, but while it is full of information it is also something of a pain to deal with, so a case can be made that there's an economic rent (alpha) to be earned by doing a good job at using the Web effectively. This was suggested at the end of Chapter 4, "Where Does Alpha Come From?" This chapter gets into the specifics, showing real examples relating textual patterns and events (not just individual documents) to excess returns.

Bill Gross, of the PIMCO investment management company, described equity valuation as that mysterious fragile flower where price is part perception, part valuation, and part hope or lack thereof."[1] An old Wall Street proverb says, more tersely, "Stocks are stories, bonds are mathematics."

This chapter is based on a talk given at Fidelity Investments' Center for Applied Technology, July 2008.

This has enough truth in it that looking for the right stories is a worthwhile activity. With hundreds of billions of pages available on the surface Web (the portion covered by search engines), and even more information stashed in proprietary databases and other deep Web locations, there are plenty of places to look. It makes sense in looking at these to break them into vaguely more manageable categories. A useful way to do this is to consider four broad classifications:

1. *News.* This is the old standby, and we all know this when we see it. It is often called the mainstream media (MSM). It is written by reporters, edited by editors, and published by more or less reputable sources. News was once exclusively disseminated on paper, radio, and television, and later via expensive dedicated electronic feeds. It is now ubiquitous on the Web, and news vendors are trying to move upscale, with tagged news that is more amenable to machine understanding using intelligence amplification (IA) and artificial intelligence (AI) tools. These deluxe feeds go for deluxe prices, tens of thousands of dollars per month.

2. *Pre-news.* Pre-news is the raw material reporters read before they write news. It comes from primary sources, the originators themselves: the Securities and Exchange Commission (SEC), court documents, and other government agencies. Not every reporter knows Deep Throat, but they all talk with people who might have something newsworthy to say. In pre-Web days, primary source information was much harder to come by, so we were far more dependent on reporters and established news organizations to find it for us. Today, in yet another instance of disintermediation by the Internet, many information middlemen have been eliminated.

3. *Rumors.* Here is content with a slightly to dramatically lower pedigree than reputable, signed news reporting, or the primary source material that goes into MSM news. Internet advertising has created a means to monetize spreading rumors, and spawned a new segment of the information industry. Some blogs and web sites are driven entirely by rumors, with little or no regard for truth. Others have much higher standards, closer to the highest-minded bastions of reputation-driven journalism, and may be spawned by those news organizations as they evolve. Others have an "all Britney, all the time, except for shark attacks" attitude, but keep people coming

back by breaking an occasional legitimate true story overlooked by the mainstream media.

4. *Social media.* The barriers to entry at the low end of the "news" business on the Web are vanishingly small. Anyone can send spam, create a blog, or post on message boards for stocks or other topics. A great deal of this is genuinely useful—think of the product reviews on Amazon—and some is just noise. On stock message boards, there have been CEOs who reveal valuable information; but for the most part, the typical posting still reads like it came from some guy sitting around in his underwear in Albania at 3 A.M., on vodka number nine. A great deal of research has gone into trying to sort out the legitimate sources from the louts. Some seems to have promise, at least in identifying future volatility. But you may be better off looking for the words of the prophets on the subway walls.

The first two items on this list are the subject in this chapter; the second two are the subject of the next one.

This chapter reviews research and ideas relating to extracting investable information from news and pre-news sources. A recurring theme is *molecular search*: the idea of looking for patterns and changes in groups of documents, rather than just characterizing *atoms of information*, the individual documents or stories we find as the result of conventional search engine queries. The choice of molecules and atoms instead of the usual "forest and trees" metaphor is not just some fancy science talk; it's because there is only one basic relationship between trees and forests—spread out a bunch of the first to make the second. Molecules made from atoms have infinite variety and complexity, as do the relationships we can infer across groups of documents.

Ten Pounds of News in a Five-Pound Bag

The tagline in the corner of the paper version of the *New York Times* is "All the News That's Fit to Print." In fact, this was never true. The size of the paper is limited by many factors: press speeds, cost, and the limits of physical delivery. Editors have to pick and choose. This is true for all paper and ink publications. The *Wall Street Journal* index of companies mentioned rarely includes more than 300 names. But on the same day, Web sources will have news on thousands of firms. International and specialized news sources used to be costly and difficult to come by. Now they are as accessible as the local paper.

News is a time-honored source for investment information, and there is more of it than ever before, more than a person can handle. With the relentless march of technology to the beat of Moore's law, previously impractical computationally intense approaches to natural language can be used to parse, categorize, and understand the onslaught of news. Reporters help the process along by tagging story elements at their point of origin. They inject some valuable wetware into the mix of hardware and software involved in the modern production, dissemination, and consumption of news. There is a great deal of commercial effort in this area, applying language and Web technologies to gather, filter, and rank individual news by type, sentiment, or intensity. Some are available to try on the Web.[2]

The purest of efficient market purists once claimed that all news was already incorporated in prices. Someone always knew the news before you did, so there was no point in paying attention to it. This is another case of someone having to pick up that $100 bill on the sidewalk first, but those hundreds do get picked up pretty fast.

An example in the fall of 2008 shows how truly unexpected news can impact prices dramatically. At 1:37 A.M. EDT on Sunday, September 7, 2008, Google's newsbots picked up a 2002 story about United Airlines possibly filing for bankruptcy. Apparently, activity at 1:36 A.M. on the web site of the *Orlando Sentinel* caused an old story to resurface on the list of "most viewed stories." In Orlando, in the middle of the night, with Mickey sound asleep and Gatorland closed, a single viewing of the story was enough to do this, and attract the attention of the newsbot, one of many search agent programs that populates Google's news database. In a cascade of errors, the story was picked up by a person, who, failing to notice that the date on the story was six years gone, put it on Bloomberg, which then set off a chain reaction on services that monitor Bloomberg news. This remarkable ability of the Internet to disseminate "news" resulted in the stock of United's parent, UAL Corporation, dropping 76 percent in six minutes, with a huge spike in volume, as seen in Figure 9.1.

This looks like (at the very least) an accidental manipulation. The SEC announced an investigation into the incident by the end of the week. Trades made during the period when the price dropped were

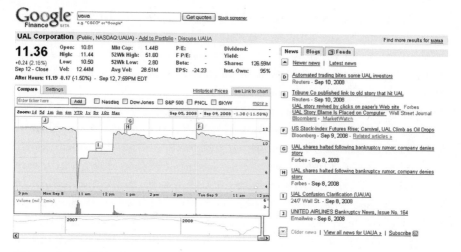

Figure 9.1   UAL Corporation on September 7, 2008. The Old news rises from the news crypt.
Source: Google Finance.

not reversed. This example, though based on what turned out to be false news, underscores the point about time acceleration of the effects of news on markets. This is an update on the "time isn't what it used to be" lesson seen in comparing pre- and postmodern Web-era market reaction to earnings surprise news, shown in Chapter 4.

In fact, it didn't take long for another major manipulation based on false news to occur. A legitimate news story followed a falsely planted one that had hammered Apple stock down by 5.4 percent, less than a month after the UAL presumed accident:

> CNN's plunge into online citizen journalism backfired yesterday when the cable-news outlet posted what turned out to be a bogus report claiming that Apple Inc. Chief Executive Officer Steve Jobs had suffered a heart attack.

> Apple shares fell as much as 5.4 percent after the post on CNN's iReport.com and rebounded after the Cupertino, California–based company said the story was false. Atlanta-based CNN, owned by Time Warner Inc., disabled the user's account and said it tried unsuccessfully to contact the individual.[3]

The effects of real news are often less dramatic. To some extent, they do reflect the efficient markets hypothesis (EMH) view that by the time news is published, it is already impounded in prices. Often, it is true that someone knew it beforehand. We can see this in a large-scale analysis of news.

In a study first published in 2006, Paul Tetlock, then at the Columbia Business School, and his coauthors[4] looked at more than 350,000 news stories about S&P 500 companies that appeared in the *Wall Street Journal* and on the Dow Jones News Service from 1984 to 2004. They used a massive program called the General Inquirer to gauge the sentiment of these stories. The General Inquirer is the result of over 20 years of research sponsored by the U.S. National Science Foundation and the British and Australian National Research Councils. It started out as PL/I programs running on IBM mainframes in the 1980s. The current version is hosted on the Web by Harvard's psychology department and is available for anyone to use there.[5] It has spawned dozens of Ph.D. dissertations, many of which have added language profiles to characterize the sentiment and content of text. There are over 70 of these. You can get a feel for how the General Inquire works by looking a simple example I've used at late-morning talks on this subject, shown in Figure 9.2.

It ingests my typing of "I'm really looking forward to lunch. This is fun, but getting long." First, it takes the sentences apart, and stems the words to identify them in a cleaner form (Figure 9.3).

Then it counts occurrences, matches them up with the many categories, and gives you the statistics of how strongly the words are associated with each category tag (Figure 9.4).

We see that *fun* matches several categories, for example, "Pos" and "Pstv," two variations on positive words (remember all those Ph.D.

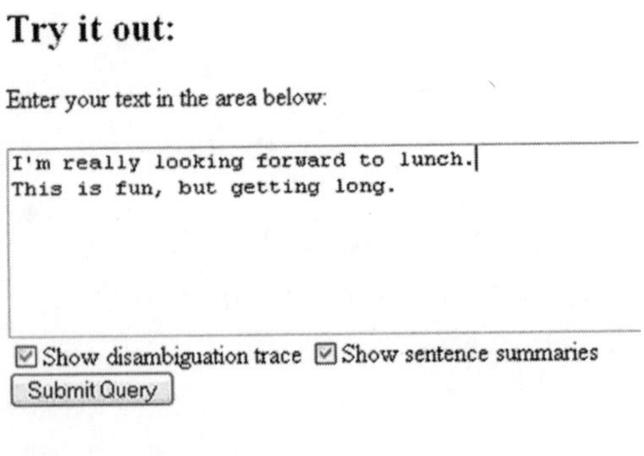

Try it out:

Enter your text in the area below:

```
I'm really looking forward to lunch.|
This is fun, but getting long.
```

☑ Show disambiguation trace ☑ Show sentence summaries
[Submit Query]

Figure 9.2 General Inquirer Test Drive

Word Stemming and Identification

Token	Word	Tags
I'm	I	PRON DEF DEF1 Singp Self+B+ROOT
really	REAL	+ LY
looking	LOOK	+ ING
forward	FORWARD	+ ROOT
to	TO	+ ROOT
lunch	LUNCH	Noun Object Food+E+ROOT
	★	+ PER PUNC EP

Figure 9.3 General Inquirer's first step is to extract stems to identify words.

Text Statistics

Tag	N	%	Words
Pos	2	16.67	FUN#1=1 REAL#1=1
Pstv	2	16.67	FUN#1=1 REAL#1=1
Virtue	1	8.33	REAL#1=1
Pleasur	1	8.33	FUN#1=1
Strng	1	8.33	LONG#1=1
Actv	1	8.33	LOOK# 10=1
Undrst	1	8.33	BUT=1
Exprs	1	8.33	FUN#1=1
Solve	1	8.33	LOOK# 10=1
Space	1	8.33	LONG#1=1
Object	1	8.33	LUNCH=1
Food	1	8.33	LUNCH=1
PRON	1	8.33	I=1
Self	1	8.33	I=1
IAV	2	16.67	GET#2=1 LOOK# 10=1
SV	1	8.33	ARE#1=1

Figure 9.4 The next step is to put the words in categories, count occurrences, and calculate the percentage of the text represented by each word.

students exploring variations on these themes). It also shows up as "Pleasur," which I suppose depends on where you eat, and also reflects the bad old days when programmers felt strongly about not wasting bits to hold extra characters. The IBM System 360 mainframes used for the General Inquirer didn't have many bits to waste.

"Pstv" and its complementary tag "Ngtv" were the two categories used by Tetlock and his colleagues to gauge the sentiment in those
350,000 news stories. There are over a thousand word stems in each of
those categories, but we can get a sense of them just by looking at the
top of the lists. Figure 9.5 shows the first of the 1,046 words in "Pstv."

All of this sounds pretty, well, positive. Statements including
the words *abundant, accomplish,* and *achieve* tend not to be bad news.
Similarly, we can look at the top of the list of the 1,165 words in
"Ngtv," seen in Figure 9.6.

Any news story, or corporate statement, containing the word *abyss*
is not likely to be good news. *Abandon, abnormal, abuse, affliction,* and

Top of General Inquirer Pstv

Pstv N=1046

Word	Tags and Definition
ABLE	Pos Modif EVAL Virtue Strng Pstv | adjective: Having necessary power, skill, resources, etc.
ABUNDANCE	Pos Noun Quan ECON Pstv Strng Ovrst |
ABUNDANT	Pos Modif Quan Pstv Strng Ovrst |
ACCEPT	IAV Pos SUPV Intrel Subm Pstv Psv | verb: To take, receive or accede to something
ACCEPTABLE	Pos Modif Virtue EVAL Pstv |
ACCEPTANCE	Pos Noun Affil Pstv Psv Intrel |
ACCOMMODATE	IAV Pos SUPV Vary Pstv Actv |
ACCOMPLISH	IAV Pos SUPV Pstv Strng Actv Power Complt | verb: To bring to its goal or conclusion
ACCOMPLISHMENT	Pos Noun Goal Pstv Strng Actv Power |
ACCORD#2	IAV Pos SUPV Intrel Pstv | 3% verb: 'Accord with' to be consistent with
ACCORD#3	IAV Pos SUPV Intrel Power Pstv | 8% verb: To grant, bestow
ACCORD#5	Pos LY Means Pstv | 3% adv.: 'Of one's own accord'--voluntarily
ACCORDANCE	Pos Noun Know Pstv |
ACCURACY	Pos Noun ABS Abs★ Virtue Pstv Ovrst |
ACCURATE	Pos Modif Virtue Pstv Ovrst |
ACHIEVE	IAV Pos SUPV Complt Pstv Strng Actv | verb: To accomplish or carry through
ACHIEVEMENT	Pos Noun Goal Pstv Actv Power |
ACQUAINT	IAV Pos SUPV Pstv Solve |

Figure 9.5 The General Inquirer word category Pstv (positive words) contains
over 1,000 entries. This is the top of the alphabetical list.

Top of General Inquirer Ngtv

Ngtv N=1165

Word	Tags and Definition
ABANDON	IAV Neg SUPV Fail Ngtv Weak|
ABNORMAL	Neg Modif Vice Ngtv|
ABOLISH	IAV Neg SUPV Intrel Hostile Ngtv Strng Actv Power|
ABRUPT	Neg Modif Time★ Ngtv|
ABSURD	Neg Modif Vice Ngtv Ovrst|
ABUSE#1	Neg Noun Vice Ngtv Hostile Actv|
ABUSE#2	IAV Neg SUPV Intrel Hostile Ngtv Strng Actv|
ABYSS	Neg Noun Ngtv PLACE Land|
ACCIDENT	Neg Noun Ngtv Causal Undrst|noun: An unfortunate happening, unintentionally caused and unexpected
ACCUSE#1	Neg Modif Legal Ngtv Comform Hostile|
ACCUSE#2	IAV Neg SUPV Hostile Ngtv Comform|
ADVERSE	Neg Modif Vice Ngtv|
AFFLICT	IAV Neg SUPV Ngtv Strng Actv Intrel Hostile|
AFFLICTION	Neg Noun Ngtv Weak Vice Psv|
AFRAID#2	Neg LY Negate Ngtv Weak|1% idiom: 'Afraid not'
AGAINST	Neg PREP Ngtv|prep: In opposition to, adverse or hostile to
AGGRAVATE	IAV Neg SUPV Intrel Hostile Ngtv Strng Actv|
AGGRAVATION	Neg Noun Hostile Ngtv Strng Actv Vice|

Figure 9.6   The General Inquirer word category Ngtv (negative words) contains over 1,100 entries. This is the top of the alphabetical list. None of these are anything you'd find on a birthday card.

aggravation are not any better. Think how much a CEO does not want to say "abyss."

Running those 350,000 stories, containing over 100 million words, through this process, and making an event study chart[6] showing the abnormal returns[7] to the stocks with positive and negative stories, gives the results shown in Figure 9.7.

These event studies aggregate the results over 20 years. The date the story appeared is indicated by the vertical line in the center of the chart. Notice there's a huge amount of what first appears to be pre-event information leakage. In the earnings surprise event studies we observed in Chapter 4 that relatively little happened before the event, maybe 10 to 15 percent of the eventual price change. In this example, we see what appears to be more like 90 percent of the motion occurring prior (to the left) of the event line. EMH fans might say, "We told you so," but that is not the full story here. A substantial portion of this is likely

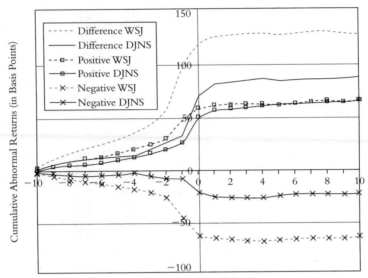

Figure 9.7   Tetlock's news event study might lead to the false conclusion that news stories hardly matter, but stories about price moves that have already happened (e.g., "XYZ Soars 53 Percent on High Earnings") are included here, diluting the results of true breaking news.
Source: Paul Tetlock, Maytal Saar-Tsechansky, and Sofus Macskassy, "More Than Words: Quantifying Language (in News) to Measure Firms' Fundamentals," Journal of Finance *63 (June 2008): 1437–1467.*

occurring due to the categorization of me-too stories, referring back to the original good or bad news, and after-the-fact reporting, that "the stock moved up sharply on news that . . . " This is another example of the need to consider textual events at a molecular level, in context with others, rather than as atomic stand-alone events.

This paints a pretty cynical picture for those who might trade blindly on news characterization—by the time you read it and trade, there's not much left for you to pocket. But even without making those distinctions, Tetlock's simulated "long on good news, short on bad news" trading strategies *do* show some simulated profits more often than not. (See Figure 9.8.)

These results, shown on a daily scale, correspond to annualized cumulative returns for the long-short strategies—21 percent. But there is a catch. No trading costs are included in that result. Recall the

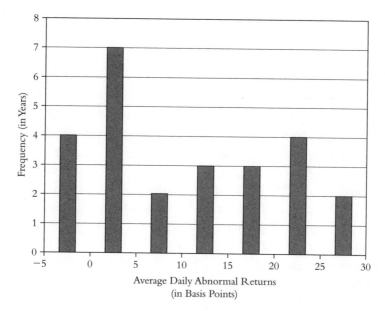

Figure 9.8   Distribution of daily abnormal returns for Tetlock's simulated news-based trading strategy, with no trading costs. Only 9 basis points of cost will eat this alpha. Institutional trading costs for US stocks average about 50 basis points. *Source: Paul Tetlock, Maytal Saar-Tsechansky, and Sofus Macskassy, "More Than Words: Quantifying Language (in News) to Measure Firms' Fundamentals," Journal of Finance 63 (June 2008): 1437–1467.*

discussion of overcoming the transaction cost hurdle in Chapter 5. When the authors factor in the cost of trading, they find that the positive 21 percent drops below zero when round-trip trading costs rise over 9 basis points. Round-trip costs of only 9 basis points would be truly spectacular trading. Most studies of actual transaction costs, including commissions and market impact, show one-way costs in the neighborhood of 50 basis points. This means that additional filtering of news would be needed for a profitable real-world strategy.

eAnalyst: "Can Computerized Language Analysis Predict the Market?"

Chapter 2 introduced the 2001 *Barron's* story that asked the question "Can computerized language analysis predict the market?" It reported on a University of Massachusetts academic project that used the idea of language models to look into the content of news stories and run a simulated portfolio based on the machine's ability to distinguish between stories that move a stock's price up and those that move it down.

Their approach, described in a paper called "Mining of Concurrent Text and Time Series,"[8] differed from Tetlock's study in important ways. They did not start with an assumption that positive or negative words would be predictive of positive or negative returns. Instead, they let the price histories of the stocks (127 of them) inform the selection of words that would affect future price. They broke the price histories, over a five-month period from October 1999 to February 2000, into three types of trend segments—plunges, surges, and flat. Then, they examined the 38,470 stories on Yahoo! News for that period to look for patterns in the stories that preceded the plunges and surges, on an intraday time scale. Thresholds were chosen to pick statistically significant price moves. The method resulted in an average of 450 plunge or surge events per stock over the in-sample five-month period. (See Figure 9.9.)

Stories preceding these surges and plunges were analyzed using methods that were adjusted to include longer and shorter reaction times, and to include stories specific to the individual stocks, or to the full set of stocks. Language models (just like the ones used to generate the tag clouds at the beginning of each chapter in this book) were formed based on these sets, and then used to evaluate "out-of-sample trading" intraday strategies over a 40-day period. Basically, the researchers used the surge and plunge language models to evaluate new incoming stories to see if they were close matches for one set or another, and to generate a long or short trading signal.

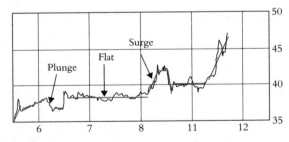

Figure 9.9 Trend extraction by fitting plunge, flat, and surge regression line segments.

The researchers found that faster reaction times were better, and that a mix of general and stock-specific language models was best. Both results seem sensible. Faster is clearly better, and some stocks have very few stories, so the combined news set is helpful on average.

The results of simulated trading on those language model signals are compared to random digital coin-toss simulated trading. Despite a clearly bone-headed trading strategy that churned the portfolio, grabbed small profits, included no transaction costs, and made no comparison with passive buy and hold, their results are intriguing. Compared to the random coin-toss trading decisions, the trades based on the news classifications resulted in profit statistically significant at the 1 percent level.

In many ways, this is a classic example of a data-mined strategy. It is classified and titled by the authors as a data mining study, so they were aware of this, but clearly not sufficiently aware to realize that after so many visits to the out-of-sample period it effectively becomes in-sample. No results were given for a true out-of-sample test, on days previously unseen, even once, by the system.

The useful takeaways from eAnalyst are the ideas of generality and specificity, and the use of returns, rather than a priori assumptions, to classify news. News systems are seeing something of a revival now, and those evaluating them can perhaps extract some ideas from this work.

Pre-News and Disintermediation

The democratization and disintermediation of information is a key part of the explanation of why news is largely reflected in prices before it appears in the newspapers and their electronic outlets. People can do for themselves much of what reporters have traditionally done. News organizations feel the same kind of pressure as brokers from disinter-mediated customers.

People can eliminate the middlemen, and go directly to primary sources. These are the same sources used by reporters to write the "just the facts" stories that have been the mainstay of the news business. When press releases came in on the Teletype, we needed the middlemen to give us the news. We don't need these middlemen in the same way when the press releases come in on the Web. Foreign publications and specialized industry journals used to be expensive and difficult to obtain. No more. Other pre-news sources include government agencies, especially the SEC and the courts, corporate communications, purchased research reports, and data collected by specialized software agents.

The New Research

David Gelertner is an accomplished computer scientist who teaches at Yale, and had the misfortune of opening a package sent by the Unabomber. He is also the author of an excellent book, *Mirror Worlds; or: The Day Software Puts the Universe in a Shoebox . . . How It Will Happen and What It Will Mean* (Oxford University Press, 1992).

What Gelertner's thesis means for investing is that we can look inside that shoebox with a new set of technologies to develop a new form of research. Grabbing more and more data, and doing more and more searches, will quickly overwhelm us, leading to advanced cases of carpal tunnel syndrome, and a shelf full of unread books with "Information Explosion" somewhere in the title.

Collectively, the new alphabet soup of technologies—AI, IA, NLP, and IR (artificial intelligence, intelligence amplification, natural language processing, and information retrieval, for those with a bigger soup bowl)—provides a means to make sense of patterns in the data collected in enterprise and global search. These means are molecular search, the use of persistent software agents so you don't have to keep doing the same thing all the time; the semantic Web, using the information associated with data at the point of origin so there is less guessing about meaning of what find; and modern user interfaces and visualizations, so you can prioritize what you find, and focus on the important and the valuable in a timely way.

The SEC: The Mother Lode of Pre-News

The Securities and Exchange Commission is a good place to start looking for pre-news. There many reasons for this. It covers all publicly traded companies, all the time. There are approximately 300 different filing types, and on an average day, 1.5 gigabytes of new data are added to the SEC web site (http://sec.gov). Prior to 1997, this was all done on paper. Erstwhile reporters would make regular trips to the local

SEC reading rooms maintained in large cities, and go over the latest filings. The most eager reporters (and many shrewd investors) would go to the Washington, D.C. headquarters of the Commission, and get a few days' lead on the people who were waiting for the mailman to arrive in Los Angeles or Atlanta. Many business news stories began "According to a new SEC filing by . . . " and many still do. Up until 1996, the SEC's information dissemination technology was based on envelopes and stamps. That was when they decided this whole computer thing might catch on and introduced the Electronic Data Gathering, Analysis, and Retrieval (EDGAR) system.

Early on, EDGAR was no prize. Electronic filing was optional, and many firms stuck with the old paper delivery. The commission hired information technology powerhouse TRW Inc. as the contractor to develop and run EDGAR. TRW was a great place to go for a satellite (its original line of work) or an automobile part (its second principal line of business), but not a place known for innovative uses of information technology, and it showed. EDGAR had a distinct Computer Museum feel to it from the beginning. It was a simple text-based system, with no indexing beyond filing type, company, and date, just the basic "name, rank, and serial number" equivalents for financial disclosure. There were no links to related filings at all. There were many exceptions, which allowed for long delays and even paper filings to be made in many circumstances, including insider trading reports.

In the TRW days, the SEC provided two kinds of access to this electronic information. Anyone could go to the SEC web site for free, using basic search facilities and tools on the site. People who paid a premium had an extensive set of tools from private resellers to analyze SEC filings. Direct premium subscribers, firms like Edgar Online, and their customers had a 24-hour lead on the public using the SEC site. It seems amazing, but subscribers willing to ante up the annual fee (roughly $40,000) and install a private line for the curiously named "Public Dissemination System" were first in line, all the time. TRW, the SEC's Web contractor, spelled it out clearly in its specification: "By design, the SEC Internet site has a 24-hour upload delay; only the SEC and PDS subscribers receive submissions in real-time."[9]

It took until the summer of 2002 for the SEC to release this information to the public in real time. This came along at the same time as other Enron (and WorldCom and Tyco)-inspired reforms in the Sarbanes-Oxley Act. The elimination of the time disadvantage for ordinary investors, paying only with their taxes and using the SEC web site, is an overdue improvement in a system that (literally) delivered yesterday's news for its first six years of existence. Other advances were slower in coming. The filings themselves remain unstructured text files, with no sign of the semantic Web and XML ideas that are used to deliver meaningful information in many other contexts.

After years of lip service to modernizing EDGAR, SEC chairman Christopher Cox (who took office in 2005) made a serious effort to do so, replacing TRW with more Internet-savvy firms and actually demonstrating prototypes that allow extraction of specific content from SEC filings. A description of the agency's plans for this "21st Century Disclosure Initiative" is now featured prominently on the home page of the SEC site.

Until the modernization is in place, it is still something of a black art to electronically dissect SEC filings into their component parts. High-end resellers do some of this, as do programmers in search of alpha at investment firms and academics in search of interesting research ideas. The latter will publish their results. Many of these are summarized in the following sections.

10-Ks: For Sentimental CEOs

Form 10-Ks are the SEC filings that correspond to annual reports. An interesting and elegantly simple piece of research was done by Feng Li, at the University of Michigan, in 2006.[10] His approach was similar to the one used by Tetlock in analyzing news. Since the 10-Ks are quite large and contain boilerplate text, tables, and other content, he wrote programs to extract the management discussion and analysis (MD&A) sections. His hypothesis was that CEOs are highly motivated to *not* sound scared, unsure, or worried in their comments on their companies.

While Tetlock used the fabulously elaborate General Inquirer linguistic analysis system, Li takes a much simpler approach. He counts the number of occurrences of the following six words:

risk	uncertain
risks	uncertainty
risky	uncertainties

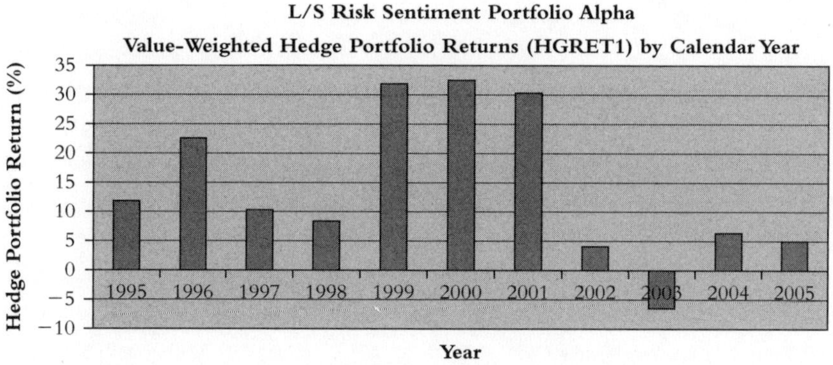

L/S Risk Sentiment Portfolio Alpha

Value–Weighted Hedge Portfolio Returns (HGRET1) by Calendar Year

Figure 9.10   Long/short risk word portfolio simulated performance: positive returns in 10 of 11 years, but smaller in recent years as this effect became known. *Source: "Do Stock Market Investors Understand the Risk Sentiment of Corporate Annual Reports?" by Feng Li, University of Michigan, 2006.*

Professor Li does this for all nonfinancial firms filing with the SEC between 1994 and 2005, a total of 34,180 firm-years. The financials are excluded since they tend to have a great deal of discussion including the six scary words.

These word counts are scaled to a "risk sentiment measure," and the firms' subsequent one-year excess returns are calculated by deciles; a long-short portfolio is formed by shorting the stocks with the most-used risk words and taking long positions in those with the fewest. The simulated performance of that portfolio over a 10-year period is shown in Figure 9.10.

It is somewhat remarkable that such a simple approach worked at all. That it does work is a measure of how badly CEOs don't want to use language that may spook investors. A number of more sophisiti-cated approaches based on similar ideas are in use, with rumors of much stronger performance. As always, when people stop talking about something, it is often a sign of success.

SEC Filing Traffic Analysis: A Barrage of BS?

Recall the Enron filings and filers example from Chapter 2. Counting the filings and filers resulted in the "Barrage of BS" result shown again in Figure 9.11.

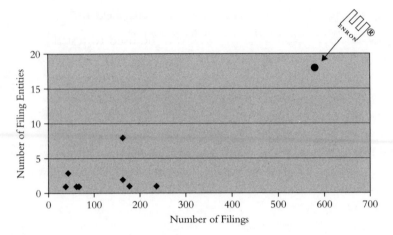

Figure 9.11   SEC Electronic Filings, 1993–2002. Compared to similar firms, Enron is a massive outlier on both scales, the number of filings and the number of filing entities (data for Wholesale Petroleum sector, 1993–2002). This turned out to be a barrage of BS.
Source: Data is from the Securities and Exchange Commission. Figure is by David Leinweber and Jacob Sisk.

This kind of aggregation and comparison is an example of what I've been calling "molecular search"—exploiting the relationships between the individual "information atoms," in this case the individual filings. This is relatively simple, but it's nothing that you can do with a search engine designed only to find one atom at a time. The process can be automated, using specialized programs designed for this task.

This example illustrates a modern investment application of one of the oldest forms of electronic surveillance: traffic analysis. It goes as far back as World War I, when battlefield commanders monitored traffic on the other side's radio frequencies to see when the other side was getting busy, even though they often didn't know the codes. These methods include no consideration whatsoever of content. Another useful application of traffic analysis in investment is to keep an eye on court actions. Bankruptcy news often shows up first in court records. With nearly 10,000 publicly traded companies, and given the reduction in research coverage for companies outside the large indexes, the collective set of financial analysts and reporters are hard-pressed to follow them all on a timely basis.

Quality of Governance and Molecular SEC Search

Another example of molecular search can be used to test the idea that better quality of corporate governance is associated with better returns. In the previous example, the related filing entities were extracted from the primary firms' 10-Ks, and the full set of filings collected. In a similar vein, we can extract the names of members of the board of directors from the 10-Ks of all filing firms, and then count up the number of boards each director sits on. The simple measure of quality of governance from this data is just the average number of boards on which all the directors of a given firm serve. For a firm whose directors sit on only the single board, that would be 1.0, whereas for firms whose directors are dispersed over many boards, we see much higher numbers. Some individual directors are on more than a dozen boards.

The idea that directors spread too thin are not helping a company as much as they might certainly rings true. I was the CEO of Codexa Corporation, a venture capital (VC)–funded information extraction service that did the kind of analysis described in this chapter. We were lucky to see the same VC director twice in a row. Those guys were on so many boards, they would make last-minute substitutions of colleagues who happened to be in the neighborhood for other board meetings. No one ever actually asked, "Which company is this?" since the name was on the door, but it was obvious that they had not read the materials sent prior to the meeting, and often had only a vague notion of what the company did. We benefited from their money, but not from their advice. Humans have a few offspring, and pay close attention to them for many years. We drive them to preschool, help with their homework, and talk to the guidance counselor. Fish spew 10,000 eggs into the ocean every month, and hope that over their reproductive years at least a few of those eggs are not eaten before the tiny fish larvae hatch, and at least a few of those larvae grow into big fish who have little fishies of their own. That is all that is needed for a stable population of the fish species. Sorry to say so, but many VC firms are like fish. If you're the CEO of a venture-funded firm, and get the sense the guy in the board meeting has no idea where he is, do not call him out on this—it will just tick him off. Instead, try to gently work some of the basics into your comments. Many of these people really do have something to offer, but they would rather sit and nod than admit ignorance or neglect.

Returning to the large-scale example, introduced in Chapter 2, we can calculate the average director concentration for each firm in the S&P 1500, and relate it to stock returns by grouping into quintiles. The picture (shown in Figure 9.12) is remarkable. Companies ranked in the top 20 percent, those with the most focused boards, outperformed companies in the worst 20 percent by over 7 percent in 2002 alone.

These SEC molecular search examples show ways to use automated collection, aggregation, linking, and analysis of pre-news. Many news stories found in major media are put together by reporters doing the same thing. In fact, tech-savvy reporters already set up agents to do this kind of ongoing repetitive research and analysis for them, and then they fill in the colorful prose and background: a textbook case of intelligence amplification at work.

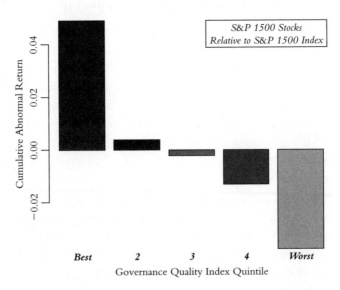

Figure 9.12 Cumulative Abnormal Return (CAR) Over 2002. Firms with boards that act like Mom and Dad do better than firms with boards that act like fish. *Source: David Leinweber and Jacob Sisk, unpublished work, 2003.*

More Pre-News on the Internet

The SEC is a mother lode of investment information because it covers all the companies all the time, and there is so much of it to mine and so many ways to cross-reference and analyze it systematically; but it is far from the only source of pre-news that is ripe for these methods.

Other government agencies are prime picking. Essentially all federal court filings are visible on the Web, including bankruptcies and securities class actions. The Commerce Business Daily announces federal contracts of all sizes. A multibillion-dollar Boeing tanker deal is something everyone waits for, but a $100 million contract awarded to a small-cap firm with revenue of $50 million can easily be overlooked. Similarly, the Food and Drug Administration, Nuclear Regulatory Commission, and Federal Aviation Administration often announce decisions that materially affect the fortunes of specific firms. If you know what to look for, and where, an intelligent research assistant agent will do the repetitive drudge work for you.

The agencies are traditional sources of pre-news, but others are new, purely creatures of the Internet. Here are a few specifics of both flavors:

- *Domain names.* Keeping an eye on domain name registrations is an early merger and acquisition warning system. It is reliably said that the first outsiders to know of the $182 billion acquisition of Time Warner by America Online (AOL) in 2000 were people monitoring domain name registrations who spotted "aoltimewarner.com" and all the permutations being registered by AOL in advance of the announcement.

- *Patents and trademarks.* Also visible on the Web, these provide early warning of new products and services. Research has shown that firms within a sector that are most innovative, reflected by high patent activity relative to their peers, are associated with better returns than their less innovative competitors in R&D–intensive sectors.[11]

- *Two-sided, company-specific labor statistics.* The volume of classified ads placed by firms looking for workers is a classic investment indicator. Counts of these ads, broken out by newspaper and locality, have been used by analysts for years. This is an aggregate measure of "job sellers" and easily visible on the Web at sites like Monster.com. But in the Web era, the "job buyers"—people looking for work—are also visible. If on average you see 100 engineers from International Widgets Unlimited, Ltd. looking to leave the firm by posting their resumes, seeing a spike to 1,000 is more than a hint of impending news in the widget sector. There is a great Gary Larson ("The Far Side") two-panel cartoon: The first panel is full of hundreds of fish feeding at a reef. The second shows a single bewildered fish looking around to see where the others have gone. The caption reads: "Nature's subtle signs of danger."

- *Web commerce firms.* The details of sales at firms like eBay, CarMax, and residential real estate can be inferred by looking at their web sites over time to see what is for sale, and what is sold (often inferred by what is no longer for sale).[12] This is yet another example of molecular search—looking at changes and relationships over time, not just at what is present at a particular moment in time. Majestic Research is an IA-driven "new research" firm that has carved out a profitable niche providing this kind of analysis.

All of these rely on more or less reputable primary sources. On the Web, access to these at the finest level of detail is easy. What about the totally new "creature of the Web" sources? Some of these used to be called rumors, but many rumors turn out to be true, or at least interesting enough to look into further. What about listening to this drum to learn how people are reacting to new products? Companies do this themselves as part of their market intelligence-gathering efforts. Investors can do the same. The next chapter examines the role of collective intelligence and these new social media as sources for Internet-centric investment research.

Notes

1. PIMCO December 2008 Market Commentary, www.pimco.com/LeftNav/Featured +Market+Commentary/IO/2008/IO+Dow+5000+Gross+Dec+08.htm.

2. Relegence was an early first-wave company that did this. It was acquired by AOL, but remains in the news machine business (www.relegence.com/). Newcomers in 2007 and 2008 include Skygrid (www.skygrid.com) and StockMood (www.stockmood. com). Firstrain.com aggregates a wide range of services.

3. James Callan, "CNN's Citizen Journalism Goes 'Awry' with False Report on Jobs," *Bloomberg News*, October 4, 2008.

4. Paul Tetlock, Maytal Saar-Tsechansky, and Sofus Macskassy, "More Than Words: Quantifying Language (in News) to Measure Firms' Fundamentals," *Journal of Finance* 63 (June 2008): 1437–1467. (An earlier working version is available at the Social Science Research Network, http://ssrn.com.)

5. General Inquirer is found at www.wjh.harvard.edu/~inquirer/.

6. Event study charts group similar events together that are actually spread out in time. In this case, the vertical line in the middle of the chart is the day the story appeared; the region to the left shows the basis point (hundredths of percent) price changes prior to publication; and the region to the right shows price changes afterward.

7. "Abnormal returns" often refer to returns in excess of the market over the period in question. This study used a slightly fancier definition of *abnormal* based on the widely used Fama-French three-factor model, a more modest version of the multifactor "Barr's better betas" approach described in Chapter 4. In addition to broad market moves, it adjusts for large-capitalization and small-capitalization companies, and for the value/growth style of the stocks, measured by book-to-price ratio.

8. "Mining of Concurrent Text and Time Series," by Victor Lavrenko, Matt Schmill, Dawn Lawrie, Paul Ogilvie, David Jensen, and James Allant, Department of Computer Science, University of Massachusetts–Amherst, 2001.

9. "Technical Interface and Operational Specification for Public Dissemination Subscribers," TRW/SEC specification by Craig Odell (TRW), May 3, 2001.

10. "Do Stock Market Investors Understand the Risk Sentiment of Corporate Annual Reports?" by Feng Li, University of Michigan, April 2006. Available at the Social Science Research Network, http://papers.ssrn.com/ (paper number 898181).

11. Zhen Deng, Baruch Lev, and Francis Narin, "Science and Technology as Predictors of Stock Performance," *Financial Analysts Journal* 55, no. 3 (May/June 1999): 20–32.

12. Majestic Research specializes in this sort thing (www.majesticresearch.com/).

MARKET many 1980's early investors world interest clients just keep correct always forecasts right money might way sites

Street site long internet board described Mr announcement well

individual fund analyst high specialist big interesting investment Earnings Codexa incentive good average SEC since became great actual iExchange

Business Wall Data INTELLIGENCE One shown much found

next Never traders Bear consensus wisdom value close Whisper Stock new back news result Groups time less even number Traffic financial firms Day COLLECTIVE message WEB Figure Investing MEDIA

Source John like people trading messages boards large now stocks approach best whispers CHAPTER seen first Numbers numbers five made

Chapter 10

Collective Intelligence, Social Media, and Web Market Monitors

The words of the prophets are written
on the subway walls.

—Simon & Garfunkel, "The Sound of Silence"

O pinions vary widely on the value of collective wisdom, with ample supporting evidence both for and against. The Internet has many positive examples: The collective ratings at consumer sites like Amazon for books (and almost anything that can be shipped in a box), Newegg for electronics, and Yelp for restaurants are almost always reliable when there is a strong consensus among a large crowd. When 95 out of 100 people say a software program doesn't work, it is probably no prize (and the other five likely work for the publisher). When 250 out of 275 people rave about the latest Asian Cajun[1] spot and the waiting line winds around the block, dinner is not likely to be too bad. When every other customer complains about meeting a man with a stomach pump, you're better off packing your own lunch.

Markets themselves are a form of collective intelligence (CI), and since transactions occur, they clearly arrive at prices seen as fair by buyers and sellers alike for everything from stocks to Pez dispensers (the first eBay merchandise). A recent book by James Surowiecki, *The Wisdom of Crowds: Why the Many Are Smarter Than the Few and How Collective Wisdom Shapes Business, Economies, Societies and Nations* (Random House, 2004) has nearly 300 pages of examples of group wisdom. One such example is the television quiz show *Who Wants to Be a Millionaire*. Contestants are asked a series of increasingly difficult

227

questions, worth increasingly large payoffs if answered correctly. At any point, they can take the money and run or proceed to the next level. If they are stumped, contestants are allowed to choose among a "lifeline,"[2] calling a friend, and polling the studio audience. Friends have provided the correct answer 65 percent of the time, but the audience has been right on 91 percent of the questions they've been asked. This is clearly an unscientific approach, since the friends and the audience have been given different questions, but it does suggest the value of collective intelligence, particularly for perky blond quiz show contestants.

That is not the case for the oft-repeated "guess the number of beans in the jar" experiment, popularized in finance circles by Jack Treynor[3] and repeated endlessly at financial conferences. A typical result was that when the jar contained 850 beans, the average estimate of the 56 students in Treynor's class was 871, and only a single student had a guess better than the collective. This game is not anywhere near as popular on campuses as beer pong, but it is still played with the same kind of positive "wisdom of the collective" result.

In contrast, H.L. Mencken, the author, reporter, and editor known as the Sage of Baltimore, wrote, "No one in this world, so far as I know, has ever lost money by underestimating the intelligence of the great masses of the plain people." Charles Mackay's *Extraordinary Popular Delusions and the Madness of Crowds*, originally published in 1841,[4] supplies ample evidence to support Mencken's thesis.

The best known events are the Dutch tulip bulb mania, when sufficiently exotic bulbs (stripes were big) sold for more than a house, and the South Sea Bubble, when utterly worthless securities came to dominate the financial markets. Imagine something like that happening today. One anonymous Amazon reviewer concisely summarizes Mackay: "Why do otherwise intelligent individuals form seething masses of idiocy when they engage in collective action? Why do financially sensible people jump lemming-like into harebrained speculative frenzies—only to jump broker-like out of windows when their fantasies dissolve?"

Both schools of thought are correct, depending on the situation. Mencken and Mackay have nothing good to say about collective intelligence, but Surowiecki writes:

Groups work well under certain circumstances, and less well under others. Groups generally need rules to maintain order and coherence, and when they are missing or malfunctioning, the result is trouble. . . . While big groups are often good at solving certain kinds of problems, big groups can also be unmanageable and inefficient. Conversely, small groups have the virtue of being easy to run, but they risk having too little diversity of thought and too much consensus.[5]

It is worthwhile to take an economic and game-theoretic view of this. When people have an incentive to be truthful, most of them will be truthful. When there is a reward for deceiving others, people will be deceptive. The studio audiences at *Who Wants to Be a Millionaire* and the bean population guessers have no reason to lie. In the case of the beans, the winner often gets to keep the jar or some other swag. For product rating scores, people feel good taking a whack at companies that sell some of the junk that passes for software and the like, and they earn a psychic payoff by sharing their positive experience with others, without risking or incurring any penalty for doing so. Scarcity issues are rare. For a restaurant reviewer, there is a slight disincentive in that raving about your favorites may result in long lines, somewhat offset by the feeling that since the half-life of new restaurants is about six months, you are helping your favorites to stick around.

If there is scarcity and competition involved, the incentives for the collective can be quite different. It becomes a game where at least some players will see a positive reward for providing false information.

Investing with Crowds

Unlike restaurant or shopping advice, collective stock recommendations on message boards and "share the love" investment sites are examples of situations where deceit can be profitable. Holders of long positions in a stock have a powerful incentive to drive up its price, and those with short positions have a powerful incentive to drive it down, irrespective of the actual merit of either position. The anonymity of the Internet and the ability to create multiple identities make this easy to do.

As long as this looks like opinions being shared and does not cross over into outright fraud, the Securities and Exchange Commission (SEC) will not come knocking on an opinion sharer's door. Many Web denizens do cross the line into criminal manipulations (some of the most egregious examples are described in the next chapter), but the distinction between the illegal and the merely malicious can be fuzzy.

During the tech bubble, a company called iExchange opened for business with a huge burst of PR, including segments on the major network news programs. The company T-shirts, which seemed to be everywhere in its hometown of Pasadena, read "BUY SELL" on the front and "TELL" on the back. It raised over $30 million from some of the biggest names in venture capital, and had one of the slickest social web sites seen up to that time. The home page from that site, www.iexchange.com, on June 20, 2000, is shown in Figure 10.1.

The business model was that the first few tastes were free, and then investor users (like H.V., J.P., and I.G. over on the right) could pay analyst users (like "The Visionary," "Big Jim," and "Biotech Believer" in the middle pane) a modest fee, usually just a few dollars, for new research. iExchange got a piece of every transaction. There were $25,000 monthly prizes for the best stock picks, which was supposed to keep everyone honest.

The Epinions.com rating site for social web sites gave iExchange four stars, "a good place to make money." The anonymous successful investors on the right are minting money. Surely they will be willing to pay the insightful analysts who let them reap these rewards? What could go wrong? Plenty. Perhaps you noticed that the screen grab is from the Internet Archive's Wayback Machine,[6] the elephant graveyard of the Internet. Either those 1,200 percent returns weren't enough to keep people happy or something went awry. The party ended, fittingly enough, just before April Fools' Day in 2001, with the following sign-off, comprising the entirety of the iExchange site:

To the iExchange Members & Analysts:

We regret to inform you that the iExchange community web site has been permanently shut down, effective March 29, 2001. While iExchange has been a great success at providing a new source of stock market intelligence, market conditions have

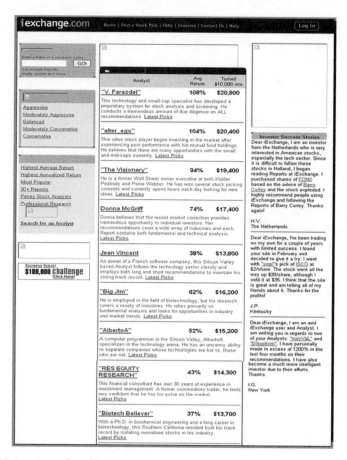

Figure 10.1   A profit of 1,200 percent in four months! Pretty soon these anonymous investment wizards will have *all* the money.
Source: The Wayback Machine (iexchange.com, on the Internet Archive site at www. archive.org).

hurt the firm's ability to develop sustainable revenue streams from the community. Payments for the March 2001 $25,000 incentive promotion program will be paid out in accordance with the contest rules.

We appreciate your patronage and wish you the best of luck in your personal investing.[7]

If I sound a tad cynical about this kind of site, it is because the grizzled old side of me that has seen the relentless search for profits on greater

Wall Street has pounded down the "peace, love, and understanding—three days of fun and music" side. I'm sure there were well-intentioned people offering sincere advice that they honestly believed in, but they were overwhelmed by shape-shifting anonymous hucksters with as many identities as they wanted.

Maybe this concept can be saved by James Surowiecki's notion about having the right sized group, with rules for good conduct. This seemed to be embodied in the Marketocracy approach. Marketocracy (www.marketocracy.com) is a social investing site that has spawned a professionally managed mutual fund, the Marketocracy Masters 100, based on the ideas on the site, allowing them (it is hoped) to sort out those with skill from those with luck and those with ill intentions. The fund trades under the symbol MOFQX. As seen in Figure 10.2, results have been mixed, with periods of outperformance relative to the S&P 500, and what appear to be remarkably bad episodes where gains are given back quickly.

Unlike iExchange, Marketocracy's approach does not seem hopelessly naive, but the fund has not had great results, earning overall Morningstar ratings of below average for returns and above average for risk. The total assets under management are less than $30 million, minuscule for a mutual fund. However, most of the recent damage seems to be due to a very bad week in December 2007, indicating an overly concentrated portfolio (see Chapter 5, "A Gentle Introduction to Computerized Investing"), so there may be hope for the Woodstock approach to investing after all. I hope that last sentence will at least partially redeem my reputation with my Temple ben Birkenstock friends and relatives.

In investment, the best use of collective intelligence may occur when you have your own nonanonymous collective. A few years back there was an issue of *CFA* magazine ("Envisioning the Future of Securities Analysis") that talked about collaboration between stock and bond analysts at huge geographically dispersed firms, like Fidelity. As someone who has mostly spent my time in smaller organizations, collaboration for me was mostly just going down the hall. But when people looking at different aspects of the same firms are located all over the world without many shared daylight hours, there are some benefits to having people work together collectively. For many individual or small-firm

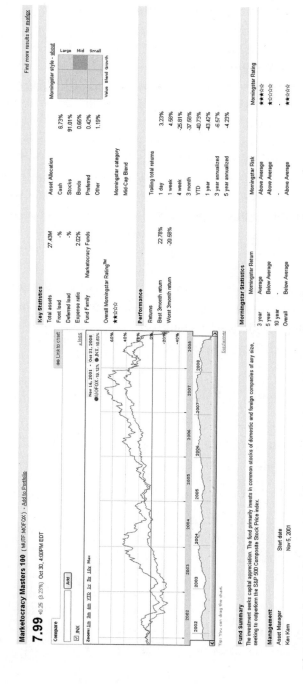

Figure 10.2 Marketocracy Fund (MOFQX) Performance and Profile, as of October 31, 2008

Source: Google Finance.

233

investors, this is not an issue; but for the megafirms, a collective, machine-assisted, but private community has many advantages.

The participants in this collective don't necessarily have to be people. Software agents assessing quantitative and textual information can post their "ideas" as well, in an application of intelligence amplification (IA) to create a unified software and wetware style of research. Quant and text agents tend to know a little about 40,000 stocks (roughly the number of investment grade names, globally), but their assessment is generally a rearview mirror effect, using models that assume things are going to be the way they were, predicting the future from patterns observed in the past. Humans can be forward-looking, more complex, and more collaborative, but there is no way an individual can pay attention to 40,000 stocks. (This would be even more overwhelming than reading all the books about information overload.)

The IA/AI human collaboration is strong on sending "this might be interesting" signals, and the CI environments enabled by the Web can do a fabulous job with that. The IA and AI people now have a valuable problem to solve. As discussed in Chapter 7 ("A Little AI Goes a Long Way on Wall Street"), this plays to the skills of computers that are extraordinarily good at using other computers.

Never Met a Data Vendor I Didn't Like

The preceding discussion about collective social investing is an outsider's view. I was never a believer in the "Kumbaya" portfolio. As the manager of $6 billion in quant equities in the 1990s, I did believe in data, and bought a great deal of it, millions of dollars' worth every year. Quality was sketchy, and since computers were ingesting the stuff instead of people, I tried to buy everything at least three times for cross-checking and error correction. Some compact single-value macro and market statistics came in over modems, while larger volumes of data on thousands of individual stocks would often arrive on tape via FedEx packages. When data vendors asked, "What's FTP?"[8] we'd go show them. By the late 1990s, along with other data hog quant managers, I'd begun to notice that the Web was changing the pace of the game (see Bob Butman's before-and-after earnings surprise charts in Chapter 4).

A particularly eye-opening moment about the shifting world of financial information came in November 1998. The Department of Labor (DoL) was scheduled to release its usual monthly job statistics data load on the 9th of the month. Then my three premium-priced macro-economic data vendors would collect it, clean it, type it in, and combine it with the rest of the day's statistics so we could retrieve it by modem overnight. But on November 5 an overeager civil servant accidentally posted the data on the DoL web site. There was a near-immediate market reaction, and the business news explained that it was due to the early Web release. The data world was clearly changing, moving faster, and moving onto the Internet. For years, all the quant managers profited by getting an electronic jump on the Greenwich suits who read *Barron's* over the weekend. Now the World Wide Web crowd was getting the jump on *us*.

My MIT roommate, Larry Russell, who was working at Sun Microsystems, had watched his colleagues streaming out the door to one dot-com start-up after another. He made a pretty persuasive case that we should do the same; I'd started a successful financial technology firm before (Integrated Analytics, later part of ITG, described in Chapter 7) so I knew lots of prospective customers, and after years of running 27 quant equity strategies across half a dozen global stock markets, I was a pretty experienced data consumer myself. By 1999, I was convinced. We started a Web-centric financial information firm called Codexa, named after an early form of book, the codex. As I recall, some porn site (the real pioneers of the Web) had grabbed the name Codex.com (think "Code X"), so we tossed an "a" on at the end and hired some bright recent college grads and a few very capable young Wall Street nerds.

Santa Claus Is Coming to Town

What should a new online financial information firm do? Waiting for the guys at the Department of Labor to screw up again didn't seem like the best plan. We wanted to offer something new, useful to customers on both the buy side (investment managers, like me) and the sell side (brokers, market makers, and specialists). I had tried to stay in touch with the clients from the MarketMind days, who were on both sides of street, particularly the friendly and interesting ones. No one was friendlier or more interesting than John Mulheren, one of the great Wall Street characters of his era. Sadly, John died too young in 2003.

At the time of his death, John was chief executive of Bear Wagner Specialists, a firm he helped grow into one of the New York Stock Exchange's largest specialist firms. John founded the arbitrage firm Jamie Securities in the 1980s, and during the mergers and acquisitions (M&A) boom of that decade he was one of the most skillful arbitrage traders on Wall Street, reportedly making over $25 million in 1986.

The *New York Times* obituary for John noted that, along with a list of his many significant Wall Street accomplishments,

> Mr. Mulheren cultivated a unique personality on Wall Street.
> A muscular man who openly displayed his emotions, he rarely
> wore a coat and tie, favoring instead open-necked shirts and
> dungarees and on special occasions, pink tuxedo shirts and cam-
> ouflage pants.[9]

Although John was charged and convicted in the infamous insider trading scandal involving Ivan Boesky in 1988, the charges were later overturned. The obit highlights that:

> In 1988, he [John] was arrested in his hometown of Rumson,
> and charged with possessing a weapon and threatening the
> life of Mr. Boesky, who had agreed to testify against him in
> exchange for a shorter sentence. Mr. Mulheren's lawyers said
> the incident was a result of his failure to take lithium prescribed
> to treat manic depression. The weapons charges were dropped.[10]

No discussion of John could fail to mention his big heart. In 2001 he was made an honorary police commissioner of New York for his charitable work related to the September 11 attacks.

At his funeral, his close friend Bruce Springsteen sang his favorite song, "Santa Claus Is Coming to Town." He wouldn't take his lithium for manic depression, because he said the highs were worth the lows. I never encountered him during a low, and always found him one of the most gregarious and interesting people on Wall Street. He loved science and math, and hired all sorts of scientific and mathematical wackos (which is probably why he was an early MarketMind customer).

There was a pair of orthodox Jewish brothers in Brooklyn who had filled their apartment from floor to ceiling with PC motherboards wired together in ways incomprehensible to anyone else in order to build a special-purpose supercomputer to solve exotic numerological problems. These are the guys who inspired the movie *Pi*. For a while, they held the world record for finding the largest known prime number. In their spare time, they worked for John.

I told John about Codexa and asked what he thought we might do with our Internet financial data machine. He had a quick answer: "Count messages." Traffic analysis, the oldest idea in electronic intelligence, would be updated for the Web era.

Counting Messages

In 1999, John was running Bear Wagner, one of the largest specialist firms on the NYSE, with a good dose of NASDAQ market making thrown in. Recall that specialists (at the time) had a central role as the buyer to nearly all sellers, and the seller to nearly all buyers. They made their living by continuously posting a two-sided quote (see the discussion of market making in Chapter 2), and in normal markets, they would buy low, at the bid, and sell high, at the ask. Keeping the spread small and the sizes large made for a liquid market and large profits for the specialists. The safest strategy for a specialist (or market maker) is to adjust the prices to keep their inventory (net long or short position in a stock) as close to zero as possible, to stay flat so as to never be left holding the bag when there was a sudden large price move in the stock. But that would conflict with maximizing volume to accommodate temporary imbalances between the flow of buyers and sellers. If a specialist or market maker had a way of anticipating which stocks might have that kind of volatility, he could "roll into a ball" and stay flat in those names, while keeping the buy low/sell high process in high gear on the others.

This is why John Mulheren was counting messages on stock message boards. His unmatched market sense told him that if there was a huge spike in overnight message traffic about a stock, it was a good bet that something volatile might happen the next trading day, and at the very least, it was worth a deeper look before commencing his usual aggressive market making. John was not counting messages himself. He'd organized an army of teenagers in Rumson to wake up early and go count traffic on their assigned message boards, then phone in their numbers to people at Bear Wagner before the open.

You can imagine how accurate a process involving teens who have to get up early to make a deadline might be. Many of the calls never happened, and spot checks of accuracy were not encouraging. So Mulheren's idea for Codexa's first Internet information-gathering service was to automate the process. He wrote us a hefty check. We wrote a bunch of code. On our end, the code was a passel of crawlers, screening the message boards at a polite pace so as not to be mistaken for a denial of service attack and consequently blocked access. On John's end, at Bear Wagner, it looked like Figure 10.3.

This worked, in contrast with the examples that opened this chapter, for two reasons: first, direction didn't matter, as it was only a

Message Volume Ratios					
Stock	PV Chart	Total Messages Previous	Total Messages Current	Ratio	Read Msg
INSO		0	24	24.00	
KEG		0	20	20.00	
XLNX		47	622	13.23	
TMCS		2	18	9.00	
CTIX		2	18	9.00	
MWD		7	56	8.00	
AFCI		15	119	7.93	
ALTR		65	515	7.92	
NDB		49	307	6.27	
MXIM		3	18	6.00	

next 10 ▼

	Ex. Return	Vol Ratio
INSO	7.6	62.5
KEG	2.8	137.5
XLNX	3.7	234.3
TMCS	-10.8	192.3
CTIX	-1.2	72.0
MWD	6.6	335.3
AFCI	-5.2	137.5
ALTR	5.1	285.5
NDB	1.4	296.7
MXIM	2.3	273.1
AvgAbs	4.7	202.7

Oct. 11, 2000
Average Abs Excess Return: **4.7%**
Average Volume Ratio: **203%**

Figure 10.3   This was the first delivery of the message traffic monitor that replaced the army of New Jersey teens. The panel on the left was the screen, showing the stocks that had the largest increases in overnight posting measured by the current (most recent) overnight count, relative to the previous five-day average. The box on the right shows the excess (net of market) returns for stocks on that day, and the volume, relative to the preceding five-day average. This was a typical day. Mulheren's intuition was, as usual, correct. If there were no messages over five days, the ratio was calculated as if there was one message, to keep it simple.
Source: Codexa.

heads-up for an outsize move; and second, motives didn't matter, as the outsize move could be the result of real news contained in the messages, or attempts to pump the price up or down for less than pristine reasons. The line between manipulation and boosterism is not always a sharp one. New Jersey high school student Jonathan Lebed made almost a million dollars on stocks he pumped with enthusiastic comments on stock message boards. After a long, hard look, he was fined by the SEC, but never charged with a crime.[11]

John Mulheren's intuition about message boards was based on his experience with how people act when they smell money. It was confirmed by traditional, and independent, academic research by Peter Wysocki, now at MIT, who examined the statistical relationships between message board postings and more traditional measures of stock market activity.[12] Wysocki's paper, "Cheap Talk on the Web," done while he was teaching at the University of Michigan, examined Yahoo! message boards for over 3,000 stocks from January to August 1998. He found that spikes in message traffic were strongly predictive of excess return, volume, and volatility. Specialists are interested in the first item on this list, trading cost control algorithms with the second, and option strategies with the third. This is particularly so for less actively traded companies. An academic study confirmed Mulheren's intuition. Spikes in overnight message traffic were the most valuable predictors of large moves that day, stronger than all the usual suspects—momentum, trends, and earnings announcements. The remarkable strength of changes in message volume as a predictor is shown in Figure 10.4.

Predictive Variable	t–statistic
Excess return on previous day, momentum	6.01
Previous day volume/ five-day average volume	4.07
Overnight message traffic/ five-day average overnight traffic	7.38
Earnings announcement on previous day	0.46
Earnings announcement on next day	3.44

Figure 10.4 Strength of predictors for absolute excess returns. Message traffic ratios are the champs.

Here, the strongest predictor of abnormal return variance is the ratio of overnight message posting to its five-day average. The t-statistic, a measure of the strength of the association, is 7.38, an extremely high value, larger than even the corresponding value for the previous day's abnormal return, volume, and proximity to an earnings announcement.

Reading message boards today can be a discouraging experience. At first, they seemed mostly to be about stocks. Now there are long political rants and ever more offers to sell you counterfeit Viagra and even more dubious products in the same SIC code. Despite this, it seems that enough people wade through this swamp to read the messages that do relate to stocks. A more recent academic study found results comparable to what we saw in the early board days, even for larger firms. In "Is All That Talk Just Noise? The Information Content of Stock Message Boards," Werner Antweiler and Murray Frank[13] find that message board activity is a significant predictor for volatility, even for the 30 very large firms in the Dow Jones Industrial Average.

Some of these studies use natural language methods, along the lines described in the previous chapter applied to news and SEC filings, to try to infer direction from messages. This seems to be a harder climb, due (I suspect) to the mixed motives and lack of accountability for message posters relative to mainstream reporters and CEOs.

Message boards, a pure creature of the Web, affect the market because people read them. This is true for other forms of Internet information as well. The Web amplifies market responses to many media and compresses the time in which those responses occur. A 2000 paper from the *Financial Analysts Journal*, "How 'Foolish' Are Internet Investors?" compared the well-known single-day effects of print media like the *Wall Street Journal*'s monthly Dartboard Portfolio[14] articles and *BusinessWeek*'s "Inside Wall Street," along with the popular televised *Wall $treet Week*, to the then-new Motley Fool investment e-mail alerts.

The authors stated, "We offer the first systematic evidence that stock recommendations published on the Internet move prices and volumes . . . [showing] statistically significant abnormal returns . . . larger than those in the print media or . . . "Wall Street Week" . . . [and with] average excess volume of 563% and average excess returns of 3.8% . . . in one day."[15]

It is likely that the continuing shift toward electronic media will continue to magnify these effects, and in fact, in the algo wars these ideas are being included in new generations of trading tools.

Blogs are a newer creature of the Web, with similar potential to affect short-term stock behavior. There are an estimated 65 million blogs. The median number of readers (other than the authors of these blogs) is zero. And from what shows up on many of them, it's far from certain that even the authors are always reading what they write. But there are many that are highly reputable for insight and timeliness, and are widely read by millions of people.

The Internet in general and the message world in particular remain active areas of interest for the SEC, which looks for abuses, and for alpha-seeking investors, who look for profit. In 2008 Dr. Richard Peterson—psychiatrist, trader, psychiatrist to traders, and author of *Inside the Investor's Brain* (John Wiley & Sons, 2007)—launched MarketPsy (www.marketpsy.com), a fund based in part on linguistic analysis of messages.

Whisper Numbers—Ruined by Success

All of the previous message tales were about anticipating volatility and large one-day moves, not about decoding the direction of those moves. For John Mulheren and Codexa's other market-making clients, this was invaluable in keeping them out of trouble, since they had firm obligations to participate on both sides of the market in all their stocks, but not necessarily to hold inventory of any significant size. For them, avoiding those nasty one-day losses was well worth the cost.

Most investors wanted to know which way the stock would move, and they were poring over the message boards for clues as well. In the late 1990s, people had begun to use stock message boards to discuss earnings; some of them seemed unusually sober and well informed on the subject. These earnings messages came to be called "whisper numbers," borrowing a term that had been used on Wall Street for years. It used to mean that an analyst would issue one set of numbers for the general public and whisper another estimate to the firm's best clients.

This behavior was due to the conflicts that big Wall Street firms had across their various lines of business. There's a lot of pressure on an analyst to keep an earnings forecast high when his colleague upstairs is trying to close a large bond deal or M&A transaction for the firm he's analyzing. This kind of shenanigan led to many of the reforms in the Sarbanes-Oxley Act, unbundled research, and the now-required disclosures of who owns what that accompany investment research.

These conflicts rattled some of the analysts, but before the message boards there wasn't much they could do about it. They would go and whisper to their better clients: "The report says the earnings will be a quarter, but I think it's really 21 cents." With the popularity of stock message boards, they had a new outlet for their frustration. During the day, the analyst might be W. Reginald von Stade IV, and wear tasseled loafers and a Brooks Brothers suit. At night, he could put on his *Star Wars* pajamas and assume an alternate identity as Frisky Bill the Truth Teller on the Yahoo! stock message boards. Frisky Bill could write, "It's really 21 cents!" without having some guy upstairs call his boss and demand his instant excommunication, crucifixion, or worse. Frisky Bill could say what he thought, and why. People noticed on the message boards that the writing style and the vocabulary often sounded like professional analysts. There were a lot of anecdotal incidents where the Internet whisper numbers seem to be more accurate than the consensus forecasts.

In 1999 Mark Bagnoli, Messod Beneish, and Sue Watts, finance professors at Purdue University (Sue and Mark) and Indiana University (Messod), decided to take a scientific look at the whisper numbers. They collected them manually for 127 stocks for two and a half years, from January 1995 to May 1997, poring over every message on Yahoo!'s stock message boards (by far the most popular, then and now). They collected 943 whisper numbers from those messages, explicit forecasts of earnings per share posted prior to the actual earnings announcements each quarter. Then they compared the message board whisper forecasts to the 3,546 forecasts for the same companies made by professional analysts.[16]

Two methods were used to do this. One was statistical, computing the mean squared error of the board whisper numbers and the professional forecasts to the actual earnings. By that measure, the whispers were approximately twice as accurate as the professionals, with an error half the size. The other was a trading simulation, which went long the stock if the whispers were higher than the First Call consensus (a weighted average of the professional estimates, packaged as a high-end data product for investment firms), and short the stock if the whispers were lower than the consensus. Positions were closed out after the announcements, when, if the whispers outperformed the analysts, the stocks would react, on average, by moving up when the whispers were higher and down when they were lower. That simulated trading produced an alpha of +1.8 percent.

Mark and his coauthors wrote: "Our analysis indicates that whispers . . . are more accurate than are First Call estimates."

This was big news. Whisper numbers were a hot topic on all the business TV channels. Sue and Mark became regulars on all of them. They made great guests. She is bigger than Tinkerbell, but not by much. Mark is a six-and-a-half-foot-tall bear of a guy. She did most of the talking. He was the straight man. In addition to being the cutest pair of academics on CNBC and the rest, everyone loved the "David beats Goliath" story of the whisper numbers.

Whisper numbers themselves became a growth industry. There were new web sites that tried to automate the process of extracting them from message boards, which the professors had done manually. It wasn't easy, since many of the messages discussed multiple earnings scenarios, and had many numbers in the vicinity of the expected earnings. To get around the difficulty of using the original message board whispers, some sites let people offer their own whispers, sometimes just with a mouse click. EarningsWhispers.com and TheWhisperNumber.com became popular destinations.

Codexa's clients caught whisper fever along with others. The system crawlers were out on the message boards anyway, counting the nongarbage messages for the traffic ratios, and we extended the program to collect and tabulate the distribution of whispers as well. Some examples of those distributions, from February 2000, are seen in Figures 10.5 through 10.7.

Soon the whisper sites began to act as a feedback loop onto the message boards, as people began to post messages about what they read on the whisper sites. The ease of voting on the whisper sites themselves distorted the process further. A Reuters story from April 24, 2000, was

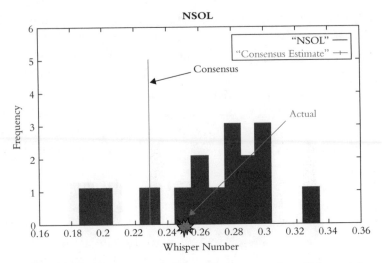

Figure 10.5 Network Solutions (NSOL) whisper numbers, February 3, 2000. The overwhelming weight of the whispers was higher than the consensus estimate of $0.23. The whispers were correct, and the stock jumped 4.7 percent on the announcement day.
Source: Codexa.

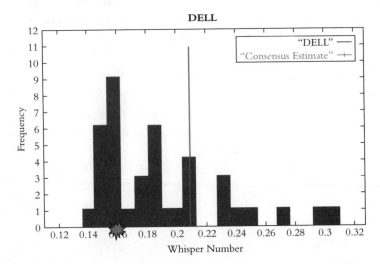

Figure 10.6 Dell, like most consumer tech stocks in the boom, had a very large number of whisper numbers, in this case, heavily weighted below the consensus. Again, the whispers were correct, and the stock dropped 2.4 percent on the announcement date.
Source: Codexa.

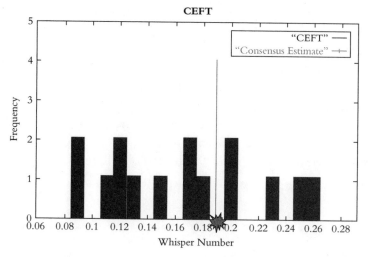

Figure 10.7 The whisper numbers weren't always right. Here whispers for Concord EFS (CEFT) averaged slightly below the consensus, which turned out to be correct. The stock dropped anyway. This stuff isn't physics.
Source: Codexa.

titled "Whisper Numbers: The Truth; How One Investor Logged on to the Web and Fabricated a 'Whisper' Number." Some excerpts:

> Matt Ruecker logged onto the Web one day last week and with a couple of clicks changed closely watched profit expectations for a hot technology company by 10%.

> The new estimate for ... Citrix Systems ... hit the Internet the next day, including the Web's most popular site ... Yahoo. ...

> The problem was that Ruecker, a 27 year-old individual investor fabricated the number. Ruecker is an auditor at a big Cincinnati accounting firm and has no special insights into Citrix. ...

> "This is just pure manipulation through the Web," Ruecker said, "It's scary."

The whisper numbers phenomenon started out in the Internet spirit of "information wants to be free," and for a time, they were seen that way. But it took less than a year for the whispers to be ruined by success.

The chief investment officer of one large mutual fund firm observed, "The psychology around the earnings report has been completely poisoned by this whisper nonsense." Sue Watts and her colleagues found that when they tried repeating the experiment, the whisper numbers had become useless, with wider variation and no value over the consensus estimates. This is yet another example of the wisdom of a collective depending on choosing the members of the collective carefully so none of them have an incentive to mislead the rest. As noted earnings analyst Yogi Berra might explain, "Nobody goes there anymore. It's too crowded."

Monitoring Web Activity: No GUI, No Glory

Chapters 9 and 10 describe some of the many examples of how and why investors and traders would want to collect, aggregate, and evaluate many flavors of content from the Web—news, pre-news, SEC filings, and messages are a small sample, and the molecular search filters to decide what is interesting are some of the simpler varieties. Turning these ideas into software was the idea behind Codexa. Unlike many dot-coms, the firm had actual paying customers and millions in revenue, but became a casualty of the bursting of the bubble just the same.

The most requested item of my cumulative efforts in financial technology is the piece about butter in Bangladesh and the S&P 500 (Chapter 6, "Stupid Data Miner Tricks"). The runner-up for most requested item is the Codexa system. Now that we've covered the motivations for gathering Web information, I'll close this chapter with those golden oldies.

Ben Schneiderman is the godfather of interactive computer graphics as an interface for modern computing systems. He founded the Human-Computer Interaction Lab (HCIL) at the University of Maryland[17] in 1983, and wrote the standard text in the field, *Designing the User Interface: Strategies for Effective Human-Computer Interaction* (Addison-Wesley, 4th ed., 2004). Anyone remotely interested in this area should spend some quality time on the HCIL web site; it is full of video examples spanning 25 years, which have inspired visual interfaces from the Map of the Market (shown in Chapter 2) to the increasingly sophisticated interactive displays we are finally beginning to see on web

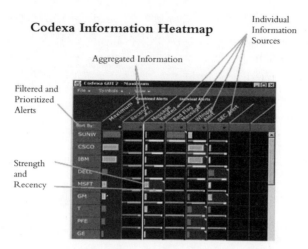

Figure 10.8   The Codexa Information Heatmap (a mockup) contained dynamic, interactive graphic elements to answer the questions "What's important?" and "What's new?" for many types of financial information. Information sources were laid out horizontally, on top: messages, whispers, SEC, and room for new or user-specific modules. The vertical axis shows the stocks of interest, which can include hundreds of names, extending below the window. This was the MarketMind/QuantEx idea, applied to text instead of numbers. *Source: Codexa.*

sites like that of the *New York Times*, which has staked out a position as a mainstream media (MSM) leader in this area.

Schneiderman's visual information-seeking mantra is the guiding principle for the Codexa approach to Web information gathering: "Overview first, zoom and filter, then details on demand." The mockup used for raising venture capital and bringing in the first clients is shown in Figure 10.8.

Each cell was envisioned as containing two graphic glyphs—upper red or green bar indicating the direction and strength of the event of interest, and a thinner "time bar" that was zero in length when the information was new, and grew longer as time passed.

The display was organized by bringing the maximum indication of interest over into the "Maximum" column, next to the stock symbols on the left, and the minimum time bars into the "Recency" column next to that. The rows, one for each stock, could then be sorted by "What's important?" (the maximum of all signals from all sources) or

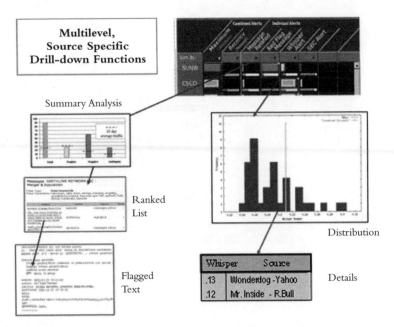

Figure 10.9 Each cell in the overview display is a drill-down point to a detailed display appropriate to each type of information. In this example (still a mockup) the message alerts drill down first to a bar chart (seen on the left) showing counts of positive, negative, and neutral messages, and further down to individual messages ranked by criteria such as "poster of interest" or those with particular text patterns. The whisper cells drill down to the distribution charts (which went from vapor to reality in the first release) and to the details on where the individual whispers were from (seen on the right).
Source: Codexa.

"What's new?" (recency, the minimum of the age of the newest signal). These sorts could cycle automatically at a schedule set by the user. This is similar in spirit to the MarketMind graphical user interface (GUI), described in Chapter 7, "A Little AI Goes a Long Way on Wall Street." It provided an intelligent assistant to monitor many stocks in multiple ways.

The screen shown in Figure 10.8 is the "overview first" part of Schneiderman's mantra. The "zoom" portion is shown in Figure 10.9, and "details on demand" in Figure 10.10.

A hefty dose of venture funding and a switch from HTML to Java made for a slicker, more elaborate display with a greater range of information sources and filters, listed along the top. In hindsight, the original

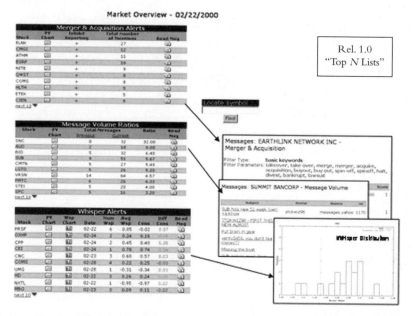

Figure 10.10 The graphically ambitious prototype was beyond the capabilities of what could be done in HTML in 1999, so the first release was a text-oriented set of tables. These are actual screen shots, not prototypes. In addition to the message traffic measures and whispers described in the chapter, another pane showing messages mentioning multiple firms with mergers and acquisitions language, a client request, is shown in the upper left.
Source: Codexa.

HTML version, implemented in the simple languages C++ and Perl, was much faster and more reliable. The "keep it simple, stupid" approach to software has much to be said in its favor.

More Web, More Warnings

The previous chapter illustrated how traditional information sources transformed by the Web can be understood by using AI and IA approaches to analyzing electronic content in rich molecular arrangements. This chapter did the same for new, nontraditional "creature of the Web" flavors of information, and how they can be delivered in a manner that turns down the data torrent coming out of the fire hose of Internet information retrieval to a manageable, understandable, filtered stream.

Earlier in the book, we saw how the similar approaches applied to quantitative, rather than textual, information could be a powerful tool for investing and trading, but this could be overdone by fooling yourself with excessive data mining. For textual information on the Web, this is still a danger, but you have help from other people in fooling yourself. On the Web, there are plenty of people willing to help you make bad decisions. Novel approaches to the old game of market manipulation appear on a regular basis—as is shown in the next chapter.

Notes

1. Asian Cajun is an actual cuisine that is suddenly all the rage in the huge Los Angeles area Asian neighborhoods of Westminster, Alhambra, and Monterey Park. Those keen on elegant presentation may want to pass. This is a meal after which you wash off with a garden hose. Tasty variants on Cajun crawfish, shrimp, lobster, and crab are all served up, with your choice of sauce (spicy, greasey, or spicy and greasey), in big clear plastic bags dropped on a table covered in brown paper, with a roll of paper towels on the side. Paper plates and plastic forks are available on request. It's much better than it sounds.

2. In Tina Fey's dead-on parody of Sarah Palin's interview with Katie Couric, the faux Palin asked "to use one of my lifelines, Katie." She would have been better off asking to poll the audience. The funniest line in that skit, a long disconnected utterance that failed to parse as English, was taken verbatim from the actual interview.

3. Treynor is widely regarded as having been a shoo-in to have shared the 1990 Nobel Prize in economics had he only published a paper that was sitting in his desk drawer.

4. Still in print after 150 years (New York: Three Rivers Press, 1995).

5. James Surowiecki, *The Wisdom of Crowds: Why the Many Are Smarter Than the Few and How Collective Wisdom Shapes Business, Economies, Societies and Nations* (New York: Random House, 2004), xix.

6. Used in other chapters, this is a fabulous site founded to allow the historians of the Internet era to have something to use. The Internet Archive is at www.archive.org, and also has an extensive collection of nearly 400,000 free music downloads. Of these, 60,000 are live concert recordings, and 6,000 of those are of the Grateful Dead.

7. Entire contents of iExchange web site, March 29, 2001. Bye-bye, Big Jim. *Source:* www.archive.org.

8. FTP is file transfer protocol, an Internet service that predates the World Wide Web and is still used for moving large chunks of information.

9. Landon Thomas Jr., "John A. Mulheren Jr., 54, Leading Trader in 80's, Dies," *New York Times*, December 17, 2003.

10. Ibid.

11. Michael Lewis, "Jonathan Lebed: Stock Manipulator, S.E.C. Nemesis—and 15," *New York Times Magazine*, February 25, 2001.

12. Peter Wysocki, "Cheap Talk on the Web: The Determinants of Postings on Stock Message Boards" (Working Paper No. 98025, University of Michigan, 1999).

13. Werner Antweiler and Murray Frank, "Is All That Talk Just Noise? The Information Content of Stock Message Boards," *Journal of Finance* 59, no. 3 (June 2004): 1259–1294.

14. Georgette Jason, who did the Dartboard articles for many years, says that while actual darts were thrown, they were never (as was alleged) thrown by monkeys. I went five rounds against the dartboard, using stocks selected by our quant methods, described in the chapters on seeking alpha and quantitative investing. I needed to explain why I'd picked a particular stock, and Georgette gently explained that "highest aggregate short-term forecast factor alpha" was too nerdy for *WSJ* readers. So I used to pick stocks near the top of our list that were amenable to having a better story backfilled as an explanation. For Home Depot (one of my winners) I explained that, having recently moved, I had personally dropped enough cash into the register to move the stock. Not keen on prison food, I never succumbed to the temptation to load up on a stock I'd picked before the story appeared in the paper. Rumor had it that not everyone in the game had the same dietary concerns.

15. Mark Hirschey, Vernon J. Richardson, and Susan Scholz, "How 'Foolish' Are Internet Investors?" *Financial Analysts Journal* 56, no. 1 (January/February 2000).

16. M. Bagnoli, M. D. Beneish, and S. G. Watts, "Whisper Forecasts of Quarterly Earnings per Share," *Journal of Accounting and Economics* 28, no. 1 (November 1999): 27–50.

17. University of Maryland Human-Computer Interaction Lab, www.cs.umd.edu/hcil/.

Chapter 11

Three Hundred Years of Stock Market Manipulations

From the Coffeehouse to the World Wide Web

n previous chapters, we saw that many of the changes in securities markets brought about by information technology in general and the Internet in particular are positive, democratizing access to markets and information. We also saw that technology is not always an unadulterated boon, and there is ample opportunity to fool yourself by blind data mining, and to find people trying to fool you using an ever-expanding bag of tricks, cons, and manipulations.

As information technology has expanded the scope of resources available to legitimate investors and traders, the Web has also become the prime new venue for the old game of market manipulation. Institutional traders and other long-term market participants often comment that they

This article originally appeared in the Summer 2001 issue of the *Journal of Investing*. It is reprinted with permission. To view the original article, please go to iijoi.com. My coauthor, Ananth Madhavan, was at the University of Southern California when we started this, was at Investment Technology Group (ITG) when we finished, and is now director of trading research at Barclays Global Investors.

see far more inexplicable price moves than they did in the pre-Web era. In many cases, these moves are tied to subtle, and not so subtle, attempts at market manipulation using the newfound power of the Internet to transmit and spread rumors, manipulate beliefs, and post incorrect information at little cost, while maintaining the cloak of anonymity.

Price distortions arising from manipulations may be short-lived, but they are real prices, and can dramatically affect the cost of trading and investment performance. The influence of the rumor machine is overlaid on the influences of more fundamental (and benign) factors that move stock prices. Therefore, interest in manipulations is not confined to the most obvious potential victims, specialists, dealers, and market makers but to all buy-side traders. This chapter examines the nature and characteristics of Internet market manipulations and their nonelectronic precedents, going back 300 years.

The Power of Manipulation

In 1999, NEI Webworld, Inc. (NEIP) was an obscure, nearly bankrupt printing company. Its stock barely had a pulse. It had been kept alive as a shell company, used by firms that wanted to access the public markets, but without the scrutiny that comes with an initial public offering (IPO). The last trade had been over a year earlier, for a penny and a half. Suddenly it rocketed up 106,600 percent in one morning. What happened? A miracle cure? A hit movie? Pokémon lunch boxes? No, none of these. NEIP's move was propelled purely by the power of Internet message boards. Two (subsequently indicted) UCLA students dramatically demonstrated how the new technology of the Internet had dramatically transformed the old game of market manipulation.

The Internet raises market manipulation to a level only dreamed of by past shysters. It used to take a real effort, a PR firm, or a major newspaper column to reach millions of potential traders. Now anyone can do it from their desktop. The Internet era is defined by the unparalleled ability of the new style of manipulator to use the Internet to affect the perceptions of vast numbers of investors at lightning speed, all the while remaining completely anonymous. This article looks at market manipulations—from early scams of the 1600s to the high-tech frauds of today—and asks how the game has changed and what you can do to protect yourself.[1]

Who cares about this, anyway? Aren't these just isolated instances of little concern to ordinary investors? Absolutely not! There are hundreds of well-documented cases involving message manipulation, with financial impacts running into the billions of dollars. And it's not just micro-cap stocks; recently multibillion-dollar Lucent Technologies was the subject of a successful manipulation attempt. When the people who get burned complain to the authorities, the Financial Industry Regulatory Authority (FINRA), the Securities and Exchange Commission (SEC), New York Stock Exchange (NYSE), and National Association of Securities Dealers (NASD), all examine messages in their investigations. The SEC set up an office back in 2000 just to deal with Internet scammers. These agencies are *reactive*—the investigators head for the message boards after someone complains that something suspicious has occurred in a stock.

Brokers, market makers, specialists, and traders, however, care in a *proactive* sense. They want early warnings of potential trouble ahead so they don't get left holding the proverbial bag. The Web has become the new prime venue for the old game of market manipulation. But it is not just the most obvious potential victims—specialists, dealers, and market makers—who care about manipulations. All good buy-side traders care about manipulations. If you have an order to trade in size—say, one day's average daily volume—you may be planning to execute the trade in parcels over three days. Price distortions arising from manipulations may be short-lived, but they are real prices, and can dramatically affect the cost of trading[2] and investment performance. The influence of the rumor machine is overlaid on the influences of more fundamental (and benign) factors that move stock prices. In an extreme case like NEIP, there are no other factors, but there are few if any stocks that are immune from these effects.

A Classic Market Manipulation

The ignoble history of stock market manipulations doubtless goes back to the most ancient markets. In one of the earliest accounts of manipulations, Joseph de la Vega, in *Confusión de Confusiones*, wrote of the Amsterdam Stock Exchange over 300 years ago (1688):

The greatest comedy is played at the Exchange. There, . . . the speculators excel in tricks, they do business and find excuses wherein hiding places, concealment of facts, quarrels, provocations, mockery, idle talk, violent desires, collusion, artful deceptions, betrayals, cheatings, and even tragic end are to be found.[3]

In the Amsterdam market at the time, market manipulations were common. De la Vega provides a comprehensive model of the various manipulations used to trick unsuspecting investors, including early versions of such perennial favorites as "painting the tape"*, making small trades to move the price. De la Vega's book, *Confusión de Confusiones*, was picked by the *Financial Times* as one of the 10 best investment books ever written.[4]

In the Amsterdam market of the late 1600s, there were two active stocks—the Dutch East India Company and the Dutch West India Company—and most of the activity revolved around speculation about the cargoes of the ships of these companies entering the port. One of the most successful stratagems was the spreading of false rumors in Amsterdam coffeehouses (*coffy huysen* in Dutch) frequented by traders and brokers. As de la Vega describes it: "The bulls spread a thousand rumors about the stocks, of which one would be enough to force up the prices."[5] Manipulators would falsely bid up the prices of stocks through a variety of artifices, including painting the tape and the spreading of overly optimistic news. Brokers would hint that ships soon to enter port carried rich cargoes ("No tea and spices—they've got furs and diamonds"), and soon the rumors would get ever more extravagant ("Lots of furs and *really* big diamonds"), leading to large price run-ups. Some things in life are fairly constant.

The Very Model of a Modern Market Manipulator

There is no de la Vega for the twenty-first century, but there is Tel212, an anonymous poster to Yahoo!'s message boards. The remarkable message that follows contains much of the same material, updated for the Internet, 320 years later.[6]

---

*Painting the tape is the illegal practice in which traders buy and sell a specific security among themselves, in order to create an illusion of high trading volume. Traders profit when unsuspecting investors, lured in by the unusual market volume, buy the stock.

Goat . . . here's the short's handbook

by: Tel212 (M/NY, NY)

3/11/00 2:48 AM

Msg: 16909 of 17535

Message boards Guidelines, used by shorters that short sell stock.

1. Be anonymous, of course.
2. Use 10% fact and 90% suggestion in one's posts. Facts give credibility, while suggestion does the "sell."
3. Let others "help" you learn about a stock thereby developing rapport and a support base.
4. Use multiple handles, but develop a unique style for each.
5. Use multiple ISPs.
6. Start each new handle slowly to build acceptance.
7. Occasionally, use two handles to "discuss" an issue.
8. Do not show all your cards at once when slamming a stock. It's a war—it's ok to lose a battle as long as you save enough ammo to win the war.
9. Know your enemies—they will end up being your best weapons.
10. Only slam until the tide starts to turn. Let doubt carry the stock back with the tide.
11. Maintain an appearance of being open minded but slant in either direction is acceptable.
12. Don't appear meek. No one follows the meek.
13. Strike just as your opponent starts to gather momentum but not before or you lose your sting.
14. Don't worry if people peg you for a slammer. The doubt will remain and that's what you are after.
15. If pegged, put up a brief fight, then let them feel they've won. This puts their guard down within a few days and your other handles can take over from there.
16. When slamming a stock, the intent is to minimize its rise, not to create an instant plunge.

17. To slam a stock requires you only to kill the dream not the company.

18. Use questions to invoke critical thinking and use statements to reinforce.

19. You can be liberal in your questions but be specific and precise in your statements.

20. Don't lie, but bend the truth.

21. When slamming, encourage research beyond calling the company. You know people are far too lazy and it's only doubt you are after, not confirmation.

22. When slamming, discourage people from taking the company's word—encourage them to seek outside proof. If the company's history is bad, point them there.

23. When slamming, refer to missed deadlines and weak financials.

24. When slamming, if the price rises, blame it on a temporary mass reaction to a press release rather than real interest in the stock. Point out low volume and emphasize the selling.

25. Pretend to share the same concerns by learning what they want to hear.

26. And above all else, be unpredictable.

Large price run-ups would in turn attract trading interest by naive investors, at which point the insiders would take their profits, selling at the top. When the bubble eventually burst, as it always did, the insiders would walk away with large profits. Such "pump and dump" strategies are still the mainstay of today's manipulator.

Bluffing

Another form of manipulation comes when a trader's intentions are deliberately misrepresented by, say, giving the impression that others are buying. Such bluffing can be very profitable. De la Vega again:

When a bull enters a coffee-house during the exchange hours, he is asked the price of the shares by the people present. He

adds one to two percent to the price of the day and he produces a notebook in which he pretends to write down orders.
The desire to buy shares increases. . . . Therefore, purchase
orders are given to the cunning broker[;] . . . he replies that he
has so many other orders he cannot be at anyone else's disposal.
The naïve questioner believes the sincerity of the statement . . .
and he gives an unrestricted order to another broker.[7]

The result of such gamesmanship is an unwarranted price increase
that favors the rumormonger, who sells at the top.

The strategies described by de la Vega faced some limitations, however. Manipulations in the seventeenth century took *time* because they
were difficult to *scale*; spreading rumors one coffeehouse at a time was
a slow way to *access* large numbers of traders. Further, it was not always
clear that the spreading of rumors would have an *impact* in the sense
that wary traders might not always act on what they heard. Finally, it
was virtually impossible for the manipulator to remain *anonymous*,
clearly a desirable feature when angry traders who had lost their shirts
were looking for revenge!

How Communication Changes
Market Manipulation

The world has changed a great deal since the late 1600s, but market
manipulations do not go out of style. All that changes really are the
details of how the rumors are spread and how bluffing is achieved.
The key is communication technology, which allows more traders to
be reached in less time.

The basic manipulations were largely unchanged from de la Vega's
time. The coffeehouse of seventeenth-century Amsterdam was replaced
with Harry's Bar or the Fraunces Tavern on Wall Street. Once again, to
have an effect, the manipulator had to go from bar to bar repeating the
rumors, as described in Edwin Lefèvre's classic *Reminiscences of a Stock
Operator* concerning the trading of Jesse Livermore in the early twentieth century.

Newspapers, telephones, telegraphy, and television all allowed gul-
lible players to be reached faster, and in greater numbers. There are

numerous examples. For instance, the classic boiler room of Wall Street used the telephone to cold-call thousands of investors, much as the broker of de la Vega's time spread rumors in coffeehouses.

A good example is the story of the manipulation of Sea World stock when it was independently traded. Manipulators who were short the stock spread rumors using the telephone that Shamu—the orca star of the theme park—had taken ill, sending the stock plunging for a quick profit.

Print and TV allow portfolio managers to reach larger audiences, creating the incentives to pump stocks that they hold. Such actions have often triggered sharp criticism since the identities of the boosters are known. In the 1980s, R. Foster Winans wrote the "Heard on the Street" column for the *Wall Street Journal*. Stocks that he recommended often rose in price the day after the newspaper hit the stands. Manipulators approached Winans and asked him to promote certain stocks in return for kickbacks. Winans was eventually caught and prosecuted for wire fraud.

Successful manipulation requires rumors to be spread widely and quickly. Communications technology allowed the manipulator to reach ever-larger audiences. However, two major problems remained. First, access to the most potent new technology (television and newspapers) was not easy. Journalists (e.g., Winans) had to be bribed, or the manipulator had to get on television, neither of which is easy to do. Second, it was still virtually impossible to remain anonymous. As the prosecution of Winans illustrates, there are some definite advantages to being anonymous.

Anatomy of a Successful Manipulation

The manipulations just described suggest five elements of a successful market manipulation. These are:

1. *Access* to large numbers of potential investors, ideally at low cost.
2. *Anonymity* for the market manipulator, who might otherwise be detected based on past reputation.
3. *Scalability*, meaning the ability of the manipulator to duplicate rumors on a large scale.

4. *Time*, the need to accomplish the whole manipulation quickly, because the danger of it being detected or found out increases with the duration.
5. *Impact*, meaning that the people who hear the rumor should be motivated to act by trading on the false information.

The Internet Era: A Manipulator's Paradise

The world moves a lot faster today. There are over 250 million people on the Internet, and more than a billion web pages (billions more if you count the ones below the surface). This is the democratization of information. Information that used to be difficult and expensive to find is widely available for low cost or no cost. Entirely new information sources are appearing. Millions of people can see and act on items of information in a hurry. For the market manipulator, this means greater access and greater impact by posting rumors anonymously on Internet message boards.

Can messages move a stock? Anecdotally, we see extraordinary events like the NEIP 106,600 percent jump. But is that evidence that far less malicious intent can move stock prices? Even unusual message traffic volumes have been shown to do this. "Cheap Talk on the Web,"[8] mentioned in the previous chapter, is a formal academic analysis of message volume by Peter Wysocki, then at the University of Michigan business school. It's based purely on traffic analysis, just counting messages. This is the earliest form of electronic intelligence gathering, dating back to World War II. Wysocki's key finding was that, after adjusting for earnings and dividend events and for market returns, the outlier events in message volume had statistically significant predictive value in forecasting subsequent excess return and subsequent volatility.

If messages can move markets, the modern rumormonger is going to be there. The task is made easier by the ability of the Internet manipulator to repeat or duplicate messages on multiple bulletin boards. The Web has become the new prime venue for the old game of market manipulation. It's easy to see why. Consider the following:

Market Manipulation Before and After the Internet Era

Attribute	Pre-Web	Post-Web
Access to media	Difficult to gain access to conventional media; often very expensive	Easy and cheap; manipulator can post messages or rumors
Anonymity	Very difficult to remain anonymous	Easy; anonymity typical on the Internet
Scalability	Difficult to repeat a rumor often	Easy and cheap through message replication and postings on multiple boards
Time	Typically slow; rumors spread through word of mouth could be repeated; more difficult for print media	Extremely fast; reaction time in seconds, facilitating pump-and-dump strategies
Impact	Depends	High, especially in stocks favored by day traders

Cyber-Manipulations

Message board scams are entirely new—a pure Internet phenomenon. Unlike in de la Vega's time, scalability is much less of an issue given the ability to post messages on multiple boards at one point in time and to replicate those messages again and again. Hundreds of thousands of messages are posted on dozens of boards every day. Some of them contain real information and some are just scams, but they change the market. There are hundreds of these cases: Raytheon, PairGain, Franklin, HealthSouth, Coho Energy, Ascend, and many others—so many, in fact, that we categorize them in what follows.

Fake News: PairGain Technologies and Aastrom Biosciences

A good example of message manipulation occurred with regard to PairGain Technologies Inc., a telecommunications firm. In April 1999, an employee of PairGain posted a message on a Yahoo! bulletin board alleging that PairGain had agreed to be acquired. The message contained a hyperlink to the supposed source of the rumor, a Bloomberg news announcement. Figure 11.1 shows what happened.

The announcement was a fake, as was the Bloomberg page, which was complete with phony advertisements. PairGain's stock price soared

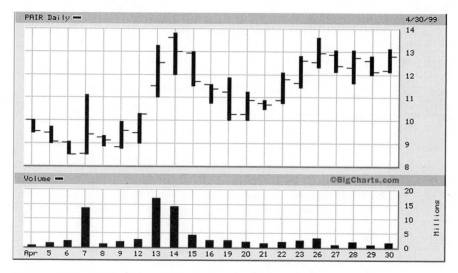

Figure 11.1   Daily Prices and Volumes in PairGain, April 1999
Reprinted with permission of BigCharts.com, © 1999 Dow Jones & Company, Inc. All Rights Reserved Worldwide.

on the announcement. An investigation by the SEC led to a guilty plea by the employee, who received five years' probation.

In February 2000, hackers posted a fake message about a merger between Aastrom Biosciences, Inc. (ASTM) and Gerno Corporation stating that the merger price would be $11.79 per share for ASTM. Shares of both companies soared on the phony news. (See Figure 11.2.) Aastrom—which had traded at about $4—was bought in after-hours trading for up to $7.50, while Gerno jumped 26 percent to a 52-week high of $59.625. As the *Wall Street Journal* noted, "Securities regulators have expressed concern and frustration about the exploding use of the Internet to defraud investors."

But you do not even need to resort to fake postings or hacking to manipulate a stock's price, as the example in Figure 11.3 of a pure message play illustrates.

Pure Message Events: Information Management Associates

Pure message events are increasingly common. Consider the wild ride of Information Management Associates, an Internet shopping site. In August 1999, the stock was trading at about $4 when "Tokyo Joe"

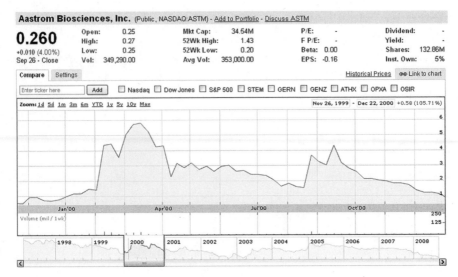

Figure 11.2 Daily Prices and Volumes in Aastrom, 2000
Source: Google Finance.

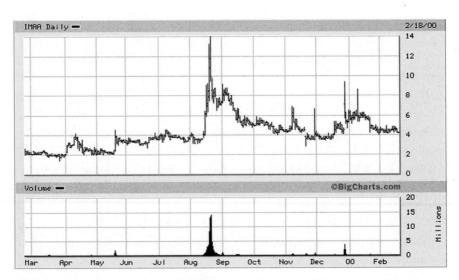

Figure 11.3 Daily Prices and Volumes in Information Management Associates
(IMAA), March 1999–March 2000
*Reprinted with permission of BigCharts.com, © 1999 Dow Jones & Company, Inc. All
Rights Reserved Worldwide.*

(who was later indicted) pushed the stock in his chat room, FastTrade. com. One participant noted: "Wait until the traders see IMAA after lunch." Joe replied: "It will be $14 when you are back." IMAA did in fact reach the high of $14 before falling significantly, as seen in the chart (Figure 11.3). Note that this was a pure message event. No real news was announced by the company.[9]

A Heavy-Handed Example: NEI Webworld, Inc.

NEI Webworld, Inc. (NEIP) is a heavy-handed example. Two manipulators, UCLA students, successfully ran up the price of the stock over 106,600 percent, from a few cents to more than $15 in a single morning. On Friday, November 12, 1999, the manipulators posted more than 500 fake messages using 50 different Web identities promoting shares of NEI Webworld, Inc., a nearly bankrupt printing company. NEIP was kept alive as a shell company, waiting for an acquiring firm looking to go public but wanting to avoid the scrutiny associated with a real IPO. The scammers used bots to simultaneously post messages like the following one on the most actively viewed Yahoo! stock message boards.

Their message: "Has anyone heard of LGC Wireless? It's the Monday high flier. They're going to buy out NEIP." They were saying that LGC Wireless, an Israeli company, was going to take over NEIP. One of the messages pumping up NEIP was:

> Has anyone heard of LGC Wireless, major customers include AT&T, Sprint, and Nokia. They are to buy out NEIP stock listing. This is called a reverse merger, LGC Wireless will buy out all remaining NEIP stock. It's a cheap way for up and coming high tech firms to go public.
>
> Buying NEIP early would entitle you to a share of LGC Wireless when it goes public next week. Look for a massive move to $5–10 as wireless stock are very hot.
>
> Look at their partners. LGC Wireless products and services deliver wireless voice, data and Internet communications throughout any facility. This stock will be a fast mover!

This had exactly the effect the manipulators wanted. The stock chart in Figure 11.4 is absolutely amazing.

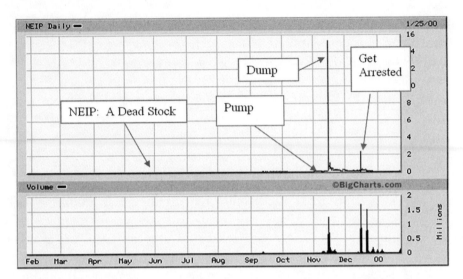

Figure 11.4 A pump and dump that de la Vega would envy—still the poster child of Web manipulations. These guys were caught in a month. What do you have to do to get caught in a week?
Reprinted with permission of BigCharts.com, © 1999 Dow Jones & Company, Inc. All Rights Reserved Worldwide.

Notice the scale—we're looking at a year period. NEIP is totally dead—just a CUSIP and an answering machine. Then, around October/November these students, the guys who posted the messages, start to buy some stock using their own brokerage accounts. They buy what they can and then they post their messages. The stock pops up 106,000 percent that morning in New York. Then, when it's morning in Israel, the alleged acquirer, LGC, says, "We don't need NEIP—we've already got a CUSIP and an answering machine." So the student perpetrators are selling all the way up. When LGC speaks up, the stock drops, but not back to where it was—some people think it's a ploy. Then a month later the manipulators are caught by the SEC. Remember, these guys are using their own computers to post the messages and their own brokerage accounts to buy the stock, like the burglar who jimmies your door with his driver's license and then leaves the license. The SEC catches them in a month. You wonder who they catch in a week. The arrest is page 1 in both the *Wall Street Journal* and the *New York Times* on December 16, 1999. The stock pops 5,000 percent. Tell me markets are efficient!

The *New York Times* noted:

> The case illustrates how easy it is to send stocks soaring by using the Internet. . . . Securities fraud has migrated to the Internet, regulators say, because stocks can be propelled there with little more than effusive talk and rosy predictions. Before the Web became stock-tip central, someone who wanted to manipulate a company's shares had to employ rooms full of stockbrokers flogging stocks to unsuspecting investors by telephone. Now an electronic message does the trick instantly.[10]

Prosecutors lauded their ability to detect the fraud, despite its heavy-handed nature. Richard H. Walker, director of enforcement at the SEC, was quoted as saying: "Let this serve as a warning to con men: if you use the Internet to manipulate our securities markets, we can and will find you. Though the perpetrators in the case went to great lengths to hide from us, we discovered them within a matter of days." It is far from clear, however, that the SEC or another agency could detect a more subtle manipulation in a more active stock.

Again, it's worth remembering that this was a pure message event. The enormous run-up in NEIP's price was being driven solely by the misleading rumors posted on various message boards by the manipulators.

Front-Running on the Web: Fast-Trades.com

Consider fast-trades.com, a free site directed at day traders set up by a Georgetown University law student, Douglas Colt. Colt took large positions in micro-cap stocks, then promoted them as attractive buys on his site. Naive traders bid up the prices of the recommended stocks and Colt sold at the peak at a large profit, just before the inevitable collapse. Although the site did reveal that its operators might trade stocks, the SEC found the disclaimer "materially misleading as to the real trading intent of the participants. . . . If fast-trades had accurately disclosed their trading intentions, subscribers would have been able to deduce that the only reason Colt offered his 'free' service was so he could further influence the market price movement initiated by his purchase of the recommended stock just before the announcement."[11]

It's Not Just Micro-Caps

Most of these examples involve thinly traded small-cap or micro-capitalization stocks. They are easier targets, but larger names are not immune from these shenanigans. In March 2000, a day trader posted a fake announcement regarding the earnings of Lucent Technologies:

> MURRAY HILL, N.J., March 22 /PRNewswire/ — Lucent Technologies (NYSE: LU - news) said today that, based on preliminary estimates, it expects operating results for its second fiscal quarter of 2000 to be lower than analysts' estimates. The company expects to report revenues in the range of $9.4 to $9.5 billion for the quarter, which will end Mar. 31, 2000, flat with the prior year period.

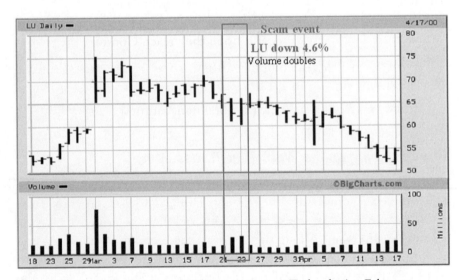

Figure 11.5 Daily Prices and Volumes in Lucent Technologies, February 2000–April 2000. Even large-cap names are subject to Web manipulations. *Reprinted with permission of BigCharts.com, © 1999 Dow Jones & Company, Inc. All Rights Reserved Worldwide.*

The effect was dramatic. As seen in Figure 11.5, over $7 billion of market capitalization evaporated within a few hours, all driven by a dozen messages repeating the false rumor. It did not matter that the perpetrator was eventually caught; the damage was done.

Where Are We Headed?

Today traders can be blindsided and left holding the bag more often than in the past. What's going on here is a profound change in the information food chain. The Internet disseminates information very rapidly, to millions of people who can act on it in a hurry. Any particular individual is concerned with only a few stocks. But collectively, they are interested in all of them, just like institutions.

These examples are just the ones that were detected. At this very moment, there are undoubtedly other manipulations under way in even more creative ways, what we term cyber-sleaze. For example, one might imagine a manipulator systematically altering the whisper number forecasts for a stock with a view toward moving the stock price. Another example of cyber-sleaze is the misdirected e-mail strategy.

A variant of this approach is to direct some apparently confidential e-mail to potential investors and hope they react. Consider the following message, complete with typos, which was actually received by one of the authors (Leinweber) while we were writing this article:

> From: brakrchi@att.net [mailto:brakrchi@att.net]
>
> Sent: Saturday, February 19, 2000 9:56 PM
>
> To: brakrchi@home.com
>
> Subject: ISFB is Climbing !!!
>
> James,
>
> This is ISFB info and the projection, that you wanted. I think this is definitly the big one we wanted. KEEP THIS UNDER YOUR HAT . . . for now . . . OK?
>
> Call me well go over it all.
>
> M.Hilton

http://moneycentral.msn.com/scripts/webquote
.dll?iPage=lqd&Symbol=isfb

INTERNET SOLUTIONS FOR BUSINESS OTCBB:ISFB

INVESTMENT SUMMARY

Current price: $6.00

Shares outstanding: 14,729,000

Public Float: 1,100,000

NASD Symbol:ISFB

Short term target: $12–15

1. INTERNET SOLUTIONS COMPANY WITH ESTABLISHED REVENUE BASE
2. STRONG MANAGEMENT AND TECHNICAL TEAM
3. MAJOR BLUE CHIP CLIENTS
4. TECHNICAL LEADER WITH 60 MAN-YEARS OF PRODUCT DEVELOPMENT

While the stock exists, as does the URL, the author of the e-mail, despite the return address, remains fully anonymous, and it is highly unlikely that the message really was misdirected by accident. Indeed, a subsequent check of the stock showed it trading below the price listed on the e-mail and well below the "target" of $12 to $15.

As past history shows, there is nothing new about the form of manipulations. Pump and dump never seems to go out of style. But what has changed now is the speed with which rumors can spread through the Internet and the fast response of stock prices due to the presence of large numbers of day traders who respond to news on Internet message boards. Scalability is no longer a problem, and the result is going to be more and more sophisticated market manipulation.[12] The ongoing battle between the spammers and the SEC resembles the seemingly endless series of *Mad* magazine "Spy vs. Spy" measures and countermeasures.

As always, the best advice is caveat emptor. Never, under any circumstances, should you buy stock recommended by your newfound e-mail friend in Nigeria.

Notes

1. Corners and short squeezes, including various railroad manipulations by Cornelius Vanderbilt and others at the turn of the twentieth century, represent another form of manipulation through scarcity as opposed to redirecting people's beliefs. This chapter focuses on manipulations based on false information of one type or another.

2. The real cost of trading is the difference between the price at the time you decide to trade and the total price at the time you actually trade. Commissions are usually the smallest part of this. Market impact and the opportunity cost of delay far outweigh the commissions. See the discussion in Chapter 5.

3. Joseph de la Vega, *Confusión de Confusiones* (New York: John Wiley & Sons, 1995), p. 169.

4. *Confusión de Confusiones* and Charles Mackay's *Extraordinary Popular Delusions and the Madness of Crowds* (another of the *FT* editors' top 10) are published together in the Wiley Investment Classics Series.

5. De la Vega, *Confusión*, p. 203.

6. The URL at the time the article was written was http://messages.yahoo.com/bbs?action=m&board=18185330&tid=wgat&sid=18185330&mid=16909. However, this guide seems to have wisely been removed.

7. De la Vega, *Confusión*, p. 199.

8. Peter Wysocki, "Cheap Talk on the Web: The Determinants of Postings on Stock Message Boards" (Working Paper No. 98025, University of Michigan, 1999).

9. Tokyo Joe eventually settled with the SEC, paying $748,000 in fines but not admitting guilt. Gretchen Morgenson, "'Tokyo Joe' Settles Suit with S.E.C. over Web Site," *New York Times*, March 9, 2001.

10. Gretchen Morgenson, "Internet's Role Is Implicated in Stock Fraud," *New York Times*, December 16, 1999.

11. SEC, Release No. 42483, March 2, 2000, Administrative Proceeding, File No. 3-10154.

12. This was written in 2001, and the prediction has proven correct. The entire genre of so-called pictograms—pictures of text touting a stock in spam e-mail—rose to a minor industry, and vanished as better antispam measures took hold.

Part Four

Nerds
Gone Wild

*Wired Markets
in Distress*

T he original plan for this book stopped after the three parts that you've just read. These parts are about how markets became machines, and about using more machines to pick stocks and trade them electronically, bringing in an assortment of nifty ideas from finance and computer science along the way.

By the fall of 2008, it was clear that stopping there would have made for a book that seemed quaint. How could any financial author ignore what has happened since then? The problem was that I had spent my entire financial career in the stock markets, and the stock market was a victim, not a cause, of the Great Mess of '08.* The causes came not from the stock side of Wall Street, but from a mix of abuses, greed, and sheer stupidity from the people who created, repackaged, and sold overly complex derivatives that started with mortgage loans that should never have been made, and were assembled into an over-leveraged financial house of cards that is still collapsing today.

These final chapters are about that collapse.

Chapter 12, "Shooting the Moon: Stupid Financial Technology Tricks," is about how wildly complex derivatives traded in opaque markets, and the misuse of mathematical models to value them, contributed to the mess. This is informative on how responsible use of market technology might have avoided the crisis and can help avoid an even more dreadful sequel in the future. Technology errors of omission and commission have contributed to our present woes. Stock markets are almost perfectly transparent, with full information available to all, and the best electronic clearing and settlement in history. These technologies were omitted in building the skyscraper of cards ("house of cards" seems too mild) out of collateralized debt obligations (CDOs), credit default swaps (CDSs), synthetic collateralized debt obligations (SCDOs), and the rest.

The Hall of Shame for those guilty of incompetent engineering features collapsing bridges, flaming dirigibles, exploding spacecraft, and melting reactors. We can add a new wing for overly complex derivatives, modeled in exquisite detail by myopic nerds with Ph.D.'s who got lost in the ever more complex simulations but ignored the basic principles, and their lavishly paid bosses who ignored the warnings from the best of them so they could be even more lavishly paid.

Chapter 13, "Structural Ideas for the Economic Rescue," expresses the view that as structural flaws in the current recovery plan become increasingly apparent, it seems clear that there is a need for a coherent systems approach to these problems. At first, I felt a great deal of trepidation about delving into this. As a longtime stock guy, I felt I didn't know what I was talking about in this area. It has become increasingly clear that the people who are in charge don't know what they are talking about, either. They try to solve problems charging up one hill with $700 billion of our money, drop a couple of hundred billion, then charge back down leaving the same problems in place.

Many aspects of the plans put forth are overly complex, and seem to ignore central aspects of the problem to protect and further enrich the people and institutions that created the mess. This chapter describes two original ideas suggested by my colleagues that address key issues in the economic recovery in a simple, straightforward way. Both have a near circuit designer's approach, removing "gain" in a system that makes it unstable, and bypassing systemic flaws that impede the desired goals. These ideas are:

- *Fractional home ownership.* My Berkeley office-mate John O'Brien is one of the founders of the field of financial engineering. His idea, which expands on a suggestion from Fed Chairman Ben Bernanke, has the potential to address the crisis where it started, in the housing market.
- *New American bank initiative.* This is an idea for getting ourselves out of the hole we are in. With my coauthor for this chapter, Sal Khan, I describe a structural solution, free of the inherent flaws and conflicts that have resulted in a tragic waste of time and money in recent months.

Chapter 14, "Nerds Gone Green," discusses how many nerds are finding themselves cast out of Wall Street. Some will find their way back, but many will not. What's a former Wall Street nerd to do? The answer may lie in market technology that is valuable outside of financial markets. Just as the Internet started out as a way for the Department of Defense to link military computers, there are future uses for market technology that may rival or surpass those involving traditional financial instruments. Efficient, environmentally sound use of energy is one of the most important. We hear from voices as diverse as Thomas Friedman, T. Boone Pickens, and Ted Turner that energy technology is the next big thing. It is not just about making energy; it is about matching the consumers and the producers of this resource. For oil, the markets are there. For electricity, they are not, at least not in a useful way (unless you were Enron in 1999). Matching consumers, at the individual and business level, and producers, including small alternative suppliers of solar panels, is an allocation and communication problem.

Wired markets have developed to a remarkable level in finance, giving individual buyers and sellers the capabilities to interact with each other and with market makers using direct electronic access that was once found only in large institutions. There is a parallel path in energy markets. Simple real-time spot pricing is not a full solution. Consumers need to know that cutting back today to help producers produce less pollution or greenhouse gases will not cost them more tomorrow. They effectively need software to manage trade futures, and it needs to be simple and reliable—a considerable technology challenge. Nerds with pink slips may find they go well with green.

---

*Jon Stewart has a much better non–politically correct name for what has transpired lately. It begins with "Cluster." But everyone tells me I can't put it in the book or use it at conferences. I think you need to watch the *Daily Show* to pick up on its continuing economic coverage. Stephen Colbert, whose show follows Stewart's, says the financial markets are like a roller-coaster ride where you vomit money. This brand of fake news has its share of dumb gags, to be sure, but there is more "truthiness" to be found there than in much of what passes for serious broadcast journalism. Recent guests include Barack Obama, Bill Clinton, John McCain, and Tony Blair. There are frequent appearances by Al Gore, that pesky rascal responsible for all the weird weather lately, who is a huge *Daily Show* fan. In *The Assault on Reason* (Penguin Press, 2007) Gore praises Stewart to the sky, and quotes Dan Rather in pointing out that a great deal of mainstream television news is "dumbed down and tarted up . . . to glue eyeballs to the screen . . . and sell advertising." (p. 17)

derivatives today less better extreme

engineering MIT assets business use

Wall Transparency

Stock crisis NERDS OTC

futures figure Investors

known started

CDOs Management SOMETHING CDO bad finance large new time

others people started participants including problem first let just

book Chapter like Emilie need

held prices even loans borrowers described

Great two transparent problems commission little Simple also risk Trading models three back

options found turned credit electronic WANT

understand securities errors Mess Technology often may energy Source complex information

PWG well best now means Infrastructure

ice money garbage

markets financia

sh place years Report AU many USED

commodity much money Fann mortgage Street make

Chapter 12

Shooting the Moon

Stupid Financial Technology Tricks

L ike many others from the stock side of greater Wall Street, I felt blindsided by the events of 2008. "Blindsided" is actually a gross understatement; I felt like the guy who comes home and finds the neighbors were running a meth lab that has exploded and flattened the block. I have tried to moderate this "mad as hell" attitude in writing this, and recognize that many participants did in fact realize that something was very wrong. One commented, "Bit by bit, we iterated toward more danger-ous things, and each step seemed okay."

It is an understatement to say the steps were okay. This was not a natural event, like Hurricane Katrina, or an external attack, like 9/11. This was a case of "Honey, I think I broke the world financial system."

To repeat the disclaimer of professional expertise on this subject: Of the billions in institutional assets I managed in the 1990s, exactly *zero* were invested in collateralized debt obligations (CDOs), credit default swaps (CDSs), and mortgage-backed securities (MBSs). I knew what they were, and particularly enjoyed the stories in Michael Lewis's book *Liar's Poker* of how the inventors of mortgage-backed securities at Salomon Brothers would shut down the market occasionally for food orgies of Roman proportions.

Our market neutral portfolios would often be equitized, putting back the market return with a simple futures position. Sometimes clients would want so-called portable alpha using futures in a market other than the one used for the stock portfolio, so we could add our return to a bond market, or an international stock market, as described in Chapter 5 ("A Gentle Introduction to Computerized Investing"). That was as far as we went with derivatives. There was little or no leverage due to the institutional constraints we had for pension accounts, and our strong desire not to blow up our clients' portfolios and our income stream by turning what would be a moderate drawdown into a disaster. Lehman Brothers' leverage was widely reported to be more than 30:1 when they turned out the lights, and other firms were equally overextended, which, while not without precedent, proved particularly toxic when applied to what proved to be nearly incomprehensible securities.

Robert Merton, who shared the Nobel Prize for economics in 1997, was also one of the founders of Long Term Capital Management, the firm at the center of a $5 billion crisis in 1998. At the time there was a sense of great peril, and the size of the rescue, which now seems quaint, seemed overwhelming. Merton wrote,

> As we all know, there have been financial "incidents" and even crises that cause some to raise questions about the innovations and scientific soundness of the financial theories used to engineer them. There have surely been individual cases of faulty engineering designs and faulty implementations of those designs in building bridges, airplanes, and silicon chips. Indeed, learning from (sometimes even tragic) mistakes is an integral part of the process of technical progress.[1]

This is not the place and I am not the person to fully explain the morass we have fallen into. I did ask the people I knew, at Berkeley and on Wall Street, to give me a crash course so I could understand how technology contributed to the crisis, how it could help get us out of it, and how to avoid a repetition. I have real and virtual stacks of articles, papers, books, and links; it would take a book this size to cover them all. A particularly clear and incisive nontechnical discussion can be found in *Vanity Fair*, by historian Niall Ferguson ("Wall Street Lays Another Egg," December 2008).

One resource stands out for an audience looking to get some traction on the global financial mess, and looking for pointers to current quality material from primary and media sources: the Baseline Scenario web site[2] started for exactly this purpose by MIT Sloan School of Management professor Simon Johnson, who returned to MIT in August 2008 after a year as director of research for the International Monetary Fund. Instead of picking up where he left off in his research and teaching, he devoted his energy to starting and maintaining the Baseline Scenario site. The place to start there is "The Financial Crisis for Beginners." It begins:

> We believe that everyone should be able to understand how the financial crisis came about, what it means for all of us, and what our options are for getting out of it. Unfortunately, the vast majority of all writing about the crisis—including this blog— assumes some familiarity with the world of mortgage-backed securities, collateralized debt obligations, credit default swaps, and so on. You've probably heard dozens of journalists use these terms without explaining what they mean. If you're confused, this page is for you.[3]

At this site you'll find links to radio programs, mostly National Public Radio (NPR), and video material that will bring you up to speed quickly. The main portion of the site, also used for an MIT course on the subject, is updated regularly with more in-depth material on the latest turns in the financial crisis.

Having franchised out the discussion of the origins of the crisis, and the larger issues around it, we can turn to the subject of this chapter, the role of technology in this mess.

To Protect and to Serve: Market Transparency

In financial theory, market transparency is a necessary condition for a free market to be efficient. In practice, at a micro scale it means that we can see the prices to buy and to sell securities (quotes) and the prices at which transactions actually occur (trades). A macro view of market transparency is that information about the securities being traded should be similarly reliable. Assuring that markets are transparent is a key role for regulators.

Public participation in the stock market grew dramatically in the early part of the twentieth century, and without regulation, abuses such as fraudulent information, extravagant fees, and extreme leverage became common. The last financial crisis of the magnitude we are seeing today made the need for regulation apparent. The Securities and Exchange Commission (SEC) explains its origins on its web site (http://sec.gov):

> When the stock market crashed in October 1929, public confidence in the markets plummeted. Investors large and small, as well as the banks who had loaned to them, lost great sums of money in the ensuing Great Depression. There was a consensus that for the economy to recover, the public's faith in the capital markets needed to be restored. Congress held hearings to identify the problems and search for solutions.
>
> Based on the findings in these hearings, Congress—during the peak year of the Depression—passed the Securities Act of 1933. This law, together with the Securities Exchange Act of 1934, which created the SEC, was designed to restore investor confidence in our capital markets by providing investors and the markets with more reliable information and clear rules of honest dealing.

The mission to provide investors with reliable information is what makes all of the quant-textual approaches based on SEC filings (described in Chapter 9 and elsewhere in this book) both possible and valuable. It is why the micro-scale market data—trades and quotes—are visible on the bottom of every business television station and financial web site.[4] (See Figure 12.1.)

Simple derivative securities like futures and put or call options transfer risk in readily understood ways. Futures markets started so farmers could protect themselves from a drop in crop prices that might keep them from covering their costs and being able to keep their farms for another harvest season. Consumers of agricultural commodities (e.g., wheat) could lock in prices that would let them fill their commitments

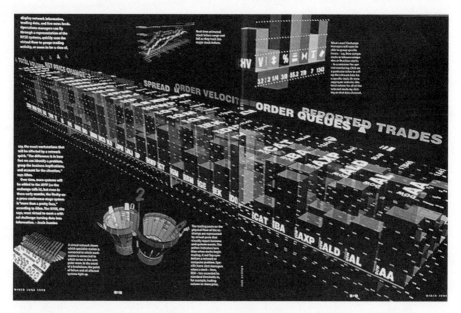

Figure 12.1 All levels of detail are available for stock and option markets, down to individual trades and quotes. Market transparency to the max. Nothing remotely like this exists for CDOs, CDSs, and the rest.
Source: NYSE.

to deliver products made with those commodities (e.g., bread) at the prices they had agreed to sell them, without risk of ruin. These commodity derivatives were also used by pure speculators with no underlying business interest in the price of wheat (or silver or oil) to make large bets on the direction of prices, since the futures markets could be many times larger than the actual physical supply of the underlying commodity. Speculative misbehavior was the inevitable result, and again, the federal government stepped in to regulate the market, this time by creating the Commodity Futures Trading Commission (CFTC), as explained on its web site at http://cftc.gov:

> Congress created the Commodity Futures Trading Commission (CFTC) in 1974 as an independent agency with the mandate to regulate commodity futures and option markets in the United States. The agency's mandate has been renewed and expanded several times since then, most recently by the Commodity Futures Modernization Act of 2000.

In 1974 the majority of futures trading took place in the agricultural sector. The CFTC's history demonstrates, among other things, how the futures industry has become increasingly varied over time and today encompasses a vast array of highly complex financial futures contracts.

Options and futures trades and quotes are also transparent, available as easily as those for stocks, and the contracts underlying the instruments themselves are standardized, simple, and transparent.

None of this transparency, in structure or in trading, is found in the world of the highly complex exotic derivatives at the root of our current problems. These toxic creations sprang from the feverish imaginations of nerds gone wild—financial instruments that were outside the authority of either the SEC or the CFTC, and in contrast to those regulated instruments, traded without scrutiny and with no requirements or standards on information for investors.

There was little or no information on what they were worth, and little understanding of what they were. These financial Rube Goldberg machines were so complex that some of their provisions were unknown even to the most senior and experienced executives of the firms that held them. So-called liquidity puts are an arcane provision of some CDOs that allows purchasers to sell them back to the issuer at the original value, a provision that did an estimated $25 billion in damage to Citigroup. In a *Fortune* magazine interview, Robert Rubin, the chairman of Citi and former secretary of the Treasury, underscored the lack of transparency. The interviewer wrote, "But it is testimony to the obscurity of this term that Rubin says he had never heard of liquidity puts until they started harassing Citi last summer."[5]

The high degree of transparency seen in the stock market lets investors measure the value of their portfolios and the quality of their trading with an extreme degree of accuracy. The little old lady in Pasadena who sells a hundred shares for $10.25 at noon can see that the bid price for the stock was $10.26 at 11:59:59 and can (and often does) complain about the poor execution, and the brokers know this. Her portfolio can be marked to market, to the penny, in real time.[6] None of this is remotely possible for the trillions in CDOs and the like that are at the root of the crisis, and this allowed the banks to ignore (or, if you are in a very charitable mood, be unaware of) the profound depth of the hole they were in. Instead of marked-to-market valuations, they relied on flawed models, the second component of technology's contribution to the Great Mess of '08.

The good news is that there is near unanimity that this must not be allowed to happen again. There is a giant scramble under way to build the highly transparent electronic markets and clearing systems that are a key piece of the solution. In a speech at the Federal Reserve Bank of Kansas City's Annual Economic Symposium, Fed Chairman Ben S. Bernanke himself said on the subject:

> An effective means of increasing the resilience of the financial system is to strengthen its infrastructure. For my purposes today, I want to construe "financial infrastructure" very broadly, to include not only the "hardware" components of that infrastructure— the physical systems on which market participants rely for the quick and accurate execution, clearing, and settlement of transactions—but also the associated "software," including the statutory, regulatory, and contractual frameworks and the business practices that govern the actions and obligations of market participants on both sides of each transaction.
>
> Of course, a robust financial infrastructure has many benefits even in normal times, including lower transactions costs and greater market liquidity. In periods of extreme stress, however, the quality of the financial infrastructure may prove critical. For example, it greatly affects the ability of market participants to quickly determine their own positions and exposures, including exposures to key counterparties, and to adjust their positions as necessary.[7]

Unlike other aspects of the often muddled rescue plans, this is not mired in debate or paralyzed by the "charge up the hill and charge back down again" behavior seen elsewhere. On November 14, 2008, the President's Working Group (PWG) on Financial Markets said its "top near-term OTC derivatives priority" is to oversee the successful implementation of central counterparty services for credit default swaps:

> A well-regulated and prudently managed CDS central counterparty can provide immediate benefits to the market by

reducing the systemic risk associated with counterparty credit exposures. . . . It also can help facilitate greater market transparency and be a catalyst for a more competitive trading environment that includes exchange trading of CDSs.

In light of recent developments, the PWG is issuing broader objectives than those that motivated the PWG's previous OTC derivatives recommendations in the March 13 PWG Policy Statement on Financial Market Developments.

The PWG has established the following policy objectives:

1. improve the transparency and integrity of the credit default swaps market;
2. enhance risk management of OTC derivatives;
3. further strengthen the OTC derivatives market infrastructure;
4. strengthen cooperation among regulatory authorities.[8]

The President's Working Group brings together the scattered agencies that can make this happen. Chaired by the Treasury, it includes the Federal Reserve, the Securities and Exchange Commission, and the Commodity Futures Trading Commission. The PWG is reviewing multiple system proposals and anticipates that at least one will commence operations in 2009.

All the usual suspects are involved—the Intercontinental Exchange, NYSE Euronext, Eurex, and the Chicago Mercantile Exchange have all submitted plans. The global aspects are being addressed as well, with a year-end deadline set by the European Commission for financial market participants to make similar plans.

Broader proposals, more controversial and less formed, include provisions for monitoring the leverage of parties involved in these transactions. The levels of extreme overleverage used turned bad ideas into major catastrophes. No less a culprit than Lehman's Dick Fuld spoke of the need for such a monitor in his testimony to Congress. Regrettably, this seems to be getting less attention than it deserves, but it is a second story on the foundation of trading, clearing, and settlement systems that can give early warning of larger problems.

Electronic market technology lowers the barriers to entry for creating this new infrastructure, as seen in the fragmentation of the equity markets described in Chapter 3 ("Algorithm Wars"). For stocks, futures, and options, this has let a thousand flowers (well, about 40) bloom, and there is a great race under way to create the systems needed for a broader class of securities. Many of the contestants appeared at a conference on global exchanges held in October 2008, organized by Rosenblatt Securities, a small firm with a large profile in electronic markets. Attendees included all the major exchanges, and new players who saw this as the opportunity of a lifetime. Citadel's Matt Andresen and other attendees considered the opportunity to move over-the-counter (OTC)-traded CDSs onto electronic exchanges as the single best product opportunity in many years—a high standard, given the electronic transformation of markets in the recent past."[9]

The mandates of federal regulation, combined with a high-octane mix of the standard Wall Street motivators of fear and greed, give us hope that this element of the technology solution will happen quickly.

Stupid Engineering Tricks

Engineers have had some great ideas. History's greatest technological advances are often cited as fire, the wheel, and storing instructions as data. The first is arguably a discovery, but the others are inventions. We can add a few more—the time value of money, the automobile, the transistor, and the World Wide Web. In the Introduction, the structure of Mutually Assured Survival (dreadfully mislabeled as Mutually Assured Destruction) was given high marks.

Not all military technology ideas had similar merit. In *Imaginary Weapons: A Journey Through the Pentagon's Scientific Underworld*, *Defense Technology International* editor Sharon Weinberger tells the remarkable story of how tens of millions of dollars were spent on a crackpot idea for what amounted to a nuclear hand grenade, despite the efforts of the most senior Pentagon scientists to scuttle the project, and the dubious utility of such a weapon. Who would want to throw it? Does the world need a nuke that fits in a lunch bag?[10]

My personal favorite for a bad technology idea, now in second place after the models that helped create the financial meltdown (but only because it was never built), was described at a RAND Corporation seminar in the early 1980s by then Undersecretary of

Defense Bill Perry (later Secretary of Defense in the Clinton years, and not to be confused with the Fridge of the Chicago Bears).

I asked him what the worst idea ever to cross his desk at the Pentagon was. Without hesitation, he said that, to his consternation, a proposal had gotten as far as his office to place a huge array of nuclear-powered rocket engines on the far side of the moon, and in the event of hostilities, fire the rockets to plunge the moon into the Soviet Union. He explained to the authors that this would drastically perturb the earth's orbit into a range where water was no longer a liquid, and thus "was neither feasible nor desirable."

There are many civilian examples of bad engineering, ranging from simple miscalculation to astounding idiocy. Some had relatively minor consequences, as in the photogenic 1895 train disaster at Montparnasse Station, Paris, seen in Figure 12.2.

Figure 12.2   The 1895 train disaster at Montparnasse Station: If only the other errors discussed in this chapter could have been avoided by a heavier foot on the brake.
Source: Wikimedia.

The collapse of the first Tacoma Narrows Bridge in November 1940 (depicted in Figure 12.3) just four months after it opened is an example of the kind of bad modeling we have seen lately in asset pricing models.[11] The mathematical model used to design the bridge, like those used to price mortgage-backed CDOs, was fatally flawed. What worked in light breezes (normal housing lending) failed spectacularly in a storm (no-income, no-job, no-assets undocumented lending).

No one was killed in the bridge collapse. Other errors of this sort have been more consequential. The *Hindenberg* explosion (Figure 12.4) in 1937 killed 36 people and ended the era of lighter-than-air travel. There are a multitude of theories regarding the cause of the explosion. Many involve management's head-in-the-sand desire to avoid the expense of better safety. Parallels are found in many stories related by Wall Street quantitative risk analysts of their interactions with their bosses in 2007 and 2008.

This kind of screw-up remains distressingly common.[12] A multilevel Kansas City Hyatt Regency hotel walkway collapsed in 1981, killing

Figure 12.3 Still from a video of the collapse of the Tacoma Narrows Bridge, which has been dear to engineering and physics students ever since. This is another still that really needs to be seen as part of a movie.
Source: Wikimedia.

Figure 12.4   The *Hindenberg*, a potentially avoidable disaster. Our financial meltdown was avoidable too.
Source: Wikimedia.

114 people. The walkways on floors two, three, and four of the hotel were supported by multiple steel rods tied end to end, instead of a single long rod passing through all three levels. Think of different ways for three people to hang off a rope. You could let the first one hang off the rope from the ceiling, then tie another rope to his feet, and let the second person hang from that, then tie another rope to the feet of person number two, and let the third person hang from that one. Someone's going to let go. Someone did.

Stupid Financial Engineering Tricks

Alas, the same kind of careless design flaws found in engineered physical objects are also evident in engineered financial structures, plus a few special design flaws of their own. Foremost on that list are what seem to many observers to be a taste for excessive and seemingly pointless complexity.

Shortly after I moved from financial technology into investment management in 1993, I was glad to be able to attend a weeklong boot camp for financial executives that Andre Perold, head of finance at the Harvard Business School, organized for the Association for Investment

Management and Research (AIMR) (now the CFA Institute). Coming from the stock world, I was stunned to see some of the Frankenstein derivatives that were being sold even then. Some depended on ridiculous factors, like the cube of the difference of two interest rates. Andre's harsh critique pointed out there was no imaginable economic justification for these freakish creations; they were Byzantine casino games, sold by fast-talking Wall Streeters to less sophisticated investors. The small-town managers in places like Orange County took the bait—in its case, in sufficient quantities to drive the county into bankruptcy in 1994.

Over the years, I remained somewhat mystified by much of what was going on in derivatives, and not particularly thrilled with the "what a rube" attitude I got from some of my colleagues when I expressed these doubts. I tended to keep quiet on the subject, and did not use them professionally except in very simple ways. It was gratifying to see occasional reports that at least a few much larger financial fish had similar misgivings. George Soros was often quoted saying his firm avoided derivatives "because we don't really understand how they work." Felix Rohatyn, who started out as a physics student and in the 1970s was credited with saving New York City from bankruptcy, described derivatives as potential "hydrogen bombs." The most common sound bite was a pithy and prescient comment by Warren Buffett that derivatives were "financial weapons of mass destruction, carrying dangers that, while now latent, are potentially lethal."

Buffett's warning was contained in the chairman's letter in the 2002 Berkshire Hathaway Annual Report. A longer excerpt is equally remarkable in its prescience:

> [Berkshire Hathaway Vice Chairman] Charlie [Munger] and I are of one mind in how we feel about derivatives and the trading activities that go with them: We view them as time bombs, both for the parties that deal in them and for the economic system. . . .
>
> The range of derivatives contracts is limited only by the imagination of man (or sometimes, so it seems, madmen). At Enron, for example, newsprint and broadband derivatives, due to be settled many years in the future, were put on the books. Or say you want to write a contract speculating on the number of

twins to be born in Nebraska in 2020. No problem—at a price, you will easily find an obliging counterparty.

When we purchased Gen Re, it came with General Re Securities, a derivatives dealer that Charlie and I didn't want, judging it to be dangerous. We . . . are now terminating it.

But closing down a derivatives business is easier said than done. It will be a great many years before we are totally out of this operation (though we reduce our exposure daily). In fact, the reinsurance and derivatives businesses are similar: Like Hell, both are easy to enter and almost impossible to exit. . . .

Errors will usually be honest, reflecting only the human tendency to take an optimistic view of one's commitments. But the parties to derivatives also have enormous incentives to cheat in accounting for them.

Those who trade derivatives are usually paid (in whole or part) on "earnings" calculated by mark-to-market accounting. But often there is no real market (think about our contract involving twins) and "mark-to-model" is utilized. This substitution can bring on large-scale mischief.

As a general rule, contracts involving multiple reference items and distant settlement dates increase the opportunities for counterparties to use fanciful assumptions. In the twins scenario, for example, the two parties to the contract might well use differing models allowing both to show substantial profits for many years. In extreme cases, mark-to-model degenerates into what I would call mark-to-myth.

The valuation problem is far from academic: In recent years, some huge-scale frauds and near-frauds have been facilitated by derivatives trades. . . . "Mark-to-market" then turned out to be truly "mark-to-myth."

I can assure you that the marking errors in the derivatives business have not been symmetrical. Almost invariably, they have favored either the trader who was eyeing a multi-million dollar bonus or the CEO who wanted to report impressive "earnings" (or both). The bonuses were paid, and the CEO profited from his options. Only much later did shareholders learn that the reported earnings were a sham. . . .

Many people argue that derivatives reduce systemic problems, in that participants who can't bear certain risks are able to transfer them to stronger hands. These people believe that derivatives act to . . . eliminate bumps for individual participants. And, on a micro level, what they say is often true. . . .

Charlie and I believe, however, that the macro picture is dangerous and getting more so. Large amounts of risk, particularly credit risk, have become concentrated in the hands of relatively few derivatives dealers, who in addition trade extensively with one other. The troubles of one could quickly infect the others.[13]

These fears, from some of the most sophisticated people in finance, were more than fully realized. Monstrously complex derivatives became even more monstrously complex. Are CDOs not bad enough? Look at synthetic collateralized debt obligations (SCDOs). Many discussions of these claim that no one really understands them, that they were so intricate and subject to interpretation that it may be the case that no one *could* understand them. The legal documents for these are several inches thick. SCDOs are numbingly obscure. In the NPR *Planet Money* series, found on Baseline Scenario, some of their creators say as much themselves. The worst of these things seem to involve skirting banking regulations in four countries at once. All of them have the magical feature of allowing unlimited amounts to be put at risk tied to a particular asset, irrespective of how much of that asset actually exists, a deadly form of synthetic leverage. Analogies use examples of allowing everyone in town to take out insurance on one house. In normal practice, the insurer would be out the cost of the house after a fire. When there are thousands of policies, the normal single fire event can bankrupt the insurer. SCDOs in particular seem to be a toxic mix of leverage, phantom assets, and many-times-removed counterparties that clearly establishes the inability of our current system to deal with the level of complexity and risk they embody. The legal and financial engineering hoops that are must be jumped through to do this are illustrated in Figure 12.5.

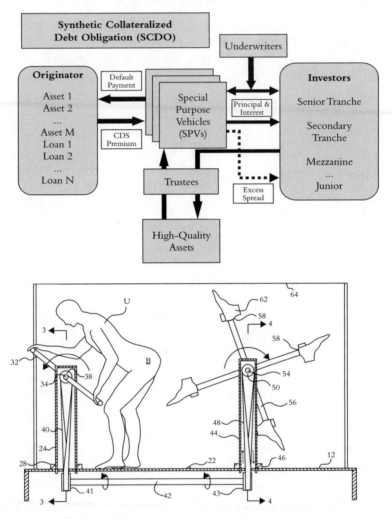

Figure 12.5 The upper panel is a simplified schematic of a synthetic collateralized debt obligation (SCDO) drawn based on various sources who for some reason seem reluctant to have their original work further exposed. The lower panel, taken from an actual U.S. patent for a "User Operated Amusement Apparatus for Kicking the User's Buttocks" is a nonsimplified schematic of the effects of SCDOs on the world's financial system.
Source: Original figure (top), U.S. Patent Number 6,283,874 (bottom).

If you and a dozen friends are at a loss as to what to wear next Halloween, you can go in a group as an SCDO. Try not to scare the children, or the adults, or me.

Take Them Out and Shoot Them

The designers of these complex derivatives created a vast edifice for derivatives analysts who had the task of building models to price them. There were many such programs, but one that seems to deserve the booby prize for being central to the crisis, and for inspiring equally dreadful imitators, made its home at Fannie Mae:

> Fannie constructed a vast network of computer programs and mathematical formulas that analyzed its millions of daily trans-actions and ranked borrowers according to their risk.
>
> Those computer programs seemingly turned Fannie into a divining rod, capable of separating pools of similar-seem-ing borrowers into safe and risky bets. The riskier the loan, the more Fannie charged to handle it. In theory, those high fees would offset any losses.
>
> With that self-assurance, the company announced in 2000 that it would buy $2 trillion in loans from low-income, minor-ity and risky borrowers by 2010.[14]

As it turned out, if this was a divining rod, it was held by a suicide bomber. Fannie (and others) built an edifice of enormous complexity and then fed it garbage. Noted systems analyst Alan Greenspan eluci-dated the old garbage in, garbage out maxim for a congressional com-mittee, to share the blame with the monster models of Fannie Mae:

> It was the failure to properly price such risky assets that precipitated the crisis. . . . In recent decades, a vast risk management and pricing system has evolved, combining the best insights of mathematicians and finance experts supported by major advances in computer and communications technol-ogy. A Nobel Prize was awarded for the discovery of the

pricing model that underpins much of the advance in derivates markets.

This modern risk management paradigm held sway for decades. The whole intellectual edifice, however, collapsed in the summer of last year because the data inputted into the risk management models generally covered only the past two decades, a period of euphoria. Had instead the models been fitted more appropriately to historic periods of stress, capital requirements would have been much higher and the financial world would be in far better shape today, in my judgment.[15]

This is a complicated way of saying they screwed up, and they should have known better. A pithy truth offered up in one of the first courses I took at MIT was that "engineering is the linearization of everything." Figures 12.6 through 12.9 are a thousand-fold simplification of what went wrong, in pictures.

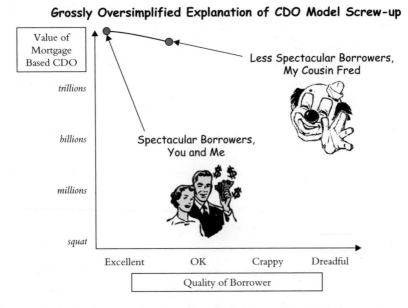

Figure 12.6 In the past, mortgage-based CDO securities built from mortgages issued to stellar borrowers, like you and me, had very high values. Less spectacular borrowers, like my cousin Fred, who drinks a bit and misses the occasional payment, made for slightly lower-value CDOs.

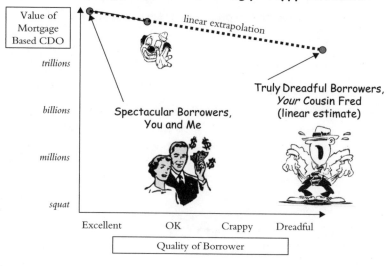

Figure 12.7 In the past, no one in his or her right mind would actually issue a mortgage to *your* cousin Fred, who previously lived in a Dumpster and traded his payment coupons for crystal meth. So modelers (in effect) used the extrapolated data from spectacular and decent borrowers to model the value of securities made from mortgages issued to deadbeats like Fred 2.

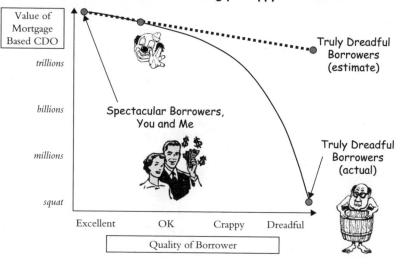

Figure 12.8 Lo and behold, evil Fred didn't make a single payment! And worse, he got six more mortgages and set up four crack houses and two indoor pot farms, making no payments on any of those, either. (Something like this actually happened in Diamond Bar, California.)

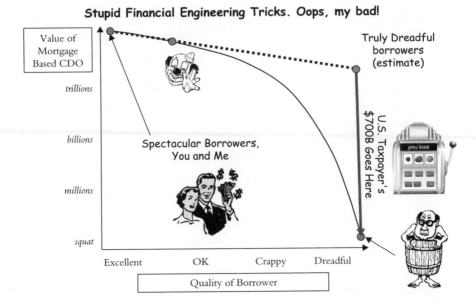

Figure 12.9   Oops. Greenspan was right. Garbage in, garbage out. Throw in 30-to-1 leverage and hope you're too big to fail! Send U.S. taxpayers bill for $700 billion.

This is an oversimplified, wise-ass version of a much more complicated story. But sadly, it is the low-tech version of Greenspan's correct high-tech explanation: These guys should have known better.

Tech Hall of Shame

We've pinned part of the blame for the meltdown on three technological screw-ups:

- One of omission—a lack of transparency that let the problem be ignored for too long.
- And two of commission:
  - Creation of excessively complex, nearly incomprehensible derivative securities.
  - Creation of even more complex, more incomprehensible pricing models, driven by the wrong data.

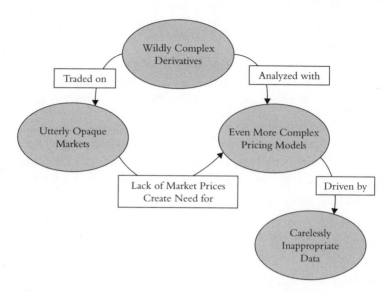

Figure 12.10 An interconnected structure for disaster: uses and abuses of technology in bringing on the Great Mess of '08. There are many other causes, over-leverage, moral hazard ("heads, I win, tails, you lose"), and heads in the sand. These are the ones that involve wires.

Figure 12.10 shows the vicious circle of financial technology errors that contributed to our sorry situation today—the design of monstrously complex incomprehensible derivatives, which then required monstrously complex valuation models, since there was no transparent market to provide this information.

This is far from a complete picture, as it omits reckless rating behavior, AWOL regulation, head-in-the-sand management, and transfer of risk from those who created it to one counterparty and then the next, and ultimately to all of us.

Quants Who Saw It Coming

There was an e-mail thread that was passed around among a group of MIT people working in quantitative finance. It seems to have disappeared, along with many other lists of this sort, replaced by discussions on the Web. Most of the time, the thread was comprised of requests for open source mathematical code, technical questions, and an occasional puzzle. Toward the end of 2007, inspired by a couple of "blame the quants" articles in *Technology Review* and *Forbes*, the topics turned to the stressed financial system. By 2008, the list appeared to have vanished. Here are some excerpts from the 2007 discussion, which give a sense of what it was like when the sky started to fall.

It didn't take a quant to realize the inordinate risks being generated. Some of these guidelines were blatant, creating notes commonly referred to as "liar loans."

Everyone was simply crossing their fingers that the accidents wouldn't happen all at once or all in the same place. Everyone knew there would be accidents; they were just hoping for them to be spread out in time and geography.

It was commonly known by industry insiders that these loans would blow up. You could go to any mortgage conference and hear the jokes and labels they gave to these loans and underwriting guidelines. Believe me, this was no surprise to anyone in the industry. The only surprise was how fast investors walked away from buying this crap.

For quants in control functions (or rating agencies), there's often a culture that your job is to produce reports saying everything's fine rather than to make sensible assessments of risk.

I certainly used to come under pressure not to look at things that were worrying so I could write a report saying that I had found no problems.

A little over five years ago, I headed up a Ph.D.–level analytics subprime department at one of the largest Wall Street firms. I received a request to value a portfolio. My group provided a best, worst, and expected valuation. Three levels up, the report was sent back to me to eliminate the expected and worst case scenarios in the report. I asked who the report was ultimately for. I was told "investors." I told my boss that I didn't feel comfortable providing an incomplete picture. A few days later, I was called in to speak to my boss's boss's boss. He told me not to worry about it. He said no one takes projections seriously and if something negative affects the projection down the road, you can always point to something in the environment that nobody would have expected you to have known. Well, consequently, I stuck to my guns and refused to cut out of the report the downside scenarios. I told them that I would supply the complete report and if they wanted to alter it, then that was up to them, not me.

Upton Sinclair wrote, "It is difficult to get a man to understand something when his salary depends upon his not understanding it."

When I first tried to get some traction on understanding these issues, I hoped that this would turn out to be an unforeseeable, unavoidable confluence of independent events. It wasn't. If Apollo 11 had ended up a pile of wreckage in the Sea of Tranquility, we might attribute it to a random accident or a bad component. If the same thing happened to Apollo 12, 13, 14, 15, 16, and 17, that conclusion would be unsupportable. Alan Greenspan and a few others are to be commended, if not applauded, for acknowledging their errors.

This chapter is essentially an educated lay outsider's viewpoint. Believe it or not, based on comments from insiders, I have tried to moderate and qualify the harsher judgments here, but as a society we must not let this happen again.

Notes

1. Robert C. Merton and Zvi Bodie, "The Design of Financial Systems: Toward a Synthesis of Function and Structure," *Journal of Investment Management* 3, no. 1 (First Quarter 2005):http://www.people.hbs.edu/rmerton/Designpaperfinal.pdf

2. http://baselinescenario.com.

3. "Financial Crisis for Beginners," Baseline Scenario, http://baselinescenario.com/financial-crisis-for-beginners/.

4. OTC markets are not inherently a bad idea; they work for corporate debt and other securities. A lack of reporting for these toxic derivative securities created a dark market on an unprecedented scale.

5. Carol Loomis, "Robert Rubin on the Job He Never Wanted," *Fortune*, November 28, 2007, http://money.cnn.com/2007/11/09/news/newsmakers/merrill_rubin.fortune/index.htm.

6. Marking to market is the process of evaluating a security to reflect its current market value instead of its purchase price or book value. Marking to market is generally a good idea, but there are circumstances when it can serve to amplify the effect of what might otherwise be a short-lived mini-panic. A discussion is beyond the scope of this chapter.

7. Ben Bernanke, "Reducing Systemic Risk," Jackson Hole, Wyoming, August 22, 2008, http://federalreserve.gov/newsevents/speech/bernanke20080822a.htm.

8. "PWG Announces Initiatives to Strengthen OTC Derivatives Oversight and Infrastructure," November 14, 2008, www.ustreas.gov/press/releases/hp1272.htm.

9. Rosenblatt Securities, "Trading Talk," October 17, 2008, http://rblt.com/newsletter_details.aspx?id=38.

10. Sharon Weinberger, *Imaginary Weapons: A Journey Through the Pentagon's Scientific Underworld* (New York: Nation Books, 2006).

11. The 1940 newsreel of the collapse is not to be missed; see it here: www.youtube.com/watch?v=HxTZ446tbzE, or just search YouTube for "Tacoma Narrows Newsreel."

12. See the "Top 10 Worst Engineering Disasters" at http://listverse.com/science/top-10-worst-engineering-disasters/.

13. Chairman's Letter, 2002 Berkshire Hathaway Annual Report, pp. 13–15, www.berkshirehathaway.com/2002ar/2002ar.pdf.

14. Charles Duhigg, "Pressured to Take More Risk, Fannie Reached a Tipping Point," *New York Times*, October 4, 2008.

15. Alan Greenspan, October 24, 2008, hearing, House Committee on Oversight and Government Reform, http://oversight.house.gov/story.asp?id=2256.

Chapter 13

Structural Ideas for the Economic Rescue

Fractional Homes and New Banks

Mom used to say, "If you don't have something nice to say, don't say anything at all." I clearly ignored that advice in the previous chapter, with the "mad as hell" opening and analogies to an exploding meth lab run by the neighbors. This chapter is more polite and more positive. It is about two ideas that can help us out of the mess we are in. Both have a systems analysis flavor, and both are from MIT graduates, who have the predilection and training to think this way.

The two ideas discussed here, fractional home ownership and a new American bank initiative, each have a great systems analysis soul—removing unnecessary complexity and negative feedback loops and creating positive feedback via incentive structures to make them work. One of the best examples of a structural approach to societal problems occurred in Germany in the 1970s. Some German rivers had become so polluted with factory waste that they would catch fire. Some were paved over and declared industrial sewers. Plants were simply required to take in their water just downstream from where they pumped out their waste. The garbage became their problem instead of everyone else's. River fires became a thing of the past, and the concrete covers were removed.

Fractional Home Ownership

John O'Brien is one of the founding fathers of the field of financial engineering. He understands the field as well as anyone, from both academic and practical experience. As a founder of Leland, O'Brien, and Rubinstein (LOR), he was one of the inventors of portfolio insurance, a dynamic hedging strategy for equity portfolios to reduce downside risk.[1] Portfolio insurance worked very well in relatively stable markets, and by October 1987, firms managing over $60 billion in assets were using the system. The basic idea was to sell futures in declining markets to protect the underlying assets, and the desired results were achieved. However, when the stock market tanked on October 19, 1987, there was insufficient liquidity in the futures markets to absorb the selling by portfolio insurers and others, and the volume of selling drove down the futures prices and in turn the stocks themselves. Portfolio insurance was not the only or even the principal cause of the crash, but it may have contributed to the speed and size of the decline.

John has taken the lessons of portfolio insurance to heart, and perhaps more than others, considers the unintended consequences of financial ideas. In that spirit, he proposed what I believe is a particularly well thought out approach to dealing with the underlying cause of the Mess of '08—the collapse of home prices. His idea lets people remain in their homes, avoiding the displacement, grief, and blight that are plaguing many communities. This is possible by creating simple, transparent securities that allow the vast collection of investors to participate in solving this problem. Fed Chairman Bernanke (yet another MIT grad, Ph.D. in economics, 1979) suggested the general outline of this plan in his March 2008 speech entitled "Reducing Preventable Mortgage Foreclosures":[2]

> The fact that many troubled borrowers have little or no equity suggests that greater use of principal write-downs or short payoffs, perhaps with shared appreciation features, would be in the best interests of both borrowers and lenders.

John has put meat on the bones of this suggestion. The remainder of this section is from his exposition of this idea.[3]

Sharing the Risk, Sharing the Rewards

Stabilizing the housing market effectively and equitably requires more innovative approaches than just lowering mortgage interest rates and extending mortgage maturities. The two key objectives should be: (1) avoiding preventable foreclosures, and (2) increasing the affordability of the existing housing stock, thus increasing housing demand. Both of these issues can be addressed by allowing home financing to include a minority, passive equity partner. With such a partner, homeowners can rightsize, i.e. adjust to an affordable level, their financial obligations by owning less than 100 percent of their homes, while maintaining all the benefits of home ownership. With a properly standardized fractional home ownership security, institutional investors could and would be that partner.

The Innovation: A Home Equity Fractional Interest (HEFI) Security

Currently home purchases are financed entirely with the owner's personal capital (down payment) and debt (mortgage). There is no opportunity for the homeowner to get external *equity* financing, where a passive investor shares in the financial gains and losses of the home's value.

At present, therefore, a homeowner who wants to live in a $300,000 home must bear $300,000 of exposure (and expense) to the housing market. The homeowner's consumption of housing equals the homeowner's investment in housing. Arguably, this makes no sense, because owning a home—rather than renting—is partly a lifestyle choice and partly an investment choice. Choosing home ownership should be possible either as a 100 percent owner with a large mortgage or a majority/controlling owner with a smaller mortgage, with the exact mix determined by the homeowner's financial circumstances and personal preferences. There is no reason why home ownership must be all or nothing.

A home equity fractional interest (HEFI) security would separate the consumption and investment decisions. For example, a homeowner might own 80 percent of a $300,000 home (with $240,000 financed by a down payment and mortgage) and an outside, passive equity investor would own the other 20 percent. The homeowner consumes housing at the $300,000 level, but has only $240,000 of exposure (and expense) to the housing market.

This innovation would have major short-term benefits for foreclosure mitigation and long-term benefits for stabilizing home prices. And it is possible now.

Mitigating the Foreclosure Crisis—Avoiding Preventable Foreclosures

The majority of *preventable* foreclosures consist of an owner-occupied home where the owner wishes to remain in the home, but only has the financial capacity to maintain a mortgage of, say, 80 percent of the home's *current* market value. A foreclosure could be prevented if the lender restructured the current mortgage to 80 percent of the *current* market value *plus* an HEFI security.

The homeowner pays for the mortgage reduction with the HEFI. Because the homeowner now has equity in the home (previously, the mortgage likely exceeded the home's *current* market value) and a sustainable mortgage expense, foreclosure is unlikely. This restructuring is not a bailout, doesn't risk taxpayer money, and is not unfair to responsible homeowners or renters.

Stabilizing Home Prices—Balancing Housing Supply and Demand

Traditionally, a home seller must find a buyer who *both* wants to consume the shelter and amenities provided by the home *and* has the means and desire to purchase it. This double-match problem makes it harder to match buyers and sellers, thus reducing effective housing demand and putting added pressure on home prices. The HEFI solves this problem—if the buyer wants to own a large house without taking large exposure to the market (and the resulting added cost), passive equity investors can make up the difference. This increases effective housing demand, which would help absorb the nation's excess housing supply, thereby stabilizing prices at a higher equilibrium price than would otherwise be possible.

A Capital Market for Home Equity Fractional Interest Securities

The HEFI security represents a passive investor interest in a home— just as a share of stock represents a passive investment in a company. Institutional investors such as pension and endowment funds would be interested in HEFIs to achieve diversification beyond stocks and bonds.

The single-family, owner-occupied (SFOO) equity asset class is as large as the entire U.S. stock market, around $10 trillion. To be properly diversified, institutional investors should hold about as much in the SFOO equity asset class as they do in stocks. Institutional investors acknowledge interest in these assets. Right now there is no practical way for institutional investors to invest in SFOO equity; HEFIs and a HEFI trading market would change this unhappy situation by creating a practical way for them to take part in this market.

New American Bank Initiative

October 2008 was a tense month, and November was no better. Was the financial sky falling? Would there be a sequel to the 2004 October election surprise message from Osama bin Laden, or worse? Would Sarah-cuda have to revert to her old Wasilla thrift store wardrobe and flat shoes? Like many other people, I kept at least one anxious eye on the news. It wasn't pretty:

> U.S. banks getting more than $163 billion from the Treasury Department for new lending are on pace to pay more than half of that sum to their shareholders, with government permission, over the next three years.
> —**Binyamin Appelbaum,** *"Banks to Continue Paying Dividends"* (**Washington Post,** *October 30, 2008*)

> Banks getting $125 billion from U.S. taxpayers to unlock the credit crunch are saying they'd rather hoard the money than use it for loans.
> —**Jody Shenn,** *"Banks Hoard Money Meant to Boost Economy, Lender Says"* (**Bloomberg.com, November 7, 2008**)

Watching CNN (with the sound off, as I tried to work on this book), I noticed Sal Khan, an earnest-looking young man, drawing colorful diagrams about the banking crisis. The Dow Jones Industrial Average, which had dropped over 450 points earlier in the day when the soon-to-be-ex-president reassured the country everything was under control, moved up more than 400 points as Sal spoke. This warranted turning on the sound and rolling back the TiVo to see what was going on. I was blown away by the simplicity and obvious merit of his proposal, and the clarity of his explanation. I was surprised that the market seemed equally impressed, since CNN is not all that big in the trading room television ratings war.[4]

Sal pointed out the reason for the problems mentioned earlier are that the banks being infused with taxpayer cash not only had no requirement to put that money back into the real economy, they had ample incentive *not* to do so. Keeping the federal cash invested in their firms for themselves was better for the bankers in terms of income, job security, and prospects to acquire other banks (plus a massive tax incentive for that, as it turned out). Hoarding the cash would reduce their risk, even though it didn't do much to improve the country's economic situation, which was the intent of the federal investment in the first place. CYA trumped USA.

I watched Sal's 15 minutes,[5] and then called in my lovely and charming wife to watch them again. "I have socks older than that guy," she said. I have seen her sock drawer, and this may be true, but it takes nothing away from the idea Sal described. I looked Sal up on the Web, and was pleased to find that he was something of a nerd on Wall Street himself, an MIT graduate (in math and computer science, two dozen graduating classes after mine) and a Harvard MBA.

He's the portfolio manager at Khan Capital Management in Palo Alto, and the founder of a free educational YouTube channel, the KhanAcademy,[6] where he has honed his teaching and colorful diagram drawing skills in over 650 videos on mathematical and financial subjects—including over a hundred on SAT preparation, and another hundred on physics. In all of them, there are tens of thousands of views, and every one I saw was rated five stars—all well-deserved raves.

It turned out that the 400-point Dow rise was a coincidence, which didn't surprise me. What did surprise me was that it also turned out there was not much follow-up interest in the idea of a system of new American banks, unencumbered by the mistakes of the past and owned by the taxpayers. It had seemed to me to be one of those Occam's razor moments, where the simplest solution is the best solution, but Sal told me it had apparently gotten lost in the 500 channels of daytime television. The idea is simple: Use part of the ocean of cash to create a newly capitalized group of regional banks that will move funds into productive, job-creating investments, without paying for the mistakes of those who created these problems or allowing them to hoard funds to cover future mistakes. Some institutions are too large and complex for this (blurring the line between government and business) but most are not.

It deserved to be heard, so Sal and I decided to rescue the new American bank idea from soap opera oblivion. We put together a paper version, with more serious-looking diagrams. We passed it around to our serious friends for serious comments, and added answers to their questions, or rethought aspects of the plan based on them. After a month, we put it up on the Berkeley Center for Innovative Financial Technology (CIFT) web site[7] and let it loose on the Web. Tim O'Reilly, the best publisher of all things digital and organizer of the Money:Tech conferences, put it on his O'Reilly Radar Blog, where a lively discussion ensued. Paul Kedrosky put it on his widely read "Infectious Greed: Technology, Finance, Venture Capital, and the Money Culture" web site[8] and daily e-mail. The *Financial Times* picked it up from there. We got lots of e-mail, and an invitation to appear in a documentary film. Slightly buffed for the book, here is the paper.

Introduction

We propose a clean, innovative, and simple approach to move capital into the investments needed to help rescue the struggling U.S. economy: Use part of the $700 billion in government funds to capitalize new banks and distribute the shares of the new entities to the American people. These new banks would then acquire the operational and human capital assets of failed banks in Federal Deposit Insurance Corporation (FDIC) receivership.

New structural flaws in the government's rescue plans are revealed on an almost daily basis. The incentives for these plans to work to the benefit of the country, and not the failed firms, are poorly aligned. The new American bank initiative (NABI) would involve no moral hazard,* no hoarding banks, no government ownership, and no throwing good money after bad. Most important, it will immediately provide $7 trillion or more in unencumbered lending capacity to real projects—green energy, infrastructure, and auto and other manufacturing. It is also the best plan for preserving the operational and human assets of failed banks and saving existing solvent institutions by making everyone confident in the availability of funds again.

Dysfunctional Finance

A core issue in the current crisis is that the financial system is no longer functioning properly as a conduit of capital from savers to investment projects that generate real economic growth. The focus of every major proposal to date has been to inject liquidity and capital into current institutions in the hope that it will build confidence and start banks lending again to real projects (i.e., unclog the conduit). Unfortunately, these solutions ignore the fact that every relevant institution is in survival mode and will only use any liquidity or capital injections as a cushion in case their sources of funding dry up or their assets have to be further written down (very likely considering where we are in the economic cycle). Even worse, they all involve some type of moral hazard by cushioning the losses for equity and unsecured debt holders (who are to varying degrees responsible for the crisis). The recent reports of capital injections effectively being used for dividends and deferred compensation are perhaps the most heinous examples of taxpayer funds being used to directly pay existing equity holders and management.

Here we briefly evaluate each of the bailout variations so far, their intended effect, why they are unlikely to work, and why they will probably lead to an extension of the crisis. Finally, we propose an alternate plan based on capitalizing new banks with clean balance sheets and discuss its potential effects.

---

*Moral hazard is the prospect that a party insulated from risk may behave differently from the way it would behave if it were fully exposed to the risk.

Zombie Banks

One of the major functions of banks is to act as a capital conduit from those with savings to those needing capital for investment projects. The banks generate returns for their investors by borrowing money at low rates and lending at higher rates. (See Figure 13.1.) This process, however, begins to break down if the banks' access to capital becomes uncertain or the banks believe that their assets may have to be written down further (probably both since no one wants to lend to or invest in someone with shrinking assets).

If a bank is fundamentally insolvent (i.e., its assets are worth less than its liabilities) or thinks it might eventually be insolvent, it will delay writing down its assets as much as possible to give the appearance of solvency and attempt to raise new equity capital in the interim. Any new capital injected into the bank will not be used to take on new risk (make new loans), but will instead be used as an equity cushion as further asset write-downs are taken. The net effect is that the bank neither lends (lives) nor declares bankruptcy (dies) and thus becomes a zombie bank. Any capital injected into the bank (which could be used for real nonbank investment projects but is not) will only slow the bank's death and help cushion the losses that the equity and unsecured credit holders would eventually take. Even worse, delaying its death only prolongs the crisis by extending the period of uncertainty regarding whether more failures are imminent and who is next. (See Figure 13.2.)

Even if a bank is confident of its solvency (i.e., that after all is said and done, its assets will still be larger than its liabilities), it needs to be acutely aware of its ongoing access to credit. No bank can be certain

Figure 13.1   In a normally functioning economy, the financial system (commercial banks, investment banks, mutual funds, etc.) acts as the conduit between savers who have individual pools of capital and the investment projects (like building factories or investing in engineering) that need the capital to grow the economy.

Figure 13.2   Once banks become uncertain of the degree of future write-downs and their access to funding, they begin hoarding cash, and the real investment projects starve for capital.

that, as its current debt matures (often imminently), it will be able to replace the debt with new funding. To avoid a future liquidity crisis, the bank will hoard any capital it is given through new loans or equity injections and thus become a bank that does not make new loans (still a zombie, albeit one that is less likely to die).

The bottom line is that it would be irrational and irresponsible (to a bank's shareholders) for any bank with shrinking assets and uncertain access to credit to take on new risk (make new loans) no matter how much new capital is provided to it. Given this, no plan that involves injecting arbitrary amounts of capital into existing banks has a reasonable chance of undoing this zombie logjam in our financial system. If anything, these capital injections are more likely to prolong the problem. (See Figure 13.3.)

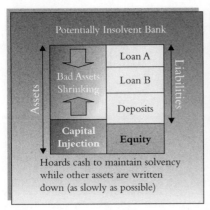
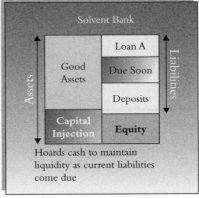

Figure 13.3   Banks with shrinking assets due to write-downs hoard capital injections to prolong the appearance of solvency. Solvent banks also hoard cash to preserve liquidity in case loans that come due cannot be renewed. It would, in fact, be irrational for any bank to take on new risk (i.e., make new loans) when things are so uncertain.

Troubled Asset Relief Program (TARP)

The Troubled Asset Relief Program (TARP) is the incarnation of the so-called bailout bill (the Emergency Economic Stabilization Act of 2008), passed on October 3, 2008, along with various baubles like subsidies for makers of wooden arrows and operators of racetracks. The bill was much larger than the original three-page "Trust me, really" version initially sent to Congress by the Treasury, but given the changes since the passage, what was actually in the bill doesn't matter (unless you're in the arrow business). The government has its $700 billion, and is still charging up and down hills trying to decide what to do with it.

TARP—Plan A The first substantive version proposed was for the Treasury to spend $700 billion buying toxic assets from banks. This was based on two premises:

1. The banks holding these assets are truly solvent, but the uncertainty around the value of the assets makes other banks less willing to lend to them (since if the assets are written down enough, it may make the holding banks insolvent).
2. The markets for assets are somehow broken, which has prevented the banks from selling the assets for fair prices.

Both of these arguments are marginal at best, considering the continuing degradation in the quality of the underlying assets (mainly mortgages), the ongoing rate of write-downs, and what these assets have been sold for in recent transactions between sophisticated parties (all more sophisticated than the government). Even if the two aforementioned assumptions were correct, they did absolutely nothing to address the zombie-but-rational bank behavior described in the previous section. Perhaps the most damning aspect of this plan was the fact that Secretary Paulson and Chairman Bernanke had to "scare the heck out of everyone and destroy all confidence in the financial system" to pass a bill whose purpose was ostensibly "to inject confidence into the financial system."

As it was initially marketed, the TARP was most probably just an attempt to push the CDO (toxic assets) markets back into operation by convincing potential investors that the government was about to go in and start throwing around $700 billion willy-nilly. If people believed that this was indeed going to happen, the rational thing to do would be to attempt to front-run the government and buy the assets before the government raised the market price (through the $700 billion of artificial demand), and then offload them (possibly to the government itself) at a higher price. It is clear that no one bought Paulson's bluff, which explains why the focus was shifted to buying preferred equity shortly after the bill was passed.

TARP—Plan B Plan A vanished when the realization hit that it was unworkable and impractical. The Treasury now intends to use the $700 billion to buy preferred equity in banks based on two premises:

1. These banks are solvent and liquid.
2. Because they are solvent and liquid, they will use the new capital to make new loans.

First, the government is in no position to be able to determine which banks are solvent, since the write-downs are likely to continue at an increasing pace as the economy worsens (and many of the banks themselves do not know if they are solvent). Even more, any bank that is truly solvent and liquid and willing to make loans needs no new capital to do so. This plan is clearly an attempt to just stave off another Lehman Brothers scenario with little hope of making the zombie institutions alive again. The government claims that it is forcing banks to participate to lessen the stigma of being associated with the investments. This statement alone implies that much of the money is going to banks that need it to stay afloat and are thus likely to hoard it.

This variation of the TARP is, at best, a temporary stopgap to prevent another major institution from failing in the short term. Besides wasting taxpayer money with limited upside, it will continue to muddle the picture as to which banks are truly insolvent and not worth saving. By not allowing the bad banks to die, the government (like Japan in the 1990s) is extending the period of time over which the financial sector will be a capital sink versus a capital conduit and over which we are all forced to muddle through in a zombie economy.

European Variations on the TARP Theme By taking controlling interests in the banks, the Europeans have injected equity capital in a much more forcible way. This is arguably better than the TARP variations for three reasons:

1. The governments now have control and can force lending by the institutions.
2. The European taxpayers will participate in any future upside (not likely since many of the banks are probably insolvent).
3. It properly dilutes the common shareholders and management of the firms in question.

Unfortunately, these actions will still bail out the unsecured creditors of these banks. Even more, they have a low likelihood of working and may cause more long-term damage than good since they are akin to moving around the limbs of a dead body to make it look alive.

These governments do not have the expertise or resources to force the lending into areas of the real economy where it is needed most. Most likely, they will throw good money after bad investments (in order to avoid further write-downs), causing these banks to become an even bigger black hole of taxpayer money than in the TARP variations. Most damningly, it exacerbates the too-big-to-fail problem and will crowd out new, healthy private banks that may have otherwise emerged in the next few years.

A Simple Structural Solution

The $700 billion is a huge amount of money—more than the equity book values of Goldman Sachs, Morgan Stanley, JPMorgan, Citigroup, Washington Mutual, Bank of America, and Wachovia *combined*. This money should be used to capitalize new banks throughout the country. To be operational as quickly as possible and to preserve valuable human and operational capital, these banks will buy good operational assets from insolvent banks in FDIC receivership. To avoid a concentration of risk, the capital should be distributed among at least 20 new institutions. To avoid the hazards of government ownership or sponsorship, the shares of these institutions should be distributed to the American people (each bank can have 300 million shares—one for every American man, woman, and child). Rather than using taxpayer money to cushion losses of previous bad investments, this will allow all of the capital to facilitate lending to the real economy, where it will prevent the current recession from becoming a depression and expedite the recovery, which would otherwise be many years away. This plan is akin to preserving the body of banks while replacing their old brains (senior management and risk management policies) and their old hearts (balance sheets). (See Figure 13.4.)

Newly capitalized banks with clean balance sheets have no reason to hoard capital. If capitalized with $700 billion, they would have the ability to make $7 trillion in new loans. By being distributed across the country, they will be close to the real projects that need investment. The shares of the new banks will be distributed to the American

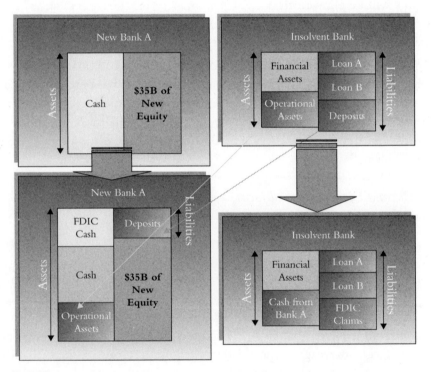

Figure 13.4 Once an insolvent bank enters FDIC receivership, the deposits, operational assets, and employees will be taken over by newly capitalized Bank A. It will pay book value for the assets. The rest of the assets will stay in receivership and be divided between the creditors and the FDIC. Bank A is able to become quickly operational with its share of the NABI $300B+ of lending capacity. Even more, the operational and human assets of the insolvent bank are preserved rather than liquidated.

people, and they will be traded on current exchanges, thus avoiding government control and giving private citizens a direct stake in the financial system. Existing solvent banks will benefit from funding from the new banks and are more likely to start lending again as the new banks make access to funding more certain.

As mentioned, $700 billion of new equity capital in new balance sheets could be directly used to fund $7 trillion in lending in the real economy. Not only would it directly address the crux of the problem, but it is actually the best way to save the good current banks. If the risk-reward trade-off is there, these new banks could lend directly to the old banks that are solvent. As existing solvent banks regain confidence in the availability of funds, they too will start lending. The insolvent old banks will be allowed to fail gracefully, and many of their good operational, human, and intangible assets will be preserved as they are bought by the new banks. Perhaps most importantly, there is a considerable amount of private capital on the sidelines (both at home and abroad) that would love to invest in the American financial system, just not in banks with shrinking/toxic assets and uncertain access to credit. Given this, these new banks could easily attract private capital and deposits extending their lending capacity well beyond $7 trillion. More than the capital, the government's real value added would be streamlining new bank charters, Federal Reserve membership, and the transfer of operational assets out of receivership.

This plan involves no moral hazard of taxpayers taking the downside for imprudent decisions (thus encouraging future bubbles and imprudent decisions), since the old equity and debt holders are left to fight over the financial assets of the insolvent banks (like a normal bankruptcy). It involves no government ownership. It is also much more salable to the American people than any alternative since they get to partake in the success of the new institutions. Even if the powers that be are insistent on proceeding with the TARP variations, there needs to be a plan B for the likely case that the TARP fails (although we would save several hundred billion dollars if this were plan A). Our economy and financial system will emerge from the malaise only once new, clean banks of respectable scale emerge unfettered by an ugly past. We can wait perhaps 10 years or more for this to happen naturally, or we can seed the process immediately and save the country (and probably the world) from at least a decade of economic stagnation.

Not a Wild and Crazy Idea

What we propose may initially seem drastic, overly ambitious, logistically difficult, or insensitive to the importance of current financial institutions. On further thought, however, it is no more drastic than a small cadre of Treasury officials directly managing $700 billion with no controls or oversight or real, overarching direction. Logistically, a government that can orchestrate the complex Bear Stearns, AIG, and Fannie Mae/Freddie Mac deals almost overnight should be able to quickly orchestrate the formation of new, clean banks and the transfer of operational assets into them. As far as the present institutions are concerned, nothing will work better to stop the writing-down of assets and to halt further financial bankruptcies than real lending from new institutions with the confidence to act.

Sal and I may have seriously damaged our career opportunities at certain financial institutions by promulgating this idea, and I do check my pillow for a horse's head more often than I used to, but it is for the best of reasons. Even more important than the notion that this plan will actually work is the deeper idea that it is a bold project that will capture the imagination of the American people. This country has no shortage of ethical financial management talent, and they will be attracted to these banks by their sense of patriotic duty and the chance to partake in something of historical significance. It will, in fact, make Americans once again feel that they have a real stake in the financial future of our country.

NABI: Frequently Asked Questions

Isn't this plan dismissive of the systemic importance of existing banks and the need to keep them afloat?

No, if anything, we strongly believe that this is the best plan for making sure that existing solvent banks will survive in a non-zombie state since it will make them comfortable with their own access to short-term capital. We also need to come to terms with the idea that much of the current banking system is in fact collectively insolvent and the problem is much, much deeper than one of liquidity and confidence. If the current banking system is solvent, this plan will help save it. If it is not solvent, then this plan prevents a financial system collapse from turning into an economic collapse since we will still have new conduit institutions between savers of capital and businesses that need it.

If these new banks can make money in this environment, why isn't the private sector (hedge funds, private equity funds, etc.) starting new banks on its own?

The private sector will eventually do this over many years, but only the government can coordinate this type of activity (streamline charters, Federal Reserve membership, and transfer of assets from FDIC receivership) and provide capital on the scale necessary to seed entities that will be of sufficient size in the near term. Large private equity funds may be natural partners with the government (their expertise being the takeover/restructuring of operational assets with new capital structures), but they could not do this on their own. Even more, any individual new bank will be overwhelmed by the systemic failures of the current financial system. Only a large number of new banks of scale formed through government coordination can collectively weather this storm (and make positive-return investments, which are critical for preserving the injected capital and making sure that the investments are made where they are most needed).

How can a new, large bank be started from scratch in a short amount of time?

Several hundred commercial banks are expected to fail in the next few years, and they will go into receivership by the FDIC. The operational hard assets (branches, IT systems, etc.) and the majority of the employees are perfectly good and would most likely be let go or liquidated even if the FDIC were to arrange a shotgun wedding with an existing bank. Rather than dissolving these valuable operational and human capital assets, they could be bought at book value by one of the new banks (which would also take over the deposits). Not only will this allow New Bank A to be operational very quickly, but the day-to-day operations of the bank assets could continue uninterrupted (preventing interruptions to capital access by small businesses and access to deposits). The New Bank A team would then replace senior management, define new risk guidelines, and do some restructuring, and it will then be a good, operational bank with a clean balance sheet formed in a very short amount of time.

What about directly helping homeowners restructure their mortgages to prevent further asset price contraction?

There is room for restructuring some mortgages (it will probably benefit the lender), but the bulk of recent mortgages (and older ones where the homeowners took on home equity loans) are just flat-out worth more than the house and it would actually be in the borrower's best interest to walk away. It will also be very logistically difficult to renegotiate these mortgages on a one-off basis. Housing prices are still well above both the long-term trend line and what they need to be to make sense as an investment, and any government intervention now will, at best, temporarily distort markets and prolong the crisis. The single best way that we can help the average American (including renters) is to provide capital to real-world investments with the highest return for their given level of risk (since they arguably add the most value to the economy), which is exactly what these new banks will do. A quick housing price correction will be less painful than one drawn out by government intervention.

The Resolution Trust Corporation after the savings and loan (S&L) crisis was successful. Isn't the TARP a similar idea?

The original TARP proposal has been marketed as a plan similar to the seemingly successful Resolution Trust Corporation (RTC) that handled the assets of the failed savings and loans in the early 1990s. There is, however, one glaring difference: The RTC took over assets *after* the S&Ls failed, whereas the TARP proposes to take over assets *before* the banks fail in an attempt to "inject confidence" and prop them up. There was no moral hazard issue with the RTC since the guilty parties were all wiped out and it did not attempt to prop up zombie S&Ls. The NABI proposal this paper advocates is actually much closer to the RTC since it advocates preserving the systemic value of banks' operational and human assets while punishing those who made inappropriate decisions. It goes one step further by quickly placing the assets in the hands of multiple private managers (who would be accountable to the American people, the shareholders) rather than a small cadre of government officials.

What about the $60+ trillion in credit default swaps?

Many people fear that if major insolvent institutions are allowed to fail and potentially default on their derivative contracts insuring bonds (credit default swaps), that it would create a chain reaction of derivative defaults, asset write-downs, and further bank failures. This is a valid concern, but existing bailout plans only defer the problem. This could be the subject of another paper, but the government should create a clearinghouse for these contracts as quickly as possible so that we can begin to unwind offsetting claims and have a clearer picture of the net liability. This could be done in conjunction with the initiative described in this paper.

It looks like short-term credit between banks is thawing. Doesn't this mean that the TARP is beginning to work?

There are some indicators that rates for short-term interbank loans have come off their highs. This is more due to the liquidity injections from the Federal Reserve, which has increased the size of its balance sheet by $800 billion relative to only a few months ago. This has nothing to do with the TARP and is an unsustainable situation.

Some people have suggested that the larger banks will use the TARP equity injections to buy weaker banks. Doesn't this solve the problem?

Larger banks' buying weaker banks just defers and worsens the problem. If the weaker bank is insolvent and has negative equity (likely), then the acquisition will just infect the balance sheet of the stronger bank (making it potentially insolvent). We will then be left with a more structurally important bank being at risk—a bank that is possibly considered too big to fail. Also, as the balance sheets are merged, asset values will become further muddled and opaque, which will only increase market uncertainty. Bottom line: this is akin to placing a burning match under a flammable carpet and pretending that it is not there.

Still Mad, but Ever Hopeful

It took great deal of imagination, in a negative sense, to create the Great Mess of '08, and we will need a great deal of positive imagination to get out of it. The magnitude of the problem is staggering. Previous financial crises have involved dollar amounts that are lost in the round-off for this one. Long Term Capital Management's near failure was a $3.5 billion problem. The size of the federal rescue goes well beyond the $700 billion in the initial rescue plan. One estimate,[9] including the hidden tax breaks for banks and the Citigroup rescue, totals $4.62 trillion through November 2008, and compares this figure to total inflation-adjusted dollar equivalents for virtually every major federal project in the history of the country, which add up to less than $4 trillion:

	Cost	Inflation-Adjusted Cost
Marshall Plan	$12.7 billion	$115.3 billion
Louisiana Purchase	$15 million	$217 billion
Race to the moon	$36.4 billion	$237 billion
S&L crisis	$153 billion	$256 billion
Korean War	$54 billion	$454 billion
New Deal	$32 billion (est.)	$500 billion
Invasion of Iraq	$551 billion	$597 billion
Vietnam War	$111 billion	$698 billion
NASA	$416.7 billion	$851.2 billion
Total		**$3.92 trillion**

This is an amazing number, roughly 40 percent of the national debt and 30 percent of gross domestic product (GDP). To comprehend this using the visual side of your brain, look at Figure 13.5.

Dealing with a multifaceted problem of this scale is unprecedented. It will require unprecedented imagination. The ideas in this chapter

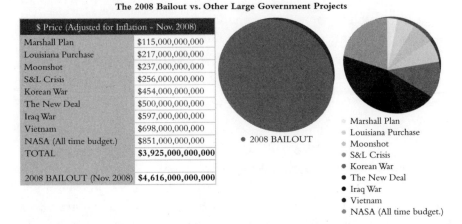

The 2008 Bailout vs. Other Large Government Projects

$ Price (Adjusted for Inflation - Nov. 2008)	
Marshall Plan	$115,000,000,000
Louisiana Purchase	$217,000,000,000
Moonshot	$237,000,000,000
S&L Crisis	$256,000,000,000
Korean War	$454,000,000,000
The New Deal	$500,000,000,000
Iraq War	$597,000,000,000
Vietnam	$698,000,000,000
NASA (All time budget.)	$851,000,000,000
TOTAL	$3,925,000,000,000
2008 BAILOUT (Nov. 2008)	$4,616,000,000,000

- 2008 BAILOUT

- Marshall Plan
- Louisiana Purchase
- Moonshot
- S&L Crisis
- Korean War
- The New Deal
- Iraq War
- Vietnam
- NASA (All time budget.)

Figure 13.5 Visualizing the bailout.
Source: Courtesy of VoltageCreative.com. Copyright 2008.

show that there is no deficit there. I am grateful to Sal Khan and John O'Brien for their efforts. Too many good ideas (and, thankfully, a planet-load of junk) are lost in the ephemera of the Web, so I am hopeful that including them here will help. I expect that much of this conversation will continue on NerdsOnWallStreet.com.

Notes

1. Andrew Kupfer, "Leland, O'Brien, and Rubinstein: The Guys Who Gave Us Portfolio Insurance," *Fortune*, January 4, 1988, http://money.cnn.com/magazines/fortune/fortune_archive/1988/01/04/70047/index.htm.

2. Ben S. Bernanke, speaking at the Independent Community Bankers of America Annual Convention, Orlando, Florida, March 4, 2008, www.federalreserve.gov/newsevents/speech/bernanke20080304a.htm.

3. John O'Brien, "Stabilizing the Housing Market," working paper, November 11, 2008. A similar article appeared in the *Christian Science Monitor*, November 26, 2008, www.csmonitor.com/2008/1126/p09s02-coop.html. Links to further discussion of this topic are found at CIFT Berkeley, http://cift.haas.berkeley.edu/systemsview.html and at Home Equity Securities LLC, www.homeequitysecurities.com/.

4. It's ahead of the Home Shopping channel, but way behind CNBC and Bloomberg, and, on most days, ESPN.

5. You can watch those 15 minutes here: www.youtube.com/watch?v=_ZAlj2gu0eM, or search YouTube for "CNN: Understanding the Crisis." A variation of this idea was first suggested to Sal Khan by Todd Plutsky, his friend and classmate from Harvard Business School.

6. All 650 videos can be seen at www.youtube.com/user/kahnacademy.

7. http://cift.haas.berkeley.edu/nabi-intro.html. This will doubtlessly evolve further past the date of this writing; the current version will be kept at the CIFT page.

8. http://paul.kedrosky.com.

9. Barry Ritholtz, *Bailout Nation: How Easy Money Corrupted Wall Street and Shook the World Economy* (New York: McGraw-Hill, 2009), excerpted here: www.boingboing.net/2008/11/25/bailout-costs-more-t.html.

today
Much
GridPoint
work
Research
Brattle
generation
want
carbon
already
first
plants
NERDS
consumers
energy
way
competitive
simple
Smart
pricing
load
one
meters
new
distribution
BTUs
Figure
WALL
briefing
tates
need
many
percent
technology
use
technologies
duration
GREEN
curve
solar
distributed
Department
utilities
devices
Emilie
market
next
power
area
dropped
decisions
trading
STREET
industry
may
efficiency
demand
Bits billion
U.S
Systems
source
markets
paper
small
CHAPTER
control
years
large
electricity
Bucks
designed
RAND
building
now
last
time
done
create
customers
electric
using
cost
savings
financial
back
allow

Chapter 14

Nerds Gone Green

Nerds on Wall Street, off Wall Street

This book closes with another chapter that, like the previous two, I didn't expect to be writing. Recent headlines (Wall Street layoffs could reach 200,000, Citigroup is cutting 50,000 jobs) imply that many nerds on Wall Street (NOWS), mostly innocent bystanders in the meltdown, may soon find themselves on the real street. The scramble to create electronic markets for the stealth securities that caused the mess will allow some to find their way back to applying their experience in finance, but many NOWS will not.

Technology has a way of spreading outside its original zone of application. The Internet started out as a way for the Department of Defense to link military computers. Similarly, there are future uses for market technology that may rival those involving CUSIPs.[1] Efficient environmentally sound use of energy is one of the most important. We hear from voices as diverse as Thomas Friedman, T. Boone Pickens, and Ted Turner that energy technology is the next big thing. The last two so-called next big things, dot-coms and extreme finance, turned into fabulously bursting bubbles, so pessimists may want to stockpile long-dated batteries.

There is no denying that clean energy is a critical issue for the future. Actually, though, that is only true in the reality-based community.

327

The Governor Caribou Barbie wing of the Republican Party maintains that global warming is just a run of bad weather caused by Al Gore and gassy polar bears, but the rest of us remain concerned and want to do something about it. The area of the energy and environmental complex where financial market technology is likely to have the largest payoff is the electric power sector. There are some strong commonalities across electricity and financial markets.

First, innovation is accelerating. We are just beginning to see the decentralized use of information technology in this industry. The laws of Moore and Metcalfe are only now starting to be felt outside of the control room. Go look at your electric meter. It is probably just like the meter your parents had, a spinning disk device with dials. This won't be the case for your kids.

Second, there are multiple buyers and sellers. The multiple buyers obviously include everyone who gets an electric bill. The multiple sellers side is more subtle. Most of us can only find one place to purchase electricity. At a household level, today, this is true. In many states, the distribution and generation of power are separate, so distribution and generation firms already participate in a market. Recall the tapes of the Enron power traders cackling as they manipulated prices paid by distribution utilities.

A proliferation of small and cottage-scale providers is emerging as solar, wind, and other technologies that produce a small amount of power become more important. No one builds a small nuclear reactor or coal plant, but just about anyone can have a wind generator in the yard, or an array of solar cells on the roof.

Third, regulators loom large. People who complain about the fragmented regulation of the securities industry by the Commodity Futures Trading Commission and the SEC will get little sympathy from the electric power people. There are 50 state agencies to deal with, many with an independent streak, with the feds at the Environmental Protection Agency (EPA) and the Department of Energy thrown in as well. Much of the regulatory structure is badly in need of rethinking.

Many states create incentives for exactly the wasteful behavior we want to eliminate. The Electric Power Research Institute reports that "in all states except California and Hawaii, utilities are now, in effect, rewarded for selling energy and penalized for reducing customer

sales. . . . Profits must be decoupled from energy sales. We need to provide incentives to utilities to lower customer energy use so that energy
efficiency can be measured as part of a profitable business."[2]

**Fourth, there are so-called fat tails that are extremely sig-
nificant.** Over the past 10 years, an investor who was fully and broadly
invested in U.S. stocks (the Wilshire 5000) would have gained 13 percent (up to the end of October 2008). If he or she missed the market's
20 best days, the portfolio would have lost 57 percent—a minus 70
percent difference just by missing the market's 20 best days. That is a fat
tail in the distribution of returns.

A Brattle Group discussion paper[3] describes a similar fat tail effect
in electricity markets: "The demand for electricity is highly concentrated in the top one percent of hours [during a year]. In most parts
of the U.S., these 80–100 hours account for roughly 8 to 12 percent
of the maximum or peak demand. In the 12 Midwestern and
Northeastern states . . . they account for 16 percent." Note that these
percentages are not referring to total *energy consumption*, but to the level
of total *power* (the rate of delivering energy) that has to be provided
over the year. In the electric world, this is called lowering the peak of
the load duration curve.

Understanding load duration curves is the first lecture in Power
101 class. If you want to understand bonds, you need to know about
the yield curve. The load duration curve is equally important if you
want to understand electricity. Figure 14.1 shows a load duration curve
and how it would shift with the use of the technologies discussed in
this chapter. Lowering the peaks on these curves is important economically, environmentally, and geopolitically, because the plants needed to
meet them are expensive, and often oil fueled.

Software applied to the electric grid offers unprecedented flexibility in reshaping the load duration curve. Utilities can either reduce
customers' nonessential loads or discharge distributed stored power,
separately or in concert, to manage peak periods in a cost-effective,
energy-efficient manner. Lowering the peaks (on the left of the chart)
has tremendous value in cutting both cost and carbon emissions.

The commonalities between electronic financial markets and
electronic energy markets suggest that skills in the former can be applied
in the latter. The state of both means that there are likely to be more than

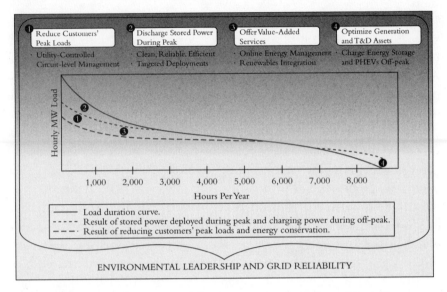

Figure 14.1 Reshaping the load duration curve. Bonds have the yield curve. Power has this.
Source: GridPoint.

a few readers contemplating this transition. This last chapter is a gentle introduction to and a survey of more in-depth resources on this topic.

Accelerating Innovation

There are over a million hybrid Toyota Prius vehicles on the road, and in Berkeley, California, it often seems that they are all parked on the same street. With only one model and a handful of colors, you need a distinctive bumper sticker to find yours. "Obama '08" does nothing to help here. "Support Your Right to Arm Bears" with a rifle-toting polar bear is a little better, but still not that unusual in these parts. "2B or D4" is more distinctive.[4]

The current generation of hybrids makes its own electricity using a small generator under the hood. They have no impact on the demand for electricity from utilities. The next wave of fully electric vehicles and plug-in hybrids will be different. A movie trailer for a scenario from the Union of Concerned Scientists (www.ucsusa.com) might be "Imagine a society with ten million electric cars. Suddenly, they all pull into their garages between 5:30 and 7:00, and plug in to recharge. Imagine the

160 new power plants we need to keep the lights on while this happens. Be afraid. Be very afraid. Drill, baby, drill!" Something has to give. In this case, the "something" is immediacy for the consumers of power. A simple timer system, spreading out the scheduled power over 10 night hours (allocated by last digit of street or IP address) reduces the number of power plants needed by an order of magnitude.

Electric vehicles are only part of the changing power scene. New suppliers using solar, wind, storage, or many other approaches are emerging. Often, they supply power only to themselves. The ski hotel with a roof full of photovoltaics doesn't have much need for them in the summer, when the rooms are empty. The economics for individual ecologically minded homeowners to put that personal windmill generator in the yard or those solar cells on the garage change if the power can be easily sold to others.

Research on Wall Street is done by individual firms and is closely held, driven by the highly competitive zero-sum nature of the market. This is not the case in the utility industry. In trading, decisions about where to put your money are made on time scales going down to microseconds. When was the last time you thought about which utility to use? Research in electricity has become more accessible. There are multiple venues to share the love. This makes it easy for NOWS on the street looking to go green to get up to speed rapidly. Here's a short list:

- *Electric Power Research Institute (EPRI, www.epri.com)*. The 800-pound gorilla of global electric research. "An independent, nonprofit organization, EPRI brings together experts from academia and industry as well as its own. EPRI members represent more than 90 percent of the electricity generated and delivered in the United States, and international participation extends to 40 countries." Includes resources for job seekers.
- *Edison Electric Institute (EEI, www.eei.org)*. The association of U.S. shareholder-owned electric companies. It sponsors and disseminates research, but is primarily a lobbying organization. "Organized in 1933, EEI works closely with all of its members, representing their interests and advocating equitable policies in legislative and regulatory arenas. In its leadership role, EEI provides advocacy, authoritative analysis, and critical industry data to its members, Congress,

government agencies, the financial community, and other opinion-leader audiences."

- *Power Systems Engineering Research Center (PSERC, www.pserc.org).* A collaboration between U.S. universities and the electric industry, designed to engage in forward-oriented thinking about future scenarios for the industry and to conduct research for innovative solutions to these challenges using multidisciplinary research expertise in a unique multicampus work environment.
- *The Brattle Group (www.brattle.com).* A Cambridge, Massachusetts—based international consulting firm with a long history of work in electric power (among other issues). Founded in 1990 by five academics, the firm now has over 200 professionals. It seems to have done a remarkable job in persuading clients to provide much of the work they paid for to the public for free. (For electric power work, go to www.brattle.com/AreasExpertise/IndustryPracticeAreas/Expertise .asp?ExpertiseID=64.)

As shown in Figure 14.2, four building blocks are needed to create the smart energy control system that can unleash the next wave of efficiency potential. Innovative rates and regulation will allow pricing structures that encourage efficiency products to be incorporated into new market

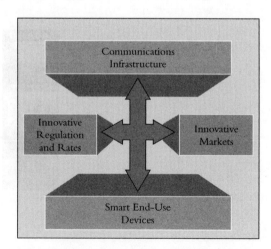

Figure 14.2 Building blocks of dynamic systems. Most frequently occurring word is "innovative".
Source: "Turning on Energy Efficiency," EPRI Journal (Summer 2006): 4–13, http://mydocs.epri.com/docs/public/000000000001013720.pdf.

offerings. Smart end-use devices will receive pricing signals directly from power suppliers through an integrated communications infrastructure and will make their own operational decisions on the basis of preset cost, efficiency, and comfort variables. (Notice that "Innovative" appears twice in the figure, indicative of the rapid pace of change, and note the foundation level position for smart end-use devices.)

These so-called smart meters are the enabling technology for intelligent engineering and market solutions to electric energy problems. Recall that electronic market access (first seen in the NYSE's DOT) was the enabling technology for disintermediation, and later, the use of information technology for algorithmic trading. Similarly, these smart meters will allow utilities, small producers, and consumers to bring the benefits of ubiquitous computation and market solutions to creating a more efficient, less polluting, low-carbon electric industry.

These smart meters exist now. GridPoint in Arlington, Virginia, is the lead dog firm in this space. It was selected as a technology pioneer by the heavies at the Davos World Economic Forum in 2007, as a top innovator by MIT's *Technology Review*, and by the Department of Energy for its model energy-efficient homes. What Apple is to music players, GridPoint is to smart meters. An overview for the controller is shown in Figure 14.3.

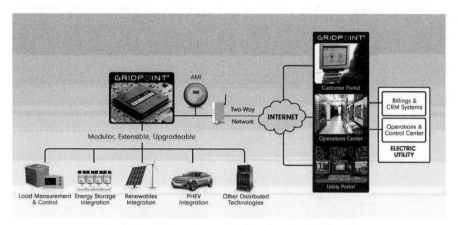

Figure 14.3   GridPoint's smart grid platform is designed to align the interests of electric utilities, consumers, and the environment through an intelligent network of distributed energy resources that controls load, stores energy, and produces power. Algo trading for electrons is coming.
Source: GridPoint (www.gridpoint.com).

GridPoint explains how its simple blue box on the wall addresses all the key issues in our electricity future:

> The platform applies information technology to the electric grid to enable distributed energy resources to perform the same as central-station generation. During peak periods, utilities efficiently balance supply and demand by discharging stored power from distributed generation assets or reducing customers' non-essential loads through demand response programs. Additionally, utilities effectively optimize baseload generation assets and relieve stress on transmission and distribution systems. The platform enables utilities to deploy proven technologies, (e.g., load control devices and advanced batteries) while creating a practical path for integrating new technologies (e.g., plug-in hybrid electric vehicles [PHEVs] and fuel cells). For consumers, the platform provides protection from power outages, increases energy efficiency through online energy management, and integrates renewable energy, paving the way for the commercial success of solar and wind energy sources.

The initial application for smart meters was simple: remote meter reading. This was the motivation for the utility vendors to install them to the limited extent that this has been done. But with greater capabilities in the newer versions the smart meters enable a much greater and more sophisticated set of applications. This could lead to savings to customers, as well as utilities, and for reductions in emissions that benefit everyone.

From Efficiency to Control to Markets

The first wave of energy conservation technologies was about energy efficiency, reducing the power demand by building better machines to plug into the wall, but with the same dumb old meter spinning outside. Under demanding federal standards, there have been some remarkable successes. The EPA's Energy Star program, responsible for those energy use labels seen on every large appliance being sold in the U.S. today, has had a significant and lasting impact. Figure 14.4 shows the price, efficiency, and size of refrigerators over a 50-year period, with a dramatic turn in the middle when the regulations took effect.

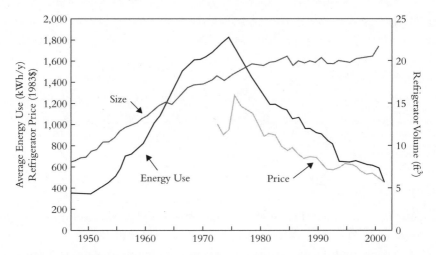

Figure 14.4   Refrigerator energy use, size, and price. Energy consumption grew along with size until the Energy Star standards became mandatory in the 1970s. Since then, efficiency has improved by nearly a factor of five, and prices have dropped by a factor of four. They became bigger better and cheaper. The unregulated fridge market was only doing bigger.
Source: Lawrence Berkeley Lab.

The U.S. automobile industry provides a marked contrast to the remarkable and rapid improvements seen in refrigerators and other appliances. The 1908 Ford Model T traveled 25 miles on a gallon of gas. Fuel efficiency subsequently declined for decades until energy and environmental concerns prompted an interest in fuel conservation. The average EPA miles per gallon for all cars sold in the United States peaked at 22.1 mpg in 1998, but dropped backed to 20.8 mpg in 2004.[5] This is a grim testimonial to the successful lobbying efforts of the auto industry and the influence of their friends in Congress, particularly John Dingell,[6] to relax the types of regulations that proved so effective for other products, and to exempt small trucks and fuel-hog SUVs from the already weak standards.

Pass the Remote Control

Efficiency standards worked as a stand-alone measure, implemented only on the customer side. Smart meters with Internet communication capabilities were the enabling technology for the next wave of technology-driven savings, designed to bring the suppliers into the process. This was done using simple command-and-control load-shedding measures that allowed utilities, with prior agreement of larger customers, to shed loads during periods of peak demand or to remotely adjust air-conditioning thermostats upward to reduce demand when needed.

The next step, still in its infancy, is to introduce real-time electricity pricing. This will allow consumers to make their own economically motivated load-shedding decisions, and to program their meters to implement those decisions for them.

Day Trading for Electrons

In the best seller *Hot, Flat, and Crowded: Why We Need a Green Revolution—and How It Can Renew America* (Farrar, Straus & Giroux, 2008), *New York Times* columnist Thomas Friedman calls the use of smart meters to create a market-based system of energy technology (ET), "when IT meets ET—day trading for electrons." This is where the expertise of former nerds on Wall Street can have a huge impact. Transparent electronic markets and algorithmic trading have dropped the cost of trading, measured by commissions, from 25 cents a share in 1976 to tenths of pennies today.

Today, simple real-time spot pricing is the state of the art, but it is not a full solution. Consumers want to know that cutting back today to help producers produce less pollution or greenhouse gases will not cost them more tomorrow. They effectively need software to manage a futures portfolio for power, and the tools that allow them to do this need to be simple and reliable. This is a considerable technology challenge, one that has been met in financial settings by trading systems that allow individuals to trade using tools and techniques that previously were available only to large institutions, but are now widely available over the Internet for little or no cost.

Sophisticated approaches to market pricing for electricity are an active area of research. Dozens of initiatives in this area are described in a 2002 PSERC report, "Market Mechanisms for Competitive Electricity."[7] The report's authors summarize the PSERC project and its many components concisely:

> This project is concerned with the design and analysis of
> market mechanisms and instruments that support competitive
> operation of electric power systems. The project emphasizes

the interaction between the economic and technical aspects of competitive electricity markets. Our research focused on several specific topics.

- Theoretical and experimental studies of alternative auction structures and their implications for participants' behavior and the efficient operation of the system.
- How market rules in conjunction with system characteristics influence market power.
- Congestion management and transmission pricing.
- Design and analysis of financial instruments for asset valuation and risk management in electricity markets.
- Understanding price formation and market operation.
- Optimal unit commitment algorithms for competitive electricity.
- Design of demand-side contracts.

This report is a rich source of ideas for realizing the potential rewards to society "when IT meets ET." However, these are largely theoretical analyses or simulations. It is reminiscent of the joke about the mathematician who wakes up in a hotel that is on fire, walks to the sink, turns on the water, says, "A solution exists," and goes back to sleep. There is a vast amount of work to be done.

From the Vault: Bits, Bucks, and BTUs

I first wrote about this subject in a RAND paper, "Real Time Pricing and Deregulating the Electricity Market,"[8] published in 1980—at the same time as the other RAND paper mentioned in the Introduction, Kevin Lewis's banned classic "The Tumescent Threat."[9] I was flattered that RAND scanned the paper version of my work and reissued it last year on its web site. This work was done at the end of the Carter administration as part of RAND's research program sponsored by the Department of Energy and the EPA.

RAND's position in the input/output view of the economy (which relates an industry's inputs and outputs) was to turn coffee into printed material and Vu-Graphs. Vu-Graphs were a Flintstone version of

PowerPoint—clear acetate sheets laboriously produced by the graphic arts department. Letters were transferred by hand, along with the slick graphics. We'd show them to our sponsors on overhead projectors. Generals used two projectors and had colonels seated at each of them to flip the charts. I had one projector and did my own flipping. If you dropped the stack of wickedly slippery acetates you were screwed.

The title Vu-Graph from the briefing version of the paper, "Information, Economics, and Energy" is shown in Figure 14.5. Note the cheeky alternative title, "Bits, Bucks, and BTUs." BTUs are not used in discussions of electricity, but "Megawatts" didn't alliterate with "Bits" and "Bucks."

Figure 14.6 shows another Vu-Graph from the "Bits, Bucks, and BTUs" briefing. Throughout the briefing there are references to the promise of using that new microprocessor technology. This was three years before the PC.

The Public Utility Regulatory Policies Act (PURPA), passed in 1978, was a set of federal guidelines designed to promote the greater use of renewable energy. However, implementation was left to the states. After President Carter left office, it was safely ignored by most states. On the last bullet point, the second "P" in the first "PURPA" is

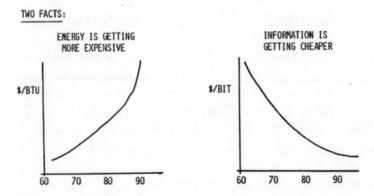

Figure 14.5   Opening Vu-Graph from author's 1980 paper, complete with cheeky subtitle.
Source: RAND Paper P-6448.

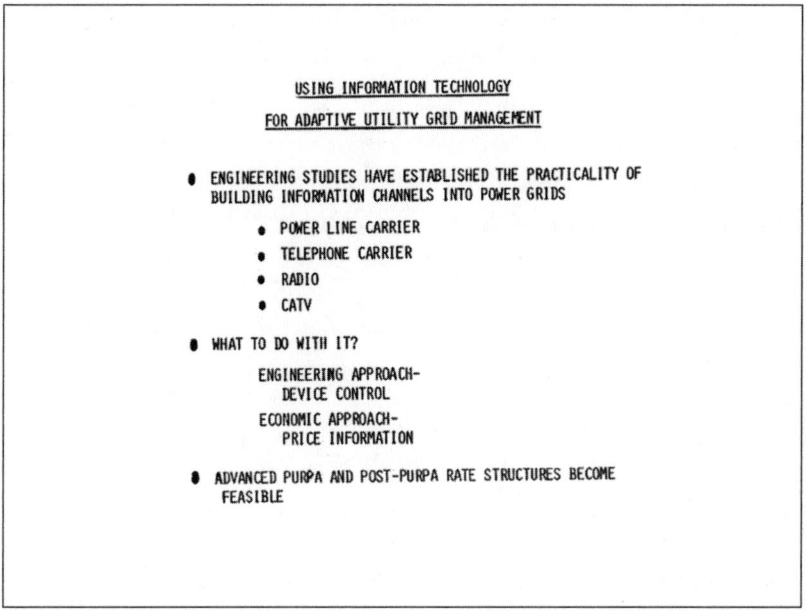

Figure 14.6   Another Vu-Graph from the 1980 briefing. Note the quaint list of communication technologies. None of them were practical for industrial or consumer use. It was hard to keep the modem and the PDP-11 next to the smelter working for very long. The Internet existed, as the ARPANET, but was utterly not ready for prime time.
Source: RAND Paper P-6448.

pretty sorry looking. The graphics guy coughed while pressing it onto the acetate, and making corrections would have involved an Exacto knife and tape, which wouldn't have looked much better. I recall being told that with all the labor and materials even the simple text Vu-Graphs cost about $50 each, so we saved a few bucks for the taxpayers.

Billions of Dollars and Millions of Tons of Carbon

Then, as now, these were valuable ideas. There is a very large, effective, and immediate payoff to electricity conservation. It takes 10 to 15 years to bring a new power plant online. Conservation is the equivalent of a zero-emission power plant you can build in a day.

It's good to see that this is finally going mainstream. Jim Rogers, CEO of Duke Energy, has it spot on:

> Efficiency programs can deliver at a lower cost than new power plants, we can deploy them faster than new power plants, and they can provide savings over relatively short periods of one to three years, as well as over the longer term. From an environmental perspective, we should view energy efficiency as a basic building block in reducing the industry's emissions profile. In 2004 alone, efficiency programs in place saved more than 29 million metric tons of carbon equivalent greenhouse gas emissions.[10]

The Brattle Group attached some numbers:

> Demand response programs based on advanced metering and dynamic pricing could reduce peak load in the United States by at least 5% over the next few years for a savings of approximately $3 billion per year in electricity costs. The discounted present value of these savings would be $35 billion over the next 20 years.[11]

Remember the good old days when $35 billion was a large number? With a return to a reality-based view of the world's problems and their solutions, there are ample opportunities for people with skills in market technology to apply them outside traditional financial markets. I hope that more than a few Wall Street nerds with pink slips can turn them green. More (or less) power to you all.

Epilogue

This book started out as a popular guide for people looking to get into financial technology. It is based in part on the kinds of questions I often get from UC Berkeley students curious about the Center for Innovative Financial Technology.[12] The financial technology globe has not stopped turning, though it has slowed a bit, and its population is not as large as it once was. I'm confident in saying that there will in fact be room in the future for new people in the wired markets of the world, whether they are trading securities, emissions, or electrons.

Ogden Nash was mildly nostalgic but mostly joking when he said, "Progress might have been all right once, but it has gone on too long." None of us will be going back to shouting under the Buttonwood tree.

Notes

1. CUSIPs are issued by the U.S. Committee on Uniform Security Identification Procedures; they are nine-character alphanumeric security identifiers. See www.cusip .com for more than you need to know.

2. Brent Barker and Lucy Sanna, "Turning on Energy Efficiency," *EPRI Journal* (Summer 2006): 4–13, http://mydocs.epri.com/docs/public/000000000001013720.pdf.

3. Ahmad Faruqui, Ryan Hledik, Samuel A. Newell, and Johannes Pfeifenberger, "The Power of Five Percent: How Dynamic Pricing Can Save $35 Billion in Electricity Costs," *Electricity Journal*, October 2007, www.brattle.com/Publications/BooksArticles .asp?PublicationID=922.

4. This book's title does start with the word *nerds*. In hexadecimal, D4 is the complement—negation—of 2B, so this is "To be or not to be."

5. "Engineers Push Fuel Economy to Front Seat at Auto Summit," *Detroit News*, April 11, 2005, www.detnews.com/2005/autosinsider/0504/12/A01-146552.htm.

6. Some things that seem to never change, change. Dingell has been replaced by Henry Waxman as chair of the House Energy and Commerce Committee.

7. "Market Mechanisms for Competitive Electricity: Final Report," Shmuel Oren, Project Leader, University of California, Berkeley, Power Systems Engineering Research Center, Publication 02-42, November 2002, www.pserc.org/ecow/get/ publicatio/reports/2002report/oren_marketmech_finalreport.pdf.

8. David Leinweber, "Real Time Pricing and Deregulating the Electricity Market," RAND Paper P-6448, www.rand.org/pubs/papers/P6448/.

9. If anyone reading this has a copy of "The Tumescent Threat," please contact me. The fact that this footnote is here says it all about how effectively this has been vanished, and about the sorry state of my garage filing system.

10. "Rogers Calls for 'Paradigm Shift' to Realize Full Potential of Energy Efficiency," Edison Electric Institute press release, February 2007.

11. Faruqui et al., "Power of Five Percent."

12. http://cift.haas.berkeley.edu/

NOWS Companion Web Site

Links to references , animations, colorful bonuses and Web extras can be found at NerdsOnWallStreet.com.

Index

About the Web Site

Many of the references in this book are URLs. Even the most dedicated nerds get tired of typing these. Someday soon, you'll point your handheld's camera at the book, it'll do some OCR and find (or offer to sell you) the material you're looking for. Absent that fancy gadget, try the web site **NerdsonWallStreet.com.** It has links in to the NOWS references, plus extras that augment the bandwidth of black ink on white paper. Color and animated versions of the printed black and white screen grabs, in addition to new and topical items, will be added often.